Invertebrate Surveys for Conservation

Invertebrate Surveys for Conservation

T. R. New
*School of Zoology, La Trobe University,
Bundoora, Victoria 3083, Australia*

OXFORD • NEW YORK • TOKYO
OXFORD UNIVERSITY PRESS
1998

This book has been printed digitally in order to ensure its continuing availability

OXFORD
UNIVERSITY PRESS

Great Clarendon Street, Oxford OX2 6DP

Oxford University Press is a department of the University of Oxford.
It furthers the University's objective of excellence in research, scholarship,
and education by publishing worldwide in

Oxford New York

Auckland Bangkok Buenos Aires Cape Town Chennai
Dar es Salaam Delhi Hong Kong Istanbul Karachi Kolkata
Kuala Lumpur Madrid Melbourne Mexico City Mumbai Nairobi
São Paulo Shanghai Singapore Taipei Tokyo Toronto

with an associated company in Berlin

Oxford is a registered trade mark of Oxford University Press
in the UK and in certain other countries

Published in the United States
by Oxford University Press Inc., New York

A catalogue record for this book is available from the British Library

Library of Congress Cataloging in Publication Data
New, T. R.
Invertebrate studies for conservation / T. R. New.
Includes bibliographical references and index.
1. Invertebrate populations—Research—Methodology.
2. Wildlife conservation. I. Title.
QL362.N435 1998 592.17'88—dc21 97-31861

ISBN 0-19-850012-2 (Hbk)
ISBN 0-19-850011-4 (Pbk)

Preface

Documenting the magnitude and distribution of the earth's biodiversity is central to planning for a sustainable world and for the needs of burgeoning human populations. The need for this short book results from one very simple conjunction, which is of great relevance in trying to make global conservation as effective as possible and in studying biodiversity at the organism and assemblage levels: most animals are invertebrates, and most conservation managers and practitioners know very little about their biology or how to study and survey them adequately in the field. They are thus commonly ignored by conservation planners, rather than accorded the importance they merit as predominant and environmentally sensitive components of animal diversity. This neglect applies equally whether invertebrates are viewed directly as conservation targets or as valuable tools for broader assessment of the characteristics and condition of communities and ecosystems, and for monitoring changes which result from human intervention.

Indeed, the immense diversity of invertebrates and of their ways of life effectively precludes anyone from having more than a superficial acquaintance with more than a few of the 25–30 phyla involved, or of their major habitats. Most specialists in invertebrates confine their interests to one such major group and, commonly, to only a small component of a phylum, such as a particular order or family of insects or molluscs. Likewise, most conservationists and ecologists work in only one major system, such as terrestrial, freshwater or marine habitats. Any such group of scientists may know little about other taxonomic groups or other major biomes.

Collectively, invertebrate animals are the major energy conduits and agents of nutrient and material recycling in marine, freshwater and terrestrial ecosystems throughout the world, and the sustainability of the earth's life-support systems depends on their well-being. Wilson's (1987) evocative categorization of invertebrates as 'the little things that run the world', and documents such as the *European Charter on Invertebrates* (Council of Europe 1986) have done much to encourage awareness of the importance of invertebrates and of needs for their conservation. A few general texts on conservation biology of invertebrates (such as Samways 1994a; New 1995a) now complement more specialized literature, and some relevant symposium volumes (Collins and Thomas 1991; Gaston, New and Samways 1994) also survey recent progress and changing attitudes. The major impetus to development of the discipline during recent years has been the pioneering *IUCN invertebrate red data book* (Wells et al. 1983), in which many of the pertinent issues were addressed for the first time.

However, the major practical theme of 'how to survey invertebrates and interpret assemblages as a basis for biodiversity assessment and conservation', and the reasons for doing so and needing such study, have not been addressed comprehensively. To judge from many queries received during the last few years, a practically orientated account is indeed needed for students and for conservationists unfamiliar with the complexities of invertebrate life. This book is not simply a 'recipe book', but I try to introduce the rationale, needs and methodology for studying invertebrate animals in a range of contexts, most of which at some level are relevant to conservation assessment, and to provide sufficient reference to more advanced or comprehensive works for the reader to pursue in greater detail, if needed, from the first principles included here. Much of the book emphasizes the needs of people coming to the intricacies of invertebrate biology from other backgrounds, and the initial chapter and some of the later discussions set out the peculiarities and practical limitations of studying invertebrates. These are commonly not appreciated adequately in designing sampling regimes and analysing the resulting accumulations of specimens, but are vital if important management decisions stem from such interpretations.

The scope of the book is deliberately restricted, not least because virtually any biological and ecological information can be relevant to some form of practical conservation. In the interests of brevity, I have not recapitulated methods of analysis which may be regarded as standard in other fields of ecology: sampling design and classical analysis (such as by ordination techniques) are treated only briefly but references are included to more comprehensive standard texts. The brief lists of 'further reading' given for each chapter include suggestions for such broader background. Many of the sampling methods treated in Chapters 3 and 4 are explained more comprehensively in texts dealing either with particular groups of invertebrates, or assessment in particular habitats. Southwood's (1978) classic text on *Ecological methods: With particular reference to the study of insect populations* remains indispensable to anyone seeking background information on the development of invertebrate sampling methods in non-marine environments. However, continued modification of well-tried methods, and attempts to improve them and quantify their properties, biases and limitations more completely, have characterized much invertebrate sampling in recent years. I note later that many published accounts are of 'one-off' modifications which can be difficult to compare with others. Conservation assessment relies to a great extent on use of comparable, standard sampling regimes and interpretation and, for invertebrates, there are many problems in doing this reliably.

One increasingly pervasive theme, resulting directly from the diversity of invertebrates and the difficulties of sampling them satisfactorily, has been moves towards 'rapid biodiversity assessment' through varying levels of approximation and 'short-cuts' to sample interpretation. This logistically attractive approach requires clear understanding of how the methods work, the limitations of the information gained from them, and precisely what information is needed to answer the questions pertinent to the study. I hope that this book will help practitioners work through the logistic morass that exists at present, and lead them towards more considered and reliable study and use of invertebrates in practical conservation. Development of reliable protocols for practical study is one of the most pressing needs in this field, and these can come only from understanding the problems we face and the methods and approaches available to solve these. Although many people are seeking straightforward answers, in the form of 'recipes' for invertebrate sampling, the discussion here should help emphasize the difficulties of formulating these.

Bundoora
October 1997

T.R.N.

Acknowledgements

The following authors and publishers are gratefully acknowledged for permission to reproduce diagrams or tabular material from the sources cited in context: American Midland Naturalist, American Society for Limnology and Oceanography, American Society of Zoologists, Australian Institute of Marine Sciences, Blackwell Science Ltd, Bombay Natural History Society, Cambridge University Press, Chapman & Hall Ltd, CSIRO Publishing, Ecological Society of America, Entomological Society of Canada, Elsevier Science-NL, European Journal of Entomology, Field Studies Council, Gustav Fischer Verlag, Kugler Publishers B.V., Kluwer Academic Publishers, Netherlands Entomological Society, Prof. R. Gadagkar, Dr P.J. Moran, Royal Society of London, Smithsonian Institution Press, SPB Academic Publishing, John Wiley & Sons Ltd. Mrs Tracey Carpenter prepared many of the figures for this book, and undertook most of the typing with her usual care: I greatly appreciate her dedication and help over many years. The constructive advice of two anonymous referees has been invaluable, as have discussions on the subject matter with Dr A.L. Yen (Museum of Victoria).

Contents

1 Introduction. Invertebrates in conservation

Introduction

Our appreciation of conservation need comes commonly from noticing decline of species' abundance or distribution, or changes to ecosystems, and the realization that these may lead to them becoming extinct or non-sustainable. The enormous variety of threats to species and habitats as a consequence of human activities leading to declines or losses at any level can stimulate massive efforts to counter them and, if necessary, to restore and manage habitats and the organisms they harbour. The basis for such practical conservation is the need to sustain ecological processes—in essence, the dynamic 'life-support systems' on which all animals and plants ultimately depend. Practical conservation should be founded on sound scientific information, and obtaining such information thus underpins many of our efforts to conserve animals and plants and the places in which they live.

Declines in species are heralded most volubly and forcefully when they are members of 'popular' groups (warm-blooded vertebrates, in particular), and are especially significant to many people when these are commercially desirable species subject to industrial (whaling) or illegal (elephant, rhinoceros) exploitation, or where livelihoods suffer directly as a consequence of decline (fisheries). As a direct consequence of the demonstrated conservation needs of mammals and birds, especially, well-documented and substantial protocols for conservation exist and the basic needs for management are often based on reliable quantitative information and reasonably accurate estimates of population size and trends in abundance and distribution. This is not so for the most abundant and diverse animals in all marine, freshwater and terrestrial ecosystems. These, the enormous variety of lineages and life forms simplistically treated as 'the invertebrates', are most commonly overlooked in conservation planning and assessment. However, considerable recent appreciation of their relevance as the most diverse constituents of animal 'biodiversity', and of the need to evaluate invertebrate assemblages in all of the earth's habitats, has occurred as an important part of setting templates for establishing conservation priorities. Deep oceans, caves, the upper soil horizons, all water bodies and vegetated zones, and montane environments each support a great variety of characteristic invertebrate life, and all these habitats and the resources they contain are subject to degradation and change from the influences of people.

There is thus a practical need to identify and overcome the problems of studying invertebrates for conservation, to evaluate their roles in holistic conservation programmes, and to set out existing and potential methods and protocols in a form which will be accessible to non-specialists. At present, most conservation managers have not been trained primarily as invertebrate zoologists, and many (most) conservation biologists and practitioners have a stronger familiarity with either vertebrates or vascular plants. Many people are thus reluctant to work with invertebrates simply because this predominant part of the animal world is viewed as a 'black hole' of daunting complexity, or is dismissed as 'bird food' (or some similar disparaging oversimplification!), without regard for the diversity of life forms present.

This account is designed to help bridge this important gap and broaden the appreciation and accessibility of invertebrates in practical conservation. It is not simply a 'recipe book', but introduces the options and importance of surveying and interpreting invertebrate assemblages, the problems and limitations of doing this, and the major gaps which exist. It will become apparent very quickly that, although we may ask questions very similar to those in, for example, mammal conservation programmes, obtaining equivalent answers for an invertebrate study may demand a very different approach, as may the ways in which the information is best utilized in practical conservation. There is increasing demand for surveyors and managers to include invertebrates in their considerations (Brooks 1993a), and for invertebrate surveys to form an integral component of many Environmental Impact Statements and similar protocols (Majer 1987) rather than the somewhat token acknowledgement of their presence which has characterized many such documents in the past.

Indeed, without this dimension much conservation assessment may be substantially the poorer. Much of the audience for conservation assessment needs clear, simplified reports of highly complex data sets involving taxonomically complex and diverse assemblages, couched in unambiguous terms and with the trends and recommendations expressed. It is easy to become overwhelmed with detail, and by the variety of sampling and analytical devices available. Clear descriptions of sampling methods and of the procedures followed in sample processing and analysis, with appreciation of the limits to interpretation, are essential. Lack of such clear background information is 'probably the most common shortcoming in many applied papers in benthic ecology' (Burd et al. 1990), and that comment could be extended easily to studies on other systems where invertebrates are the predominant life forms. Nevertheless, sampling and identification of species constitute the essential baseline for understanding animal diversity, and studies on invertebrates are an important focus for this.

Problems in studying invertebrates for conservation

Characterizing biodiversity and understanding its components and distribution is a key need for global management (Heywood 1995), and is an immensely difficult task. At any level, be it establishing the species richness (the number of species, or alpha-diversity), the taxic diversity (the taxonomic dispersion of species) or functional diversity, attempts to do so are frustrated by poor understanding of many groups and by our inability to survey them effectively. In particular, significant problems in studying biological diversity arise from the differences between invertebrates and vertebrates. Some of these are of far-reaching importance in practical conservation, and are noted here as background to much of the later content of this book. They illustrate some of the main impediments to accurate interpretation and dominate many considerations in invertebrate conservation.

Invertebrates are diverse

It is entirely feasible to produce definitive (or near-definitive) species lists of mammals or birds for inventories of natural areas cited for importance or possible protection, or to prepare such lists for protected areas such as National Parks, in order to assess their adequacy or representativeness as reservoirs of taxa and, hence, their conservation significance. Such listings are an important comparative tool in helping to rank sites of importance (Usher 1986), based on species richness or the presence of 'significant' taxa, or to select the 'best' areas for priority treatment or reservation. Preparing such lists for all invertebrates is impossible but, with considerable effort, is feasible for a few well-known groups such as butterflies, dragonflies and a few other orders or families. It is not possible to achieve complete or near-complete species lists for nearly all invertebrate groups on any broad scale, although there are local exceptions reflecting expertise of particular workers. Inability to produce definitive lists is taken by many people to reflect lack of interest or relevance of invertebrates, rather than the suite of logistic and biological problems that hamper acquisition of the necessary fundamental information.

Expertise

The amount and quality of expertise available to document invertebrate assemblages is limited. Although invertebrates are present in all natural communities, the numbers of species involved and the great variety of taxa precludes total assessment by any one specialist or group of specialists. An experienced field observer may be capable of recognizing, to species level or near and mainly at sight, all species of birds or mammals in a National Park (or, even, country or larger region) without the need to capture individuals of most taxa for closer appraisal. In contrast, an entomologist may be able to recognize many members of one order of insects, but more often only a restricted subset of these and then only after capture, preparation and microscopical examination, and it is indeed unusual for any person to be able to recognize reliably even the families of more than one large phylum or class. There are probably as many *families* of insects as there are *species* of mammals! Many invertebrate groups are largely unidentifiable beyond family level except by a very few specialists or experienced devotees, who may be too fully occupied to respond to requests without substantial prior notice.

This situation reflects a number of very basic features. First, most invertebrates are small, and not identifiable to species level with the naked eye—there are exceptions, such as many butterflies, dragonflies, some groups of molluscs and crustaceans but, even for these, confirmation of identity by specialists is needed commonly to avoid confusing similar-looking taxa, and prolonging inaccurate analyses. Second, there is often considerable taxonomic uncertainty. Discovery of a new species of mammal or bird is a relatively uncommon event, and most individuals of those groups are recognizable to species level or beyond; in contrast, many invertebrates are undescribed and difficult to identify. Many species, even of better-known groups, cannot be distinguished simply on general appearance but need to be dissected and examined by specialists. The difficulties of identification reflect the abundance of undescribed taxa, lack of knowledge of species variation and limits, and lack of identification aids.

For many groups of invertebrates, even the order of magnitude of species number is uncertain. For nematode worms, for example, Groombridge (1992) noted a possible range of 0.5–1 million species (in itself a large uncertainty for a group in which only about 15–20000 species have been described so far!), but other estimates for nematode diversity are much higher. Indeed, it has been claimed that nematodes may comprise as much as 90% of all metazoan species, and Lambshead (1993) estimated that there could be 100 000 000 deep sea species, alone. For the insects, Groombridge (1992) noted a possible range of 8–100 million species, and such figures are little more than 'guesstimates'—yet many workers now readily accept a figure of 5–10 million living insect species and the background to deriving such estimates (May 1990; Gaston 1992; summary by New 1995a) indicates the various assumptions used, mainly linked to levels of habitat specialization and restricted distribution, both important parameters in conservation assessment where species may be ranked on their vulnerability and rarity.

Even the relative diversity of invertebrates in different major habitats is uncertain. Recent work on marine benthos, for example, suggests that the common inference that marine invertebrates are far less diverse than in terrestrial faunas may be questionable (Grassle and Maciolek 1991; Poore and Wilson 1992). Most invertebrate phyla have an undescribed (or unknown) component *at least* as large as the described one, and the chances of finding numerous undescribed taxa in any reasonably comprehensive survey in any major ecosystem or habitat are high.

Lack of knowledge of species limits occurs because most invertebrate taxa have been described, necessarily, solely from dead museum specimens and often from very few individuals. The type individual or series is/are the only known material of many species, and the extent and pattern of intraspecific variation is unknown. Stork's (1994) example, citing beetles from a selection of papers in the *Zoological Record*, that 45% (of 186 species) are known from single localities and 13% from single specimens, is likely to be representative of many other groups, although the knowledge may be even worse for many of these. Beetles, after all, are a relatively popular group of animals. Likewise, no specific details of biology and ways of life are available for most species, and even the small amounts of generalized information present may be grossly misleading, because they may mask a great variety of feeding habits and life history characteristics. Many taxonomic revisions of invertebrate groups reveal a high level of new synonymy, as well as including descriptions of new species. Although it is of critical importance in delimitation of many species and higher taxa, morphology is only one criterion of species distinctiveness, and the biological limits of many invertebrate species, and the number of morphologically similar cryptic or sibling taxa in many groups are, simply, unknown.

The above uncertainties mean that the standard of field guide, or comprehensive illustrated keys to species identification, taken for granted by workers on many vertebrates, are unavailable for most invertebrate groups. Even for such popular taxa as butterflies and large gastropods, which have long been sought avidly by collectors, modern comprehensive field guides for much of the tropics and some temperate region countries do not exist. Many of the keys which *do* exist are outdated and can be used only with caution, and many contain technical vocabulary which is off-putting to non-specialists. Primary taxonomic advice is an integral part of invertebrate identification, and this may necessarily be based on incomplete knowledge of a local or regional fauna, or by specialists without first-hand practical knowledge of the fauna of the region under study.

Visibility

Many invertebrates are difficult to detect, not only because of their small size and cryptic habits which may necessitate specialized collecting techniques (Chapter 3), but also because they may be present or apparent and amenable to capture for only short periods each year.

Flight seasons of particular insects, for example, may last for only a few days or weeks each generation (commonly, each year) so that the only chance to capture them in that state is during that restricted period. The rest of their life may be passed as inconspicuous eggs, as larvae feeding in habitats where the adults do not occur normally, or as resting pupae. Any of these stages may be impossible to associate with the corresponding adult unless they are reared directly to confirm their identity. Taxonomic knowledge of the abundant immature stages of invertebrates is far poorer than for the adults. Parallels to the insect life cycle noted occur in most invertebrate groups which undergo complex metamorphosis. The planktonic larvae of many marine taxa differ greatly in appearance from their corresponding adults, for example, and may pass through several very different forms as they develop.

Such patterns of morphological and habitat change, perhaps over only a local scale or commonly more widespread and incorporating patterns of migration, mean that many invertebrates 'use' habitats on different scales to more conspicuous larger animals, and that surveys for them may need to incorporate a range of 'subhabitats' rather than just the main environment. Samways (1994a,b) stressed the different patterns of landscape use by insects, and many are indeed highly restricted within, even, an apparently homogeneous region. Problems of scale are thus an integral consideration in sampling many invertebrates, with increasing sophistication and difficulty frequent for fine-scale appraisals. Few human conservation managers think of natural environments on the scale perceived by a grasshopper or a snail, and how many such taxa may partition a complex environment to satisfy the mosaic of their needs. The amount of sampling needed to clarify even very broad patterns of diversity and distribution of large groups may be daunting. For marine nematodes, the 17 standardized data sets discussed by Boucher and Lambshead (1995) 'despite representing an enormous outlay of scientific time and expertise by various investigators are taken from only about 0.5 m^2 of sediment surface' of an environment which covers about two-thirds of the planet. It is simply unknown whether these can be taken as representative of the larger environment but, clearly, there is room for doubt.

Ecological specialization

Such distribution patterns link with patterns of resource use. Being small, even though they may be numerous, many invertebrates show ecological specializations unusual for larger animals in that whole populations can be sustained by small areas and small amounts of resources. This tendency has considerable application in conservation assessment, where particular invertebrate species or groups may exhibit very subtle responses to habitat change, and 'divide' the habitat in more extreme ways than vertebrates or major plant groups. Such specialization, also reflecting effects of scale, has important ramifications in relation to possible use of these latter groups as possible surrogates for broader diversity. Studies of correlations of invertebrates with vertebrate or plant diversity are not well-developed, and most of the results are not clear-cut.

As one such study, Yen (1987) studied the distribution of beetles, vascular plants, and vertebrates in the semiarid mallee region of western Victoria,

Australia, and recognized more distinct ecological assemblages of beetles than of either of the more conspicuous groups. Vertebrates and Coleoptera from 32 sites, representing eight vegetation communities, were classified using the ordination analysis TWINSPAN. There was no significant relationship between the richness of vertebrates (n for survey, 60 species) and the richness of Coleoptera (n for survey, 176 species) for each vegetation type. The beetles separated into 11 communities (compared with nine for the vertebrates) and reflected the vegetation communities more distinctly. There was clear inference that land management plans based on the vertebrate data alone might not lead to adequate representation of all the major communities present. Importantly, a priority site selected for vertebrate species richness may not necessarily support the highest diversity of beetles—or, by extrapolation, of other invertebrate groups. In practical conservation, site evaluation commonly focuses on relatively small, discrete, habitat patches, and the demonstration that there may be unexpectedly high faunal differences between apparently similar habitats when their invertebrate components are appraised reveals the shortcomings of this approach.

At least part of the reason for such high numbers of invertebrate species is this 'packing' of specialized taxa into a small area or habitat with diverse resources among which the species can distribute with little interference or competition. Ecological specialist taxa are especially vulnerable to habitat change, and even small or restricted change can influence some invertebrates adversely. A related problem is that it may be impossible to decide whether many of the invertebrates captured during a survey are even residents of the area, or are simply tourists. Apparently rare species in a habitat may not even live there, and be more common elsewhere.

Ecological complexity has four important consequences for practical studies on invertebrates in relation to those for many vertebrates.

1. Many vertebrates can be studied by direct observation in the field, or by reasonably straightforward and well-understood, non-destructive sampling regimes using traps, mist nets or pitfalls. By contrast, any reasonably comprehensive invertebrate field study is likely to involve a number of different techniques used in conjunction to overcome biases inherent in each. In many cases these involve trapping and killing the taxa for later determination, and sampling separately from various subdivisions of the habitat to determine their spatial distribution. As emphasized earlier, such collection is an integral part of field studies of invertebrates, and of surveys used to compare different sites, and most taxa cannot be identified to species level while they are alive.

The problems of needing to collect in order to evaluate invertebrate faunas are not overcome easily but collecting, if poorly understood, may well be a threat to species in restricted habitats, such as caves (Culver 1982), or contribute to the decline of rare taxa. In such environments, biologists should ask themselves critically if the specimens are really needed, and whether any real advance in understanding may result from their collections or surveys (Culver 1982). However, in outdoor environments, enormous numbers of individuals are commonly collected and killed indiscriminately as a normal part of sampling invertebrates, usually with scant regard to slaughter of possibly rare taxa.

2. Most vertebrates may be detectable over a reasonable short survey, so that (excepting migratory taxa), relatively complete lists of resident species may be accumulated during a few weeks. Invertebrate surveys to provide inventory data or information on numbers of species present generally need to be longer term to account for massive variations in apparency linked with differing phenologies and seasonality. Even a full year of survey may not reveal all the taxa present, especially rarer ones whose appearance may be subject to vagaries of weather pattern or food supply. Any survey needs careful planning to ensure that its duration is sufficient to answer the questions posed.

3. In many cases, some knowledge of the ecology of the vertebrates present in a habitat is likely to exist; in some groups, detailed appraisals may be available for some species and sound inferences may be possible, for example, on the trophic roles of many others. Little specific information is likely to exist on the ecology of most invertebrates which live there, beyond categorizing them very broadly as, for example, herbivore, detritivore, predator, parasitoid or parasite. Even this may be difficult, and confused by the diversity and variety present, and by imprecise or erratic identifications. Some recent work on soil nematodes, for example, used their diversity to suggest a 'community maturity index' (Bongers 1990), but analysis was possible only at the *family* level and, even then, there may be massive ecological and trophic variety among the members of any such large category. Extrapolation beyond very cautious limits may be misleading and restrictive.

4. An area reserved for the conservation of a significant vertebrate may remain suitable to sustain it for a long period, and it has commonly been assumed that this is so also for invertebrates: that simply 'locking up' an area as a reserve may be adequate practical conservation. This may not always be the case, because the specialized ecological needs of a target species (or an assemblage) may depend, for example, on regularly renewed successional stages of vegetation. If suitable management does not occur in a reserve, such species may become extinct through natural vegetational change rather than directly from human effects. Monitoring (Chapter 8) may be needed to determine this.

Psychological problems and human attitudes

Public perceptions of invertebrates are commonly unsympathetic and, although the above-mentioned impediments to conservation in relation to vertebrates are formidable, a major additional factor—perhaps just as important as any of the above—is the lack of sympathy and understanding for invertebrates, fostered in part through the impacts of relatively few pest taxa. Invertebrates are seen as harmful competitors for human needs and may arouse fear. Arachnophobia was cited by Ehrlich and Ehrlich (1981) as a barrier to conservation, and fear of getting bitten or stung may be a severe deterrent to interest, and to enrolling support for their conservation.

There are also widespread assumptions that small size equates with insignificance and lack of importance, and that invertebrates are resistant to extinction, even by determined suppression programmes. All are manifestly untrue. Determined efforts to suppress pest species commonly do not succeed, but many of the potential victims are generalist, common, highly fecund species with broad ecological ranges. They by no means typify the vast number of more specialized forms which arouse interest for conservation as they decline. The 'stereotype' images of invertebrates constitute a major barrier to communicating the needs for conservation, and education to redress this attitude is an important practical component of invertebrate conservation strategy (Yen 1994; New 1995a). Price (1988) noted the common human perception that the organisms people relate to most easily (trees, shrubs, birds, mammals) are the most important organisms on earth, but that the latter animals were only 'diminutive radiations' compared with many groups of smaller organisms. Kellert's (1993) essay on perceptions of invertebrates summarized a number of relevant points which are valuable in increasing positive attitudes toward invertebrates. These include their important ecological benefits and roles, which include many utilitarian aspects, commodities such as food and commercial items, and practical uses such as indicators of environmental quality, and massive scientific and cultural benefits. Whereas many people in Kellert's survey reacted negatively to invertebrates, many valued aesthetic, utilitarian and ecological aspects. One intriguing facet of overcoming aversion to many invertebrates is the rapidly increasing appreciation of them as 'novelty pets'. In 1995, for example, there were 108 species of tarantula spiders in the pet trade (Thomas 1995). However, additional conservation complications may then arise through depleting populations of rarer species and their release into new areas, and such trade may need to be regulated effectively to reduce such risks.

Administrative barriers

Linked with the above, and also with the need for education, are a set of 'administrative barriers' related to: (1) invertebrates being excluded, commonly by lack of specific mention, from definitions of 'wildlife' and similar terms, so that few staff in many government conservation agencies, at any level, either have knowledge of them or specific responsibilities for their conservation, and (2) their diversity putting them firmly in the 'too hard basket' for formulating management or recovery plans. The common administrative assumption that invertebrates can either take care of themselves, or are conserved automatically under the aegis of programmes for other taxa, is by no means universally true. As Yen and Butcher (1994) stated, this remains untested, but simple reservation of habitat in which many species may continue to thrive is likely to remain a high priority in invertebrate conservation activities.

Practical approaches

The above points are not comprehensive, but exemplify some of the practical problems which occur in studying and interpreting invertebrate assemblages in most parts of the world. Overcoming the various taxonomic, ecological, and bureaucratic impediments to studying invertebrates for conservation has received considerable attention in the last few years, and is a recurring theme in this book, and of others on invertebrate conservation (see New 1984, 1991, 1995a; Collins and Thomas 1991; Fry and Lonsdale 1991; Gaston *et al.* 1994; Samways 1994a).

The practical approaches to invertebrates in conservation relate to two main contexts:

(1) invertebrates as conservation targets; and

(2) invertebrates as tools in conservation assessment and monitoring.

Either may concentrate on single species, or on larger taxonomic or ecological groupings. The first usually involves focusing on single species suggested or perceived to be declining or under threat and may demand reasonably precise evaluation of numbers and distribution as components of status (Chapter 8), to form a template for understanding how relevant management or recovery programmes should be designed. Alternatively, or in addition, the status of larger groups may need to be determined through various recording or mapping schemes, leading to evaluating changes of status in relation to changes in the environment, and the use of such changes to monitor anthropogenic effects on environmental quality, such as pollution or land management practices. Such assessment may require adequate historical data (Eversham 1994). Some invertebrates may also be useful in indicating changes due to climate change (Watt *et al.* 1990). The range of contexts in which invertebrates can be used as 'tools' is clearly substantial. On the one hand, detailed autecological studies of a particular species and the factors influencing its distribution and abundance are needed; at the other extreme, estimates of diversity and the trend in abundance of particular invertebrate groups known (or believed) to respond to particular factors or processes are used commonly in the contexts of comparing assemblages or sites for their integrity or ecological complexity, as 'indicators' of habitat quality. Others may have value as 'predictor sets' (Kitching 1993), that is, as reflectors of more comprehensive species richness of an area. Some invertebrates seem to be particularly valuable in reflecting overall diversity of a habitat or site, and many species and groups have very restricted distributions and patterns of endemism. If these patterns can be clarified, they are valuable adjuncts to setting priorities in the conservation of given areas, and also for 'overlaying' with patterns of other taxa to determine areas valuable for sustaining a suite of taxa, which, therefore, may be considered of particular importance. However, as noted earlier and emphasized later, precise data may be difficult to obtain and the levels of approximation which can be accepted validly need to be assessed for each individual study (Chapter 5).

The kind of knowledge needed for practical conservation may differ considerably in different contexts, but does not obviate the need for a more general understanding of approaches to studying invertebrates for conservation. In particular, the means for sampling invertebrate species and faunas in relation to specified aims or questions, and the methods of processing and interpreting the samples for status evaluation studies or in broader studies of biodiversity are commonly unfamiliar to people wishing to use them. Disney's (1986) comments that: 'At present the use of invertebrates in the process of evaluating terrestrial sites for conservation purposes rarely moves beyond the anecdotal stage' and 'there is a dearth of quantitative data that could be used for ranking sites objectively' remain alarmingly true, although the importance of obtaining such information has indeed come to be appreciated more widely during the last decade. We need to understand how to get that information, and how to interpret it accurately and effectively, especially in the light of recent international undertakings by many countries to document the world's biota in the coming decades.

Further reading

Groombridge, B. C. (ed.) (1992). *Global biodiversity*. World Conservation Monitoring Centre, Cambridge.

Heywood, V. H. (ed.) (1995). *Global biodiversity assessment*. UNEP, Cambridge University Press, Cambridge.

Majer, J. D. (ed.) (1987). *The role of invertebrates in conservation and biological survey*. Department of Conservation and Land Management, Perth, WA.

McNeely, J. A., Miller, K. R., Reid, W. V., Mittermaier, R. A., and Werner, T. B. (1989). *Conserving the world's biological diversity*. IUCN, Gland.

National Research Council. (1995). *Understanding marine biodiversity*. National Academy Press, Washington, D.C.

New, T. R. (1995). *An introduction to invertebrate conservation biology*. Oxford University Press, Oxford.

Samways, M. J. (1994). *Insect conservation biology*. Chapman & Hall, London.

Wells, S. M., Pyle, R. M., and Collins, N. M. (1983). *The IUCN invertebrate red data book*. IUCN, Gland.

Wilson, E. O. and Peter, F. M. (ed.). (1988). Biodiversity. National Academy Press, Washington, D.C.

2 Approaches to invertebrate surveys: posing the questions

Introduction

There are several distinct levels for focus in practical conservation and invertebrate surveys. The questions posed may differ substantially both between and within each level, and on whether the invertebrates are direct targets for conservation or tools for broader environmental assessment in setting priorities among sites or assemblages. The precise questions addressed must be posed clearly in the planning phase of a study, and examples of these are noted below. In general, the steps needed to organize surveys encompass a sequence from formulating clear objectives to responsible dissemination of results and deposition of the data and specimens accumulated. These are summarized in Table 2.1 (Danks 1996).

Table 2.1
The steps needed in planning a practical survey of invertebrate diversity (after Danks 1996, referring particularly to insects)

1. Clear definition of objectives and specific questions to be answered.
2. Gathering existing background information relevant to the specific study and for its comparative appraisal.
3. Development of an overall plan to assume that the funds and personnel needed will be available for a sufficient period.
4. Defining the level of detail, especially the extent of taxonomic appraisal, needed.
5. Site selection and characterization.
6. Taxon selection.
7. Duration of the study.
8. Selection of sampling methods.
9. Quality control of sampling, including trap maintenance and replication.
10. Sorting and preparing samples.
11. Identifying material.
12. Managing the data accumulated.
13. Curation and disposition of specimens.
14. Reporting, publication and dissemination of information.

Levels of interest in practical conservation

The species

Many invertebrate taxa have been nominated on various 'Red Lists' and other listings of priority taxa for conservation because they need attention to assure their survival in relation to actual or perceived threats. The *IUCN Red List of threatened species* (1996) nominates some 2000 such taxa, and it is recognized widely that these may represent only a minute proportion of species which are likely to be threatened. Only three groups have been appraised to even a reasonable extent. The 1996 list includes more than 900 molluscs, but those assessed represent only a small proportion of the 70 000 or so known species. The other groups predominant in the Red List are insects (more than 500 species) and inland freshwater crustaceans (more than 400 species). The latter are important in reflecting the common notion that freshwater invertebrates may be generally at rather high risk.

The needs for designing conservation schemes for these species, as for others, are reflected in Fig. 2.1. Quantitative data are needed to establish the initial status of the taxon(a) as a basis for defining conservation need and, thus, for all subsequent conservation action. Such preliminary work may lead to commitment of limited financial resources and expertise for which there is substantial competitive demand, and thereby deprive other deserving taxa of badly needed support. The major need as management proceeds is to determine its success and to refine/optimize it in response to trends in the target species. As in other ecological studies, clear baseline data may be needed as a standard for assessing subsequent changes by regular monitoring.

Continued inspection is thereby of critical importance, and the components of management relate also to the kind of threat(s), their duration, and the difficulties of countering their effects, and the approaches are noted in Chapter 8. Such species-focused conservation operations need to be undertaken with considerable care, and may also involve aspects of *ex situ* conservation such as captive breeding for release to the wild after sites have been rehabilitated. Protocols for this are only gradually being developed (New 1995*a*). Each protocol necessarily draws heavily on knowledge of the species ecology and population dynamics, which is often very limited.

Essentially, for a single taxon, the problems involve trying to assess risks to survival and countering these constructively and for the long term. Examples of the practical questions asked in single species studies, most of which can be formulated as testable hypotheses, therefore include:

1. Taxonomic. How is the taxon recognized and diagnosed? Is it a discrete entity, and definable clearly as a species/subspecies or distinctive population?
2. Distributional. Where does it occur? Has its range and/or the number of populations declined and, if so, why? Does it occur along definable environmental gradients, and can any pattern of incidence be found?
3. Population size and form. How abundant is it? Are its numbers stable or declining and, if the latter, is it threatened with local or broader-scale extinction? What is the population structure? What are the patterns of 'normal' fluctuation in time and space?

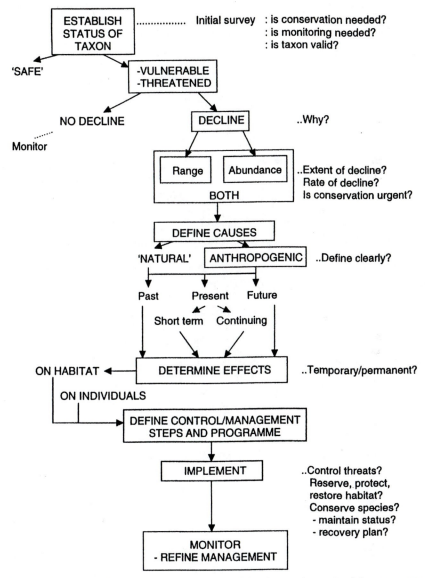

Fig. 2.1 The practical steps in planning conservation of a single species (after New 1995a), with some of the questions posed at different stages.

4. Ecology. What is the taxon's life cycle and phenology? What are its critical needs for resources, and can these be managed to promote its well-being?

5. Management. If practical management is needed for conservation, how should this be undertaken? Is any form of *ex situ* conservation (captive breeding) needed, together with translocation to new sites? Is legal

protection needed, and can it be enforced? Are the threats over, continuing or anticipated? Can threats be controlled or ameliorated? Can the taxon be monitored effectively to detect changes in status and refine management as needed?

6. Support. What field and laboratory methodology is needed to address the questions posed? Can the programme planned be supported by adequate finance and expertise? Are there local experts or interest groups whose help could be enlisted?

Additionally, it may be necessary to select objectively the 'most deserving' species for priority attention from among a wide array of possible candidates.

Much of the above scheme may be approached initially by seeking out whatever information is available in published studies, and appraising any historical data on decline. Studies on related taxa may furnish useful background information on methods and approaches to the study.

Species assemblages and local faunas

Many parameters used to evaluate the degree of distinctiveness or importance of a site or habitat depend on knowledge of the fauna present, and comparing it with that of other areas. The most useful criteria involving invertebrates are diversity, incidence and number of 'rare' species, 'naturalness' (or typicalness), and representativeness, but many other criteria are incorporated into wildlife conservation values for sites (see Margules and Usher 1981; Usher 1986). These criteria are related to area of habitat, as one of the most significant general parameters for establishing reserves. Where knowledge permits, assessment of endemicity is also important. Surveys of particular invertebrate groups are important in assessing these criteria and in helping to characterize habitats/sites with high diversity or high special conservation significance in terms of the taxa present.

The practical questions asked in studies of assemblages, communities and ecosystems include:

1. Diversity. How many species are present? What are they, and to what extent is it necessary to identify them formally? To what level? Are any taxa of particular conservation significance?

2. How can species richness be determined? What sampling methods/frequency/intensity/duration (collectively, sampling effort) is needed, and can the costs (both of sampling and sample processing) be supported? What are the precise questions which need to be answered by the sampling regime? In particular, is it possible or necessary to sample to obtain the highest possible proportion of species present (e.g. for total

inventory studies or compilation of species lists)? Can particular groups be used as some form of surrogate for more comprehensive appraisal? Can restricted samples replace a more comprehensive regime? Are sampling methods sufficiently standardized to facilitate comparison with data from other sites, or over time at the same site? Is adequate notice taken of likely seasonal differences in species richness? Are 'one-off' or repeated samples needed?

3. What is the relative abundance of the taxa present? Has this changed, or the species composition changed over the period of the study?

4. How does the richness/spectrum/abundance of the taxa present relate to the resources available in the habitat, and how does it compare with other habitats or sites?

5. Which of the higher taxonomic groups present may be incorporated into future monitoring to detect either changes in environmental quality or changes in biodiversity? How can or should these be monitored?

Critical faunas

Locally, nationally, and globally, the approach of designating 'critical faunas' has been valuable in helping to clarify priorities for designation of protected areas using invertebrates.

The approach developed for some groups of butterflies (Danainae: Ackery and Vane-Wright 1984; Papilionidae: Collins and Morris 1985) is adaptable for other groups and at a variety of geographical scales. With the Papilionidae (swallowtails and their allies), for example, Collins and Morris tabulated the numbers of species present in each country and the number of endemic species. Starting with the country with the highest number of endemic species (Indonesia) they added successively countries with the greatest numbers of endemics in a sequence of maximum complementarity (that is, of species unrepresented in higher ranked countries); part of their table (Table 2.2) shows that the 'top 5' countries contain about half of all the 573 swallowtail species, so that if *only* the faunas of those countries could be conserved effectively, a high proportion of the family would be secure. Extending the list to 10 countries incorporates nearly 68% of the species, but 51 country faunas need attention to ensure the conservation of at least one population of every species. Complex archipelagos, such as Indonesia and the Philippines, can be analysed further, at the level of island endemics to provide a finer focus, and each subregion could then be assessed by representation of species in existing protected areas to consider their adequacy in providing safe habitats. Unfortunately, though, the latter kind of information is unavailable for most invertebrates—even for such conspicuous taxa as the largest butterflies—in the tropics, and obtaining it is an urgent need to help in assessing the

Table 2.2
The principle of 'critical faunas': countries listed by sequence for swallowtail butterflies, commencing with country with the greatest number of endemic species, then adding countries with successively lower numbers of endemic species for maximum complementarity (after Collins and Morris 1985)

Order	Country	No. swallowtail species		
		Endemic	Total	Cumulative Total
1	Indonesia	53	121	121
2	Philippines	21	49	146
3	China	15	104	222
4	Brazil	11	74	296
5	Madagascar	10	13	309
6	India	6	77	323
7	Mexico	5	52	365
8	Taiwan	5	32	370
9	Malaysia	4	56	375
10	Papua New Guinea	4	37	387

conservation of many areas for invertebrates and for nominating additional priority sites. At present, it is feasible to obtain and synthesize this information for only a few invertebrate groups, but the principles and use of this approach need effective consideration, if only to corroborate or deny the more general 'hope' that areas with high diversity and/or high endemism in selected invertebrate groups will reflect similarly high values for other groups. At its simplest, only 'presence/absence' information is needed, rather than more quantitative data on absolute or relative abundance of the species.

Questions relevant to this approach include:

1. Which groups of invertebrates are suitable or sufficiently well documented for employment in interpreting broader-scale patterns of species richness, endemism or other aspects of distribution?

2. How can such knowledge be augmented most effectively? Are 'quality controls' in sampling, observation and identification adequate for comparative appraisal? If so, can they be implemented easily?

3. What scales of survey or distribution plotting are needed? Is there likely future need for this to change—for example, from a local to a national or regional survey? Is there provision for centralized or co-ordinated data recording, and for production of distributional data correlated with other environmental variables or features?

4. Can reliable templates of features such as taxon richness and levels of endemism, or the presence of characteristic subgroups, be provided?

5. Can the information be used to enhance/prioritize the selection of areas for future protection or increase levels of protective management in existing reserves?

The questions posed for any of the above approaches define the scope of the survey needed. Patterns of diversity, distribution, abundance and endemism are all important. However, assessment of all these features is problematical (for the reasons outlined in Chapter 1), but illuminating in revealing the variety of geographical and ecological scales which need to be appraised in an holistic programme to ensure ecological sustainability. The range of scales from global landscape to 'microscape' (Samways 1994*a*) is indeed vast, but appreciation of scale of species incidence and needs is vital in invertebrate conservation. A specialized taxon (species or larger group) may well occupy only small 'islands' in a sea/ocean of apparently suitable habitat, so that reservation of the major habitat (be it estuary, lake, forest or mountain) may fortuitously incorporate those needs but may not assure the security of the species unless they are understood and their provision assured. Designation of 'critical habitat' (incorporating the totality of resources essential to the well-being of the target taxon) in this way is an important need in practical species-level invertebrate conservation, as is the creation or restoration of suitable microhabitats, when necessary. As one example, butterflies and other insects on the northern fringes of their European range in southern England may need to occupy south-facing slopes in order to satisfy their thermal needs (Warren 1993), and creation of additional sites (perhaps involving substantial physical alteration using explosives or bulldozers in reserves: Thomas 1983) may be an important management tool. Creation of 'refuge habitats' is often important in maintaining invertebrate diversity in areas subject to change. Consideration of key environmental needs is an integral part of such management.

Approaches to invertebrate surveys

Surveys for invertebrates differ substantially in purpose and emphasis, and range from general to highly specific (Table 2.3; Sheppard 1991). Two rather different approaches to multispecies survey dominate considerations of invertebrates in conservation, and both emphasize the species richness and abundance in communities. The first approach, the more comprehensive, aims to indicate the *total fauna* of selected groups present, to provide an inventory for a habitat or site. For most groups, this is extraordinarily difficult and complete data can be approached only for well-known and easily sampled taxa for which specialist aid may be available, and by sampling by a variety of methods over an extended period. The second approach, the more usual, is *sample-based* and relies on interpreting standard (or, at least, replicable) samples in which diversity and abundance is taken to represent that of the site, and which can be extrapolated to compare or rank sites. This may form the basis of 'baseline' or 'pre-impact' data for evaluating effects of later changes, be repeated as the disturbance ensues, or be used to monitor

Table 2.3
Categories of invertegrate surveys (after Sheppard 1991)

Inventory surveys	Aim to determine what is there, and whether there are significant features of species incidence, diversity or community size/ structure.
Site comparisons	Comparison of series of sites. Ranking of sites in terms of invertebrate fauna or some taxonomic subset(s) of this.
Management evaluation	Aim to evaluate the influence of planned management on invertebrates.
Impact assessment	Requires predictions about the effect of specified proposed activities on invertebrates.
Rare species surveys	Evaluation of current status of particular rare or notable taxa on sites, perhaps in relation to defining critical habitat or reservation or other protection.

restoration or rehabilitation after disturbance. It follows that the extent of quantification of samples is critical, and this must be addressed early in planning because of the costs involved and generated by later analysis and sorting. At one extreme, simple confirmation of the presence of particular taxa may be adequate. At the other, much more extensive and rigid sampling regimes may be needed to provide for quantifying relative abundance of all (or a substantial subset) of the taxa present.

The major objectives of an initial survey are to discover what species (or higher groups) are present at a site, and their abundance. Commonly, a general, more superficial survey of a large area may precede quantitative sampling (Elliott 1977), and results from such preliminary work may be very helpful in formulating the final sampling regime. The number and size of samples needed can often be decided confidently only after such initial investigation. Preliminary insight into densities, diversity, distribution trends and ecological gradients in the system under study can markedly improve the final design of a sampling regime.

In general, three basic questions have dominated much research on invertebrate assemblages in recent years (after Burd et al. 1990):

1. What is the most efficient and accurate way to identify and describe the faunal status of a sample?

2. How can the faunal representation of samples be differentiated from each other over time and space?

3. How do natural and anthropogenic variables affect the faunal status of samples, and how can these be distinguished?

Answers to these depend on reliable sampling, but that reliability is often assumed rather than measured directly. Among the major sources of error in sampling, Resh (1979) noted the four major categories as:

(1) Choice and operation of sampling devices;

(2) Physical features of the environment;

(3) Field and laboratory sorting procedures; and

(4) Biological features of the study organisms themselves.

Although he was writing particularly on benthic taxa, similar caveats are universal.

Definition of scope

The aims of the survey and the target group(s) of taxa to be appraised will dictate the range of sampling techniques and designs which can be employed, but each group of invertebrates can be collected by a range of different methods and it is not always easy to define the 'best' one(s) for a given context. The scope and objectives of the study help to determine the optimal methods needed (Table 2.1).

The two major contexts may be thought of as 'extensive studies' and 'intensive studies'. The former are undertaken over a large area (to determine the distribution or relative abundance of taxa over a range) or have a broad taxonomic or ecological base (typified by faunistic or inventory-type surveys), whereas the latter involve more detailed study of population fluctuations or distributional changes of a species in a given area. Linked with the survey objectives, details of subsequent statistical analyses to be applied and needs for comparison with other (actual or anticipated) studies must also be assessed in the planning phase. Historically, many invertebrate surveys and sampling programmes seem to have been undertaken with little consideration for subsequent analysis and comparative interpretation. Their long-term value is sometimes minimal. The need for replicated sampling is sometimes overlooked or minimized because of the high costs of sampling and analysis, but replication is essential to answer many key questions of interest (Danks 1996). As Southwood (1978) emphasized, difficulties may arise because of the virtual impossibility of sampling the many different species equally efficiently by any single method—in itself an endorsement of the need to employ a suite of methods in any extensive survey (p. 107). In addition, experts in any particular taxonomic group of invertebrates may disagree over the validity or uses of a particular sampling technique for providing realistic samples. The degree of reliance on pitfall traps for making definitive collections of ground-foraging ants, for example, is open to question, although the method is used very extensively. The same is true for carabid beetles, despite major conclusions on their distributions, and site evaluations based solely on animals captured by this method. Adis (1979) listed 18 main sources of error for pitfall traps (p. 55), and most of these are not considered objectively in most published studies, even though they may bias heavily the interpretation of results and the spectrum of taxa captured, as well as their relative numbers—so that most of the basic assumptions of the survey may be untenable. Many of the studies relying on pitfall traps to interpret local faunas are thus extremely difficult to compare—and similar cautions are needed for many invertebrate sampling methods.

The needs for site-based or sample-based surveys and plotless samples (p. 25) relate to the needs of extensive or intensive surveys, and also for absolute or relative estimates of numbers. Absolute estimates necessitate gaining information on numbers and density in relation to a definable habitat, whereas relative estimates of populations are in unknown units and involve methods yielding 'presence/absence' or 'catch/unit effort' information, or various forms of trapping without regard to habitat area. Such studies permit comparisons in space and time.

Surveys thus need to be designed in relation to the sampling methods employed or available, the duration of the study, and the levels of taxonomic and ecological analysis needed to answer specific, focused questions. These will be dictated in part by the funding available, the nature of the habitats and fauna of the sites(s) under investigation, and the expertise of the practitioners. In particular, use of 'standard' techniques allows for comparison across sites and sampling occasions but, as Yen (1993) emphasized, it is not always possible to use fully standardized techniques, and some form of adaptability is commonly needed. Techniques and protocols used in any survey should be described carefully if these depart in any significant details from published accounts. The scale of survey is usually a major consideration. Bouwman (1987) noted that, although meiofaunal surveys necessitate the same considerations as macrofaunal surveys, their scale may be in centimetres, rather than metres. 'Diversity measures' may intrinsically compare habitat heterogeneity of different sites as a determinant of the number of taxa present, rather than different site areas themselves—which may be assumed to be similar in the resources they provide.

Single species studies necessitate sufficient extensive and intensive work to determine status, and changes in status, of taxa which are usually rare and/or elusive, so that even confirming the presence of the species may involve long-term and thorough searching. In their study of a rare lycaenid butterfly in Australia, for example, Britton et al. (1995) sighted only about five individuals in three full flight seasons of field work. If searches for such elusive species are not exhaustive, as when undertaken by sampling over only part of the flight season or time they may be present, absence may be real or simply reflect sampling inadequacy—but even massively increased sampling may not guarantee discovery of the target species. Deciding how much effort is warranted to detect such species is a complex exercise (McArdle 1990).

Wherever possible the data must be quantified. At one extreme, simple numbers of taxa (species or higher group richness) may be needed to give data on relative diversity. Simple 'presence/absence' information may be all that is required and single collections may be sufficient. Information on the relative abundance of taxa demands more rigid and extensive sampling to establish quantitative baselines, and determining changes in such relative abundance or species incidence involves progressively more complex and long-term studies. Obtaining good estimates of changes in invertebrate diversity, population size, age structure or standing crop may be especially difficult and necessitate investigation of spatial distribution. Contiguous distributions (p. 33), in particular, can be associated with considerable variation between samples and their effects can be reduced by bulking samples on any sampling occasion.

There is probably no single 'right' approach to sampling invertebrates on any broad scale, but many of the methods used commonly are noted in the next chapters. Many of them merit critical scrutiny to understand them better. Even the term 'sample' needs clear definition in a survey. It may be equivalent, for example, to:

1. One unit of sampling effort, such as a single benthic grab, substrate core or pitfall trap catch.
2. The total from a series of such units, either in standard replications or amalgamated more casually; bulking of sample units may be space- or time-based, so that units from several samples or several sampling occasions may be amalgamated. Thus, an array of pitfall traps can each be treated as a single sample, or the catches of all the traps on a site or subsite (plot) bulked for a trapping occasion or a series of occasions. Such bulking leads to loss of the finer details of spatial or temporal distribution, but may be justified if the aim is inventory without need for those finer details. 'Space-bulking' can be used where effects of impacts on a large scale (such as pollution effects in estuaries versus open water) are of interest, and helps to reduce the effects of short-term variation at individual sites. 'Time-bulking' can counter influences of short-term fluctuations at any site for comparison with others. Duration of trapping is also important, and must be standardized in comparative work. A pitfall trap operated for 10 days is likely to catch more than one operated for 3 days: analyses such as 'number of organisms/trap day' are then needed to standardize for sampling effort.
3. All the data from a particular site.
4. The total complement of a taxon across all available sample units (Burd et al. 1990).

These are not always distinguished clearly in reports.

Problems of measuring and interpreting species richness, as a parameter commonly assumed to be ecologically important and (by non-practitioners) easy to determine, were discussed by Coddington *et al.* (1991). The two major approaches to collecting such data both provide problems, but are complementary. These approaches are:

1. Samples collected by systematists. These may represent the species richness of an area reasonably well, but may be difficult to appraise statistically.

2. Samples collected more specifically to answer ecological questions. Analysis of these is often reasonably straightforward, to satisfy a rigid sampling programme, but the *total* fauna may be only poorly represented, and the information gained may not be extrapolated easily to other contexts.

The details of a sampling programme therefore differ in relation to primary objectives of survey, collection or monitoring (Phillips and Segar 1986). They may include:

(1) number of sampling sites;

(2) location of sampling sites;

(3) number of samples; or

(4) period of survey.

Sampling and analytical techniques need to be developed hand-in-hand, presupposing that aims and hypotheses can be stated clearly. As for sampling methods 'researchers....can be simply overwhelmed by the variety and complexity of analytical methods available' (Burd *et al.* 1990). Emphasis on statistical analysis may predispose workers to use methods that can be controlled adequately in definable sampling units such as plots or quadrats, but such methods (which minimize variability between samples) may be unsuitable for many taxa. By contrast, 'collectors' (as exemplified by trained museum personnel in Coddington *et al.*'s 1991 essay) typically aim (and are trained) to maximize the number of taxa obtained in a site over a short period. A site may be visited only once, perhaps only for a few hours or—at most—a few days. The emphasis of collectors is to sample as many habitats as possible with little quantitative regard for sampling effort or intensity, merely changing as soon as a 'good series' is apparently captured or when the workers feel 'ready to move on'. These approaches thereby address different levels of diversity: (1) the first provides more complete 'species lists' with little other information except fortuitously, and (2) the second may provide for greater valid comparison between samples by defining sampling effort (even though the method(s) may be deficient) and allows for estimates of relative abundance and its changes between sampling occasions. For any such exercise, a primary aim is to maximize return for the efforts and cost outlayed.

Coddington and his colleagues (1991) stressed the need to develop 'hit-and-run techniques', incorporating plotless samples, to combine these approaches effectively, especially for diverse tropical faunas and areas where extended sampling may not be practicable. Despite the undoubted attractions of such approaches, Danks (1996) has cautioned that local diversity cannot be characterized unless the sample data are more-or-less comprehensive, and that hit-and-run techniques are likely to be inadequate except for superficial assessments. Such methods must be fast, reliable (to provide bases for comparison and generalization beyond the site where the information was gathered), simple, and cheap. Cheapness is important because needs are greatest in regions where sophisticated scientific infrastructure may not be available, but all these features are important guides to developing practical sampling protocols for invertebrates. The following points were regarded by Coddington *et al.* (1991) as important in doing this.

1. Collecting methods used consistently by museum systematists for any groups should be incorporated into inventory procedures with as little modification as possible.

2. The number of collecting methods should be as few as possible, and divisions of microhabitats should be as simple as possible in order to minimize sampling complexity.

3. The sampling protocol should work adequately in plotless and plot-based sampling situations. For example, time spent sampling may be a good basis for measuring sampling intensity in many cases, simply because it is easy to do in the field.

4. The sampling unit should be large enough to yield adequate numbers (individuals and/or species) within samples, but small enough that the number of separate samples can be large enough for valid statistical treatment.

5. Data should be collected in forms in which variations can be estimated and analysed.

6. Data on the numbers of individuals and species taken should be able to be combined to produce species abundance distributions, which can be used to estimate species richness.

7. If possible, the analysis should produce confidence intervals on the estimates produced.

In developing a survey or monitoring programme whose results are to be used by non-biologists, clarity of presentation is very important. Thus, for

Table 2.4
Ingredients for a clear report on benthic invertebrate surveys for use by non-biologists (from Stark 1985)

1. Descriptive analysis of macroinvertebrate communities.
2. Site descriptions and measurements of physicochemical factors likely to influence macroinvertebrate community composition.
3. Pictorial methods of data presentation (histograms, 'pie-charts', graphs) with raw data as appendices.
4. Single sample analysis (such as diversity indices) to reduce complex information to single numbers, which can be used to rank sites or evaluate site status.
5. Multivariate analyses (dendrograms, ordinations) for assessing spatial or temporal changes, and comparing control and treated sites. Where possible, at least two complementary methods of analysis are useful.
6. Identification of environment factors responsible for the observed biological patterns.
7. Interpreting the results into practical recommendations with direct application to resource management.

water management, Stark (1985) listed several means to facilitate interpretation of a study of benthic invertebrates (Table 2.4).

Setting priorities

The above criteria incorporate many of the basic needs of sound inventory surveys. However, it is impracticable—other than in the most general terms—to attempt to produce definitive data on *all* groups of invertebrates at any given site. Particular groups of invertebrates are selected for more detailed investigation in most surveys, and the choice of group(s) will reflect the kind and diversity of habitats sampled, as well as ecological and logistic considerations. This selection is a complex but important issue in many invertebrate studies. It commonly represents a compromise between scientific relevance and feasibility (Danks 1996). Many sampling techniques (Chapters 3 and 4) collect enormous numbers of individuals, representing many higher taxa, and total analysis is simply impossible without massively greater resources than are usually available. Few, if any, such surveys have been analysed completely to species level for all the invertebrate groups present.

The groups selected may be dictated by the availability of cooperating specialists, personal interests or idiosyncrasies of the practitioner, or prior selection in relation to particular aims or hypotheses demanded. Groups with different feedings habits, diversity and habitat needs may well have different values in answering the survey's focal demands. Selection of target groups is not merely expedient—even if guided by expediency in many cases; it may well dictate the kinds of sampling method to be used and the schedules for processing and analysing samples (Chapter 6). Selection of optimal groups is discussed later (Chapter 7), but it is essential that the targeted groups (or species) convey as much as possible of the information needed on the sites or habitats they frequent (Brooks 1993a). Selection of particular target groups thus incorporates ecological background, the readiness with which they can be sampled reliably, and longer-term expediency such as the ease of specimen treatment, identification and adequate interpretation. Criteria for selecting such groups from the wide array usually available vary from context to context, but New (1993, 1994, 1995a) suggested a broad 'umbrella suite' of invertebrate taxa useful in a broad range of conservation assessments, and these (all at phylum level) may be useful in providing a first-level selection by relatively de-emphasizing many other invertebrate groups because of paucity of knowledge relevant to their use in broader conservation programmes. Greatest advances in quantifying invertebrate biodiversity may well come from focusing efforts as effectively as possible to help overcome the taxonomic and ecological impediments noted in Chapter 1, and there is need to debate the merits and drawbacks of this approach rather than merely 'counting everything that is there', in the interests of effective evaluation and comparison.

Principles for selecting priority groups, and the groups of importance, have been nominated by several workers. As examples, three large groups, molluscs, crustaceans and polychaete worms, constitute high proportions of marine benthic invertebrate faunas and are sufficiently diverse and ecologically complex to reflect local conditions (Jones 1993); and for terrestrial faunas, Kremen et al. (1993) have queried whether arthropods, alone, might provide for virtually all realistic needs in conservation assessment. Brooks (1993a) stressed that the groups should include ecological specialists with exacting habitat requirements, should be accessible to sampling by standard means and must be taxonomically tractable. Di Castri et al. (1991) advocated representation of species-rich and species-poor groups and abundant and rare groups. Danks (1996) commented that 'work should normally be done on a relevant but taxonomically and ecologically diverse subset of the taxa collected', and warned of the dangers of concentrating on too few groups because they might not provide adequate answers. New's (1993, 1994) broad suite of phyla was based on a range of ecological and logistic considerations and perceived advantages over other groups: (1) all major ecosystems need to be represented, and groups selected included marine, freshwater and terrestrial taxa and ones transcending these in various combinations; (2) diverse ways of life, with trophic levels and feeding guilds replicated, and including indicator groups suitable for monitoring significant ecological interactions and roles; (3) groups mainly widespread but with large numbers of local endemics to reveal critical faunas or diversity centres, and facilitating informative comparison between different regions; (4) most groups diverse and with at least some sections well understood taxonomically; (5) amenable to standard, simple and replicable sampling techniques; (6) with defined or definable pragmatic values helpful in gaining public sympathy, and omitting many of the groups for which public prejudice is high; (7) for which there is a 'critical mass' of scientific expertise and potential for international/global cooperation and co-ordination of effort; and (8) where substantial institutional collections are available to help provide distribution and status information for determining patterns of diversity and distribution. Selection of groups for particular purposes, such as indicators in given environments (Chapter 7) should also be considered, but is often used in more restricted situations than broad assessment of diversity (Stork 1991; Pearson 1994; New 1995a).

However, two rather different contexts involving selection of focal groups tend to become conflated, and should be distinguished clearly in practical study. Any taxonomic group may be treated as an entity in its own right, and the sole focus of a study. More broadly, though, it may be taken either as some form of surrogate to mirror changes in a wider array of groups as a consequence of environmental change (that is, as indicator taxa) or to reflect overall diversity or complexity of an assemblage (that is, as 'predictors': Kitching 1993).

The level of selection may be relevant in both contexts. Because of the impracticability of assessing all members of large phyla, such as Arthropoda, concentration on particular orders, families or other defined subsets is necessary. However, *any* group will need a number of approaches to effective collecting or sampling, usually involving a combination of sampling methods as a 'sampling set' (Disney 1986) or a 'sampling package' (Stork 1994) (Chapter 5). Many collecting techniques for invertebrates are habitat-based, and the two following chapters outline many of the methods employed, to point out their principles and their relative strengths and weaknesses. For many techniques, calibrating effectiveness is difficult, despite its importance in comparative appraisal. Writing on Malaise traps (p. 41), for example, Darling and Parker (1988) commented 'it is disconcerting how few comparative studies have been done to assess their collecting efficiency', and similar remarks could be advanced for most of the other methods which are used in many attempts to sample invertebrates. Yet, 'efficiency' is assumed commonly to be high, and is the basis for much streamlining of sampling regimes for Rapid Biodiversity Assessment (RBA) and in more comprehensive analyses; this topic is discussed in Chapter 5.

Rapid biodiversity assessment

The need for RBA has arisen directly as a consequence of invertebrate diversity, with the realization that total taxonomic interpretation of large numbers of accumulated samples is impossible (Beattie *et al.* 1993), and aims, in part, to minimize formal taxonomic content (Chapter 6) in employing invertebrates as tools to assess environmental quality (perhaps especially for water: Resh *et al.* 1995) and as mirrors of overall diversity. A major aim is to try to make invertebrate surveys more cost-effective, by focusing on particular procedures or taxonomic groups (Oliver and Beattie 1996). It has important implications in biological surveys and diversity assessments, community ecology (such as integrating the series of diversity indices, and testing the value of 'umbrella groups'), environmental monitoring, and resource management but, as Beattie *et al.* (1993) emphasized, 'packages' of tested and replicable sampling procedures for most invertebrate surveys have not yet been designed or adopted. A possible exception to this is for freshwater benthic macroinvertebrates, for which a substantial number of measures and protocols for RBA exist (Resh and Jackson 1991), especially for small shallow streams. Equivalent procedures for larger streams and lakes still need development.

The measures are sometimes: (1) based on simple generalizations, such as taxon richness generally decreasing with decreasing water quality, so that the number of taxa (species, genera, families, orders), alone, is measured, or (2) that the number of species in selected orders (such as the insect orders Ephemeroptera, Plecoptera, Trichoptera (hence, the EPT index)) is assessed (with or without identification) on the basis that most taxa in these groups are pollution-sensitive. At one extreme, all macroinvertebrate specimens are counted with no identification, on the basis that low benthic abundance is correlated with poor water quality. Other RBA assessments are based on diversity indices for comparison between sites, or aspects of the relative abundance of different taxa reflecting changes presumed to be due to differential pollution tolerances, or functional groups; although these are commonly open to question because of poor ecological knowledge of the individual species in a higher group. Many of the published freshwater RBA approaches have been used in specific contexts and would need to be re-appraised if they were to be transferred elsewhere; a point of much more general relevance in invertebrate sampling methods.

The term 'rapid' has been used in several different ways (Trueman and Cranston 1997), so that RBA may mean:

(1) the need for answers to questions on biodiversity to be obtained quickly;
(2) speedy field surveys covering many taxa simultaneously by using multidisciplinary teams;
(3) basing diversity measures on formal taxonomic categories above the species level;
(4) basing species richness on recognizable taxonomic units, without the formal identification of species.

Different meanings may be implicit in the same legal documents (Trueman and Cranston 1997). However, ability to recognize the organisms collected to the desired level(s) of separation consistently and accurately remains a paramount need.

Sampling and analysis in RBA has two main objectives in relation to more comprehensive quantitative surveys:

1. Reduction of effort and cost, such as by reducing the numbers of habitats or sites and replicate samples in each of these; identifying and otherwise analysing only selected groups of animals rather than whole samples; and seeking taxonomic approximation where possible and appropriate, such as by identifying taxa only to genus, or sometimes to family or even higher taxonomic level, rather than always to species.

2. Summarizing the detailed results of surveys in ways which can be understood by non-specialists (Resh and Jackson 1991), for example by presenting results as 'scores' and placing these in categories of environmental quality.

Either or both of these objectives could lead to inadequate data gathering or simplistic evaluation, and continued emphasis on the need for economy must not replace the need for (preferably replicable) estimates of lasting scientific worth. Both objectives implicitly incorporate aspects of 'data reduction'. In any normal survey on invertebrate assemblages analysed to species level, the size of the resulting data matrix can be unmanageable. Hundreds of species may be present, each a row in a matrix, containing many columns (representing separate samples, or a time series), so that the analysis of species/sites/samples or times becomes very complex (Stephenson and Cook 1980). Approaches to data reduction, discussed by Burd *et al.* (1990), are themselves diverse and may involve pooling of the data or averaging of replicates, or eliminating rare species (those which occur infrequently in the samples), or using higher level taxonomic separations, as above. The parameters selected for analysis need careful consideration.

Invertebrates lend themselves particularly well to RBA approaches, because of their generally high species richness and diversity, but there is great variety in how these are explored and assessed. As with other sampling regimes, investigation of the accuracy of RBA measures is overall rather sparse. A survey by Resh and Jackson (1991) of 30 RBA protocols for benthic macroinvertebrates showed that about half the programmes involved only one or two quantitative assessments (QA). By contrast with qualitative approaches, several trends were apparent and involved many aspects of sampling practice and interpretation.

1. Kick nets (p. 89) are used commonly in RBA but less commonly in QA.

2. All habitats are sampled commonly in RBA, but in relatively few QA.

3. In both approaches, most samples are examined in their entirety, but there is a tendency for some subsampling (p. 123) in RBA, only.

4. In almost all QA, identifications were to genus and species, whereas in some RBA family-level identification only was undertaken.

5. RBA relies heavily on some form of 'biotic index' (that is, incorporating pre-established water quality tolerance values for taxa: see Metcalfe 1989), whereas QA does not.

6. Statistical testing is generally absent in RBA, but used in most QA to determine whether impact has occurred.

In this very common context simple techniques such as kick samples have considerable value. Dip nets were adopted for sampling by Chessman (1995) and Wright (1995). These techniques do not require elaborate apparatus and, therefore, are cheap. They usually catch a high proportion of total species present and, especially if employed throughout by the same collector, often provide reasonably comparable data over different samples and sites. Kick samples can be related to substrate area, and net samples can be standard-ized (at least in part) by time interval. However, kick samples cannot be used in deep water and, as they are not strictly area-based, they do not provide reliable data on densities even though the relative abundance of different taxa can be shown. In short, quantitative samples enable more adequate comparative analysis in the context of known number, size and location of sampling units. But one difficulty with many quantitative techniques, such as freeze-coring for benthic samples (Marchant and Lillywhite 1989; p. 84) is that they are complex and demand considerable labour, especially if they are to be used in remote areas. They are thus more expensive to deploy.

Background information to survey design

The most extensive investigations of sampling design and efficiency for invertebrates and most methods noted in later chapters for assessing their incidence and population levels come not from conservation studies, but from studies of pest species or commercially desirable taxa: in particular, from the development of accurate protocols to help forecast pest or harvestable commodity populations and implement optimal strategies to control them or exploit them. Literature on, for example, applied entomology and applied nematology provides the most extensive discussions of sampling these ani-mals, and 'fisheries literature' includes many appraisals of sampling or harvesting (especially) marine invertebrates and how to avoid non-target taxa and depleting stocks. Such accounts are often detailed because of the large investments and economic incentives involved, but the needs in conservation studies may be just as precise when they form the basis for decisions on which costly long-term management programmes or recovery plans are based. However, the funding available is usually much less, and one benefit of the detailed 'applied' studies is in providing comprehensive background information which helps selection of optimal techniques and sampling regimes and is not available commonly from conservation studies *per se*.

Many pest evaluation studies may be summed up by comments similar to that on nematodes by McSorley (1987), namely: 'Most applied work depends on a knowledge of nematode population densities in the field, and the accuracy of estimations of these is directly dependent on the sampling and extraction methods used'. Difficulties of achieving this state, even with considerable effort (McSorley's next sentence expresses the sentiment of pessimism by authors about obtaining such accurate estimates even by detailed sampling schemes!) underline the tenuous nature of the information on which important conservation management decisions may be based, and the need for optimal use of limited capability and funds available for invertebrate conservation work. Even for what appear to be extremely simple situations in ecological terms, such as populations of a single pest insect on a monoculture crop in a defined area, variations in population within the crop, between different plants or within each plant makes estimating the population difficult (Shelton and Trumble 1991), and a wide variety of sampling regimes is available. Virtually any recent issue of the numerous journals on applied entomology, pest control, ecology or fisheries management contains information which can be used to help refine sampling and monitoring of invertebrates in other contexts.

The other major impetus to development of invertebrate sampling techniques has been, simply, 'ecology'—the mass of information gathered during the last few decades in relation to studying the population dynamics and community/assemblage structure of invertebrates in all major habitats and ecosystems. Data on numbers, population fluctuations and the features determining distribution and abundance are the core of community and population ecology, and many 'pure' ecology studies contain much information of great value for conservation. Compendia of methods for collecting, studying and analysing invertebrate samples, such as Southwood (1978), Elliott (1977), Williams and Feltmate (1993), Edwards (1991), Rounsefell (1975), Hobbs and McIntyre (1984), Burd *et al.* (1990) and others, and more general volumes on ecological techniques (such as Sutherland 1996) are invaluable sources of the information often incorporated implicitly into very brief statements on methodology in published studies on invertebrate surveys. Older works on sampling methods are often still of considerable value also: Welch (1948), for example, contains critical appraisal of a wide range of limnological methods.

The case noted above, of an insect on a field crop, is pertinent in considering the range of options for plot-based sampling. The *purpose* of sampling will determine from where the samples are taken. If simply seeking to determine the insect's presence, one may be guided by previous incidences or knowledge of its ecology to select 'high likelihood' areas or times and ignore others. If the need is to estimate the overall population in the habitat (crop), it is important to obtain a representative sample which minimizes any sampling bias, so that random, stratified random, or systematic samples are taken over the area. Most commonly, transect lines or quadrats form the basis for this approach. Some methods have been used for a wide variety of purposes and such considerations are critical in interpreting published results. Pitfall traps (p. 55) for carabid beetles have been employed in faunistic studies, habitat associations, population size estimations, clarifying diurnal activity patterns and seasonal patterns, species diversity studies, and population changes between years (J. Andersen 1995, Digweed *et al.* 1995) in addition to simple surveys for monitoring taxa of conservation significance. They exemplify the group of methods that can be strictly plot-based through being set out in definable and replicable patterns on a site, with number, size, spacing and other features defined, or used on a broader, less formal scale for collecting with less regard to estimating density of the taxa collected. They are thus also useful in exploratory work.

As Shelton and Trumble (1991) stated, computer graphics programs can now render integrated pictures of such data for patterns straightforward. On a smaller scale, it may be necessary to sample whole plants, or only a small part of each plant. Such 'subsampling' is an important consideration in reducing overall sampling cost (p. 123) and has been addressed comprehensively in pest assessments. At either level, the dispersion of the target species is highly relevant, and the degree of heterogeneity will influence the spatial arrangement of the sampling plan. An initial stratified-random sampling regime may be useful if no information is available on the species' dispersion; this entails dividing the habitat into equal-sized units and taking a sample randomly from each. One feature of many conservation sampling programmes, in strong contrast to many 'pest studies', is that the biology of the target taxa may not be well-known and exploratory sampling is needed to provide information on the whole 'system' being investigated and the factors which form the basis for management.

Simplistically, a species might have one of three broad patterns of distribution at a site (Fig. 2.2)—systematic, aggregated (or contiguous), or random. Systematic distributions are rare, as are true random distributions, and by far the most common dispersion pattern includes some degree of aggregation or clumped distributions, a trend which produces the greatest degree of variation in sampling results of all three patterns. Relative mobility of organisms may be important in considering sampling. Much benthic infauna is reasonably sedentary, for example, so that much of the methodology developed for spatial sampling of plant communities may be applied directly to them (Burd *et al.* 1990). Much practical conservation management for invertebrates involves determining the critical resources which are foci for aggregation or reproduction of the target taxa and enhancing or providing these actively. It

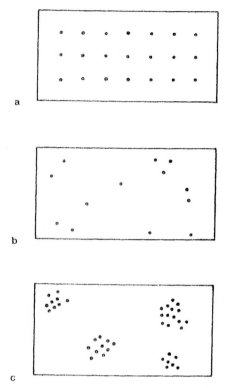

Fig. 2.2 Examples of the distribution of organisms (dots) in a sample plot (bounded). (a) Regular distribution; (b) random distribution; (c) aggregated distribution.

follows that such key resources may be reflected in a species' distribution pattern in its habitat, and one aim of sampling is often to detect such non-random distributions clearly. The number of replicate samples needed to do so will depend on the level of accuracy required, and the resources available.

If a habitat (or site) is stratified, it may be possible to use existing knowledge to eliminate patches likely to yield zero or low returns, as emphasized by Southwood (1978). Stratified random sampling is used widely in ecological surveys, and is especially useful when sampling in relation to large-scale environmental patterns, for example along gradients across a shoreline or vegetation sere, up a mountain or along a stream. Selectivity (which may or may not be desirable) and chance also play their part in designing a sampling programme.

The timing and frequency of sampling or monitoring may also be important in seeking particular invertebrates. Many taxa are very seasonal in appearance and may also show well-marked patterns of activity in relation to weather or time of day. Many butterflies, for example, are most active for only a few hours each day so that counts at the same site during different

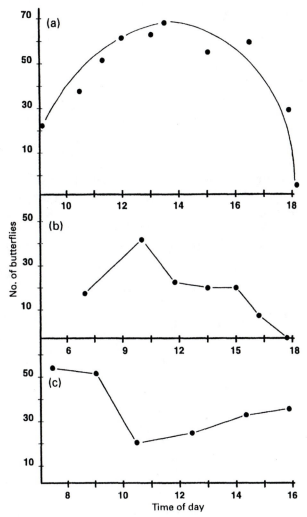

Fig. 2.3 Diurnal activity patterns of butterflies, to indicate variations in abundance estimates from counts made at different times. (a) *Aglais urticae* in Britain, 1 day, $n=465$ (after Frazer 1973); (b) *Potanthus confucius* on Anak Krakatau, Indonesia, 1 day, $n=124$ (after New and Thornton 1992); (c) *Lethe diana*, Japan, 15 days, $n=221$ (after Yamamoto 1975).

times of day may yield several-fold different results. Likewise, activity may be influenced by temperature, precipitation, wind, or sunlight, so that reliable comparative information can be obtained only under particular, similar conditions. Figure 2.3 indicates the kinds of diurnal pattern which can be exhibited by particular butterflies, and figures for species richness at a site (as well as the incidence and abundance of particular taxa) can differ at different times of the day. Parallel changes may occur in benthic assemblages in relation to tidal or daily cycles. Comparative samples must be taken at similar times, and sampling frequency may need to incorporate such variations.

To be truly representative of the environment they purport to represent, invertebrate surveys must take into account patterns of phenology and activity, as well as larger variations due to biological factors (such as migration) or environmental differences (such as seasonal flushing of aquatic systems), in addition to the overall heterogeneity of the environment at any time. Related to this is a clear understanding of the limits of the entity being sampled. In particular, some species associations may be reasonably stable and persistent and these can be particularly valuable in characterizing assemblages and as indicators of change. Others may be more transient or sporadic. Discrete communities may indeed be difficult to define, and even their incidence (versus a continuum of systems) is still debated. Sampling programmes may reflect the personal philosophy, expertise, and experience of the individual practitioner (Burd *et al.* 1990), but parameters such as 'diversity' are concerned directly with the species composition of some category of ecological unit and this must be reflected as accurately as feasible in the samples interpreted. Using accessible sites reduces costs of sampling, and using discrete habitats aids in replication. However, the sites for biodiversity surveys must be fully representative of the systems being studied in order for the questions to be answered satisfactorily (Danks 1996).

Finally, the size of any particular target animals can influence the choice of

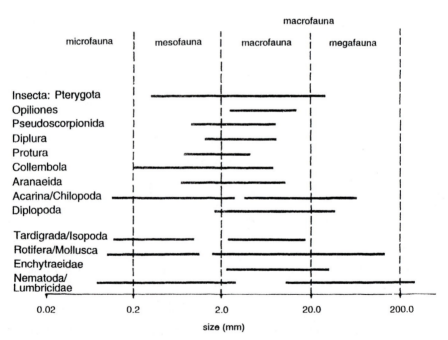

Fig. 2.4 Characterization of soil invertebrates by size into faunal groups (based on van der Drift 1951).

sampling and extraction methods and the efficiency with which they are used. Indeed, size can be the over-riding consideration in determining the sampling regime used. In benthic fauna, for example, predominant methods for 'macrofauna' (defined commonly as animals retained by a 0.5 mm mesh grid, but see p. 128) and 'meiofauna' (which pass through such a sieve) differ (Chapter 4). For soil fauna, van der Drift's (1951) artificial but functionally useful size categories are adopted widely (Fig. 2.4). 'Mesofauna' must be assessed by extraction procedures (p. 63), whereas 'macrofauna' are usually clearly visible and can be sorted adequately by hand. However, such complexity is reflected in a general lack of methods which enable simultaneous assessment of the various taxonomic groups present, and the generally high labour requirements of methods for isolating and assessing soil invertebrates (Gorny and Grum 1993). As these authors emphasized, the principle (equally true for all other habitats and taxa) is to foster flexibility and adaptation of sampling methods as necessary.

Parasites: a special case

Most of this book refers particularly to free-living invertebrates, as those predominantly involved in surveys and for practical conservation. However, parasitic invertebrates, many of them intricately linked with particular host taxa, are also diverse.

Virtually any vertebrate species hosts one or more species of parasitic invertebrate, and these have only rarely been considered in conservation. Because many are host-specific, and may depend also on one or more intermediate vector species to complete their life cycle, defining critical resource needs can be difficult. Parasite well-being depends on the well-being of their hosts. Likewise, other close associations between species, such as the many epizooic taxa found on marine and freshwater molluscs and crustaceans, are commonly dismissed in conservation considerations. However, more 'tangible' parasites, such as the louse and flea ectoparasites of mammals and birds, and the parasitoid Hymenoptera attacking early stages of Lepidoptera are starting to appear specifically on some conservation agendas. Surveys to detect incidence and abundance of such animals necessitate use of many of the techniques noted in Chapter 3. Parasitic wasps can be detected by direct collection of the adults, but rearing of hosts from field populations is needed to determine the extent of parasitization. Early stages can be detected by dissection of preserved hosts, but specific identification of the parasitoids may be uncertain.

Collection of ectoparasites usually necessitates removing them directly from the hosts, although extraction of nest and burrow debris in Tullgren funnels (p. 64) may yield many specimens.

1. Recently dead animals can be placed in separate sealable plastic bags with a wad of cotton wool soaked in chloroform or a similar anaesthetic.

Parasites then commonly leave the host and can be collected from the bag, but brushing or combing the host after an hour or so may dislodge many others.

2. Living animals such as mist-netted birds or small trapped mammals can be treated in a similar manner except that the bag is sealed around their neck to avoid asphyxiation. The white cloth bags in which such animals are commonly transported may well contain parasites from their most recent occupants. Note that special permits may be needed to trap and handle vertebrates in this way, and any such need should be investigated well in advance of any planned survey.

Collection of endoparasites, such as intestinal worms, involves direct dissection and searching of the hosts. Many such parasites decay very rapidly after the demise of the hosts, and special preservation of host organs may be necessary.

Further reading

Beattie, A. J. (ed.) (1993). *Rapid biodiversity assessment.* Macquarie University, Sydney.

Danks, H. V. (1996). *How to assess insect biodiversity without wasting your time.* Biological Survey of Canada (Terrestrial Arthropods) Document Series No. 5, Ottawa.

Elliott, J. M. (1977). *Some methods for the statistical analysis of samples of benthic invertebrates.* Freshwater Biological Association, Scientific Publication No. 25. Ambleside.

Goldsmith, F. B. and Harrison, C. M. (1976). Description and analysis of vegetation. In *Methods in plant ecology* (ed. S. B. Chapman), pp. 85–155. Blackwell Scientific, Oxford.

Green, R. H. (1979). *Sampling design and statistical methods for environmental biologists.* John Wiley, New York.

Holme, N. A. and McIntyre, A. D. (ed.) (1984). *Methods for the study of marine benthos.* Blackwell Scientific, Oxford.

Samways, M. J. (1994). A spatial and process sub-regional framework for insect and biodiversity conservation research and management. In *Perspectives on insect conservation* (ed. K. J. Gaston, T. R. New, and M. J. Samways), pp. 1–28. Intercept, Andover.

Southwood, T. R. E. (1978). *Ecological methods. With particular reference to the study of insect populations.* Chapman & Hall, London.

Sutherland, W. J. (ed.) (1996). *Ecological census techniques: a handbook.* Cambridge University Press, Cambridge.

3 Sampling invertebrates: terrestrial environments

Introduction to sampling methods

This is the first of two chapters that introduce some of the equipment and practical tools which may be used to sample invertebrates by collecting and extracting them from samples of habitat, such as soil, vegetation or freshwater or marine sediments. The separate major invertebrate habitats, which demand rather different sets of apparatus and approaches for sampling them effectively, are considered separately, but there are many similarities and parallels in the techniques adopted in each. Both for terrestrial and aquatic environments, these range from simple 'collecting tools', many of which have their antecedents as traditional collectors' accessories rather than as 'scientific apparatus', to carefully designed quantitative or semiquantitative techniques. The available techniques therefore range from the simple to the complex.

No attempt is made to provide a comprehensive appraisal of the innumerable variations which are available for some of these, and continue to proliferate in response to each perceived need or modified application. Some trap designs have undergone little change over the years, but most continue to be modified in the light of experience. Some have withstood the tests of time and detailed investigation, and are incorporated (albeit sometimes uncritically) into many sampling regimes or protocols. Others are useful only in limited, specialized contexts, or in particular habitats. Rather, I hope to explain briefly the principles involved in using a representative suite of devices in sufficient detail for the reader to assess their use, their advantages and disadvantages (including costs), and to provide sufficient background material on each to facilitate interpreting ecological literature referring to their use. Selected important references to the use of each technique and its limitations are included. Practical applications are noted in context, and use of combinations of techniques discussed in Chapter 5. A later chapter (Chapter 8) also augments these sections directly, but with less emphasis on the physical gathering of samples.

The approach adopted here follows the premise noted earlier, that sampling invertebrates will be an exercise new to many people now involved in attempts to measure and monitor organismal diversity, and that the 'essentials' are more important to communicate than every refinement of a widely used technique. Nevertheless, many of the biases noted are important in determining the integrity of results and, thus, interpreting many published data. 'Passive techniques' (which rely on the activity of the animals for capture) and 'active techniques' (where animals are actively pursued and captured) are both involved. Further, active techniques can be 'proximal' and undertaken while the investigator is present and observing the procedure (such as working on a shoreline or in a field) or 'remote' where such observations are not possible (such as sampling the benthos of deep water), and equivalent controls are difficult to incorporate. Passive techniques have the advantage, shared with remote active techniques, of removing bias due to abilities or unwitting preferences of individual collectors but their main benefit is often in reducing the labour costs of sampling.

Some of the groups of invertebrates collected regularly in sampling programmes have not yet either included specific conservation targets or been used reliably in conservation assessment. Many of the meiofauna (p. 96) seem unlikely to do so in the near future, for example, and are noted here for the sake of completeness and to indicate the full needs of invertebrate surveys, which are often not heeded. In general, at present, taxonomic subsets (p. 164) from the total sample in all major habitats provide the bulk of information relevant to practical conservation. But, with very few exceptions, the methods capture a wide variety of invertebrates, so that the information yielded from the samples would be much higher if it could be harnessed efficiently.

In practice, few biologists work in all major ecosystems, and most people seeking to sample invertebrates are likely to be operating in either terrestrial or aquatic systems, with the latter likely to be either freshwater or marine; hence the arrangement by major ecosystem adopted here. However, readers whose main interest is in one or the other of these major categories will find many parallels and similarities in approach in the other system. Although the practical opportunities for cross-linkages may be limited, broader understanding of the principles involved can be useful. In addition, as noted earlier, botanical survey techniques may be employed with little modification in studying sessile organisms or planning sampling designs. Methods for enumerating marine corals, for example, draw heavily on botanical methods and raise additional problems such as defining 'an individual' of a colonial taxon. Likewise, advances in miniaturization may soon bring techniques such as radio-tracking into the regular realm of invertebrate biology. Although such advances are more relevant to monitoring (Chapter 8), invertebrate sampling is an area of rapid development and refinement and it is important that we are not overly 'blinkered' by what has already occurred, and remain alert to any possibilities to improve sampling techniques.

Repeated references are made below to the importance of developing standardized sampling protocols and understanding the biases and inadequacies of the various techniques used. When the same apparatus is used by the same operators to compare biota in the same or similar habitats, these aspects may be standardized reasonably well. Greater difficulties arise when attempting to compare different studies, or across different habitats, as it is highly likely that the precise details of the gear employed will differ, or other aspects of sampling effort not be compared precisely. Quantitative or semi-quantitative comparison between different studies is often far more difficult than commonly assumed. The problems of formulating 'recipes' are noted later, but selection of methods for a given habitat or taxonomic group in any survey should yield the highest quality information feasible. In general '…any ideas of laying down "guide lines" or "manuals of instruction" would be unrealistic' (Muirhead-Thomson 1991) because of the continuing modifications of most techniques.

Terrestrial environments

Traps for aerial fauna

The following traps have been developed for sampling insects, the only winged invertebrates, and all are used widely in surveys. Their features are summarized in Table 3.1. Much relevant background information, including detailed descriptions of trap design and capture efficiency, is provided by Muirhead-Thomson (1991). Although used commonly for site comparisons, the principle of relying on measurements of activity and dispersal may lead to confusion because of an unknown 'tourist' component in the catches, in addition to resident taxa. All these traps depend on notoriously variable flight activity, which is often very unpredictable and influenced heavily by weather conditions. Comparisons of isolated catches must therefore be cautious, but longer periods of trapping yield data are valuable in inventory studies.

Malaise traps

The Malaise trap (Fig. 3.1) was developed as a collecting tool, and catches flying insects as they are intercepted by a vertical mesh panel. The typical pattern is of an open-sided tent, and intercepted insects fly or walk upward, under a sloping tent roof, and are guided into a collecting vessel (with or without a killing agent or preservative) at the higher end. The trap relies on the natural tendency of many phototactic insects to move upward and the essential design is a vertical central panel and a cross panel at each end, supported by poles and guy ropes with the bottom anchored by tent pegs, and a sloping roof to prevent escape of the insects as they move upward. Alternatively, it may consist of a cross of intersecting panels. Commonly, the roof is made of white mesh for light penetration, and the major panels are black or dark green so they are not as easily detected by approaching insects.

There are many variations on the basic pattern, both in size and complexity; large versions of the Malaise trap can have separate collecting vessels for

Table 3.1
Summary of advantages and disadvantages of some methods used for sampling free-living aerial insects

Method	Major target groups	Biases	Advantages	Disadvantages
Malaise traps	Flying insects	Strongly-flying larger taxa	Large catches. Cheap to maintain. Extended sampling periods	Expensive. Vulnerable to vandalism. Residents/tourists confused.
Flight intercept traps	Flying insects	Many weakly flying, smaller taxa	Large catches. High diversity. Cheap to maintain. Extended sampling periods.	May be expensive. Possible flooding of collecting vessels.
Water traps	Small insects and other arthropods; Hymenoptera, Diptera, Homoptera	Small, flying taxa:—may be colour biased;—taxa living on/near ground	Cheap. Easily standardized. Monitoring tool. Large catches.	Flooding possible. Evaporation can be high.
Bait traps	Various	Can be made specific or broader based	Highly selective for target taxa. Little 'bycatch'. Monitoring tool.	Not suitable for broader inventory surveys.
Suction traps	Flying insects	Smaller, more weakly flying insects	Large catches. High diversity. Extended sampling periods.	Expensive. Need power source. Heavy to transport.
Light traps	Nocturnal flying insects	Nocturnal fliers—used especially for moths	Large catches. Can keep alive for release. Monitoring tool.	Expensive. May need power source. Vulnerable to vandalism if unattended.

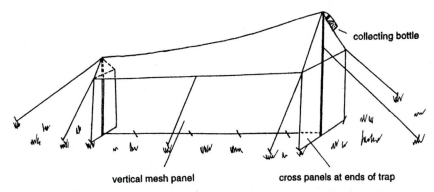

collecting bottle

vertical mesh panel   cross panels at ends of trap

Fig. 3.1 Malaise trap. A central mesh panel forms a vertical barrier into which insects fly. They move upward, under a tent roof which hampers their escape, to a roof angle and thence to the higher end of the trap where they are captured in a collecting bottle (right of diagram). The trap is supported by poles and guy ropes, and the bottom secured by tent pegs.

insects which enter from each of two or four directions, for example. Mesh size can be varied, for example to allow the escape of very small insects if these are not required, and the facility to preserve the catch in alcohol or other preservative means that the traps can be left unattended for several days to a week or more. It is therefore not labour-intensive to operate, although the relatively complex construction is expensive, and processing what can be large samples may also be costly (p. 134).

Malaise traps are conspicuous and subject to vandalism and disturbance in accessible areas; it may be necessary, for example, to fence them to exclude cattle or other large animals. They are also vulnerable to strong winds. They are useful for comparative work, if traps are standardised sufficiently (p. 113), and the very large numbers of specimens which can be captured and preserved typically include many different groups of insect. The traps are most effective if sited across natural 'flyways' such as narrow paths in woodland. More rarely, they have been erected within frames of bamboo or wooden poles for hoisting into the forest canopy on a rope and pulley system (Sweney and Jones 1975; Hammond 1991).

Many factors influence the catch composition and size. Using Malaise traps to catch Hymenoptera in Ontario, Canada, for example, Darling and Parker (1988) noted that different mesh sizes influenced the kinds of Hymenoptera captured; earlier, Townes (1972) noted that trap colour could strongly affect 'catchability' or the relative abundance of different taxonomic or functional groups of these insects, and even the cleanliness of the mesh may be important (Disney 1982). High visibility may deter some insects, and such biases are only poorly documented.

The catch is biased towards strongly flying, positively phototactic insects, and Malaise traps are usually not as effective for very small insects. However, small insects can be 'selected' by screening the catch through mesh in the collecting bottle or when removed for storage, and the bulk of samples reduced considerably.

The main uses of the Malaise trap are in initial appraisal of insect faunas in most terrestrial environments, as components of sampling in more extended surveys (including those in remote areas), and investigating patterns of seasonal variation or diversity both within and across sites.

Window traps or flight intercept traps

These, such as the one shown in Fig. 3.2 (after Peck and Davis 1980), also depend on intercepting flying or (less obviously) wind-blown insects, when they encounter a vertical panel of glass (such as house windows: Canaday 1987), clear plastic or fine mesh and drop to a sheet on the ground or into troughs of preservative or water with a 'wetting agent' (such as glycol) beneath. The vertical panel can be framed, or supported on poles or by ropes and guyed, and can be directional if needed so that catches from opposite sides can be segregated: the trap can be employed thus to estimate the relative numbers of insects entering and leaving a crop, for example. A vertical panel of netting, as used in a Malaise trap, is light and easy to transport, and collecting trays can be of light plastic or metal foil. It may be . useful to place these on a plastic sheet to avoid 'splash-back' of mud during rainy weather.

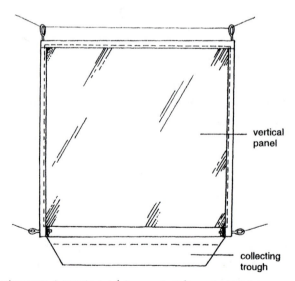

vertical panel

collecting trough

Fig. 3.2 A window trap. A translucent (glass or plastic) panel which intercepts flying insects. In this model, the frame also supports a trough of preservative into which the insects fall. The panel can be of various sizes and the trap can be placed on the ground or (as shown here) suspended on cords or a stand above the ground.

A roof, as in the Malaise trap, is incorporated into some designs, and in fine weather the trap can also be left unattended for up to a week or more. Frequent inspection may be needed in wet weather when the troughs may flood—even if fitted with drainage holes below the rim, the preservative may become too dilute to be effective. Unlike the Malaise trap, small and weakly-flying insects are captured in large numbers. The mesh wall can be treated with contact insecticide (Masner and Goulet 1981) to increase the catch of small insects such as parasitic Hymenoptera markedly.

Subject to similar possibilities of vandalism as the Malaise traps, window traps are easily standardized and cheaper to construct, although transportation of large or rigid panels in remote areas may be difficult. Non-porous panels may deflect insects in windy conditions. A combination of a small Malaise trap and a window trap was used by Basset (1988) to sample canopy arthropods in a Queensland rain forest. The two traps were suspended together in the forest canopy, so that their catches could be compared directly.

The trap is useful in broad surveys or more specific contexts, such as colonization of a habitat in which directional information is needed. It can augment Malaise trap catches in the same area by increasing representation of small flying insects.

Water traps or pan traps

Shallow glass, metal or plastic pans, trays or dishes of liquid (water or preservative) are placed on the substrate, sunk into the ground, or raised on poles above the ground; for example, at the height of a crop plant for monitoring crop pests. They can be raised at intervals as the plants grow. They can be round or angular, and of various colours and depths, standardized within a set. It is common to use traps of several different colours (such as white, yellow, green) at the same site, and organisms falling or flying into the traps are drowned and preserved. Adding soap to the water facilitates the catch sinking, and some workers have recommended supersaturated rock salt (ca. 200 g/l) as a preservative. As with the foregoing, flooding can occur, and can be countered by putting a small, mesh-covered overflow hole below the rim. Evaporation may be high in warm weather or in exposed environments and can be retarded by adding ethylene glycol, most easily in the form of commercial vehicle antifreeze. Traps may need to be inspected frequently during such weather. With these reservations though, water traps (normally 20-40 cm diameter) can be left for several days and have the advantages of being cheap, easily obtainable and readily transportable. In particularly rainy environments they can be sheltered by a 'roof' supported on sticks or pegs, and are particularly useful for small insects living near the ground or on vegetation. Large numbers of insects, together with spiders and other near-

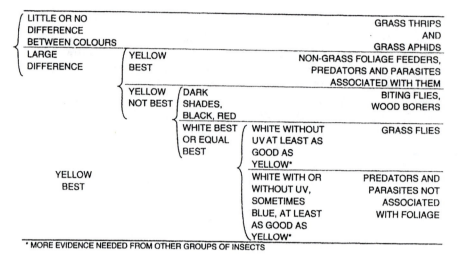

Fig. 3.3 Scheme of attractiveness of different colours of pan traps to different groups of insects (after Kirk 1984).

ground invertebrates are caught, and the colour may be critical in influencing the catch (p. 113). Large numbers of aphids and other small plant-feeding insects are attracted particularly to yellow traps, for example, and particular colours may be selected to target particular groups of insects (Fig. 3.3; Kirk 1984). Pan traps can be used both for local surveys (such as in a crop) or more extensively—such as a broad survey of peatlands in Canada (Blades and Marshall 1994), which yielded up to 870 species from each site.

Their uses therefore include surveys of many phytophagous insect groups, and small Diptera and Hymenoptera, for which colour can be an attractant. They are cheap, and can be deployed in large numbers in formal plot designs to assess distribution patterns over a site.

Bait traps

Various attractants can be employed to assess presence and abundance of selected species of invertebrates and can sometimes form the basis of surveys for broader groups. They have considerable application in monitoring some pest insects (such as fruitflies, or Lepidoptera attracted to pheromones—as are a number of important orchard pests) but can also be used in other monitoring contexts. Baits can be used independently or to increase attraction to other forms of trap, such as pitfall traps (p. 55).

Fine details of the attractant principles are not well understood for many insect groups, and baiting for many taxa is an empirical method. Functions of baits or attractant chemicals such as pheromones are complex (Ridgway *et al.* 1990). Some species of moths which are attracted to light do not come to

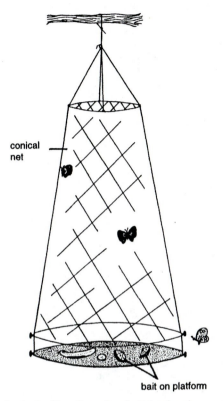

conical
net

bait on platform

Fig. 3.4 A bait trap for butterflies. Over-ripe fruit is placed on a tray suspended a short distance below a cylindrical net. Butterflies are attracted to the bait, fly upward and are trapped in the suspended net, whence they can be collected.

sugar baits, and vice versa. The operating principle is that the animals are attracted by some specific or more general chemical stimulus and move through a funnel or narrow opening into a chamber where they are held alive, or killed. Some generalized baits such as over-ripe fruits, rotting meat or fish, or dung, can attract a broad array of species. Two representative patterns are shown: Figure 3.4 shows a butterfly collector's trap, whereby butterflies (particularly, many Nymphalidae) are attracted to fruit held on a tray and then fly upward into a closed net cylinder. Figure 3.5 is a carrion trap for flies. Such traps are cheap, light, can be collapsible, and easily serviced, but are relevant in only limited conservation contexts because of their selectivity. Catches are usually small, of limited taxonomic range, and cheap to analyse. Bait traps can thus be useful in wide surveys for such insects as dung-beetles or particular families of flies. Unlike many of the other devices noted here, the material can be kept alive for release should it not be required for permanent reference.

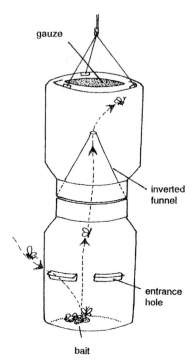

gauze

inverted
funnel

entrance
hole

bait

Fig. 3.5 A bait trap for flies. Flies are attracted to carrion or faeces in a cylindrical jar, and fly upward (towards a window panel in the roof of the trap) through a funnel into a retention chamber.

Suction traps

Suction traps (Fig. 3.6) can be used, with standardization, to provide accurate estimates of aerial insect populations, with the only critical variable being wind speed. Their operating principle is that a powered (usually, electric) fan forces air through a gauze cone which filters insects from the air column. The catch is retained either dry or in a jar of preservative. The 18-inch (45 cm) diameter propellor trap shown exemplifies the traps in which the fan unit is mounted at the bottom of a metal cylinder so that the insects are filtered before air passes through the fan. Some other patterns pass the insects through the fan first, and provide for separating the catch into hourly units by segregating the catch at intervals by a metal disc dropped into the collecting cylinder. Most flying insects are captured, although some large strongly-flying taxa may elude the fan. However, the traps are expensive, heavy, conspicuous and rely on a power source for operation. Their efficiency is also notoriously variable and extensive tests (many discussed by Muirhead-Thomson 1991) demonstrate clearly that trapping efficiency decreases with increasing wind speed and increasing insect size. Remote sensing devices, such as radar and

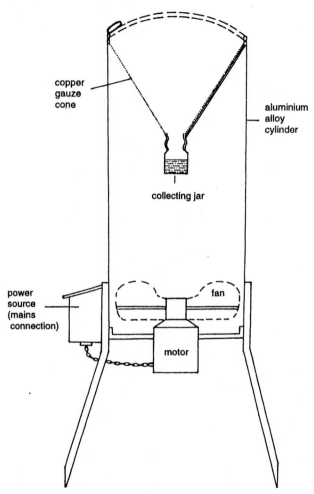

Fig. 3.6 A suction trap. This is the common '18 inch propeller' type. The upper cone is of copper gauze, through which the bottom-mounted fan pulls air. Insects in the air column are filtered out and drop into a jar of preservative at the bottom of the cone (after Southwood 1978).

infra-red detectors have revealed that only a fraction of the insects in the trap vicinity are actually captured.

Sorting the bulk catches for particular taxa can be expensive because of the large mass of insects captured. The traps are particularly valuable in sampling the 'aerial plankton'—the mass of tiny and delicate winged insects which otherwise are difficult to assess. Suction traps can, therefore, have an important role in inventory work in providing information on 'hard-to-sample groups'. As the catches can be converted into aerial densities, the traps are useful in providing 'background' faunal information in particular habitats

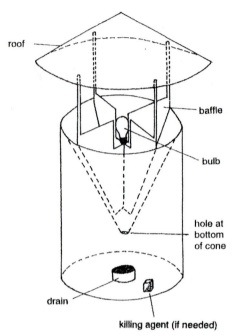

roof

baffle

bulb

hole at
bottom
of cone

drain

killing agent (if needed)

Fig. 3.7 A light trap. A high ultra-violet content light globe is suspended in the centre of metal or plastic 'baffles': moths and other insects move towards the light in a spiral flight, are intercepted by the baffles and drop through the open bottom of a cone into a retention chamber. The chamber usually has a central drainage chamber and may or may not have a killing agent. If not, it is common to provide retreats (such as egg cartons) for the moths to settle and remain quiet. A transparent roof, as shown here, is needed to keep the bulb dry.

or sites, and can be used to clarify phenological patterns and seasonal assemblage characteristics.

Light traps

Light traps (Fig. 3.7) (a particular category of bait trap) are a powerful collecting tool, but their efficiency varies greatly because of the large number of variables which influence the size and composition of the catch (p. 124). Nevertheless, it has been argued (e.g. by Holloway 1976 and Gadaghar *et al.* 1990) that they are among the best techniques for insect surveys because they collect large numbers of insects, collect well known taxa (such as nocturnal moths) efficiently, and have been important in accumulating distributional information over a long period. Extensive trials on the effectiveness of different lights and the behaviour of insects around light (Muirhead-Thomson 1991) reveal considerable differences in attractiveness and that many insects settle nearby, rather than enter the trap container. Searches of nearby vegetation (such as by sweeping, p. 59) may thus reveal numerous additional insects, including some moth species which are habitually not simply trapped.

The various patterns all involve the attraction of many flying insects to light, and many taxa are more strongly attracted to ultraviolet (short wave 'black light') or mercury vapour lights (with both long and short wave radiation) than to normal incandescent bulbs. The source of the light is the single most important determinant of the variety of insects captured, but wind conditions, temperature, precipitation and moonlight all affect insect activity and, hence, amenability to trapping. The bulbs or tubes can either be mounted between baffles, so that the spiralling insects moving to the light are intercepted and knocked into a funnel entrance to a collecting box, or suspended in an open tent or against a white sheet on which the insects settle, and from where they can be retrieved as needed. In the former arrangement, the insects can either be killed or retained alive—in which case shelters (such as corrugated paper or egg cartons) are useful to reduce activity and damage. It is necessary to protect the bulb from rain by some form of 'roof', and the trap chamber may also need drainage holes to prevent flooding.

Light traps are quite expensive, many are difficult to transport (although some lightweight collapsible models exist) and many require access to a power supply. Battery-powered models are effective for single nights of survey, and the batteries can be re-charged easily, for example by solar-powered chargers in remote areas. Some light traps, used particularly for small weakly-flying insects, combine a light with a small powered fan to combine the features of light trap and suction trap. Large active insects, such as large moths and beetles, may cause considerable damage to small, delicate specimens in light trap catches. Microlepidoptera are especially vulnerable and can often be denuded. Attempts have been made to design small light traps especially for such small insects, by providing for localized light orientation and separating large and small insects in different compartments by regulating the size of entry ports (Common 1986).

In general, light traps with retained catch need at least nightly servicing and, of course, if the insects are simply attracted to a resting surface, such as a sheet near the trap, frequent or constant attention is needed to collect the taxa of interest.

Light traps are effective for only a limited range of insect orders, but have the advantage of yielding numerous representatives of nocturnal taxa not captured by conventional daytime collecting methods, and which otherwise may be difficult to find. They are also important in monitoring particular species, including a number of agriculturally important pests.

Traps and collecting devices for ground or vegetation-frequenting invertebrates

A variety of methods is available, and their comparative features are summarized in Table 3.2. All are used for sampling from the ground or low vegetation.

Table 3.2
Features of some general methods for collecting terrestrial invertebrates from vegetation

Method	Features
Vacuum samplers	Sample animals on/near ground; high-diversity, large catches, non-selective; samples may contain much debris and be expensive to sort (flotation).
Emergence traps	Can be relatively specific, depending on habitat investigated; low tourist component in catches, but relatively low returns—not good for broad, inventory sampling.
Sweep netting	Mainly captures arthropods on low vegetation; cheap and (as other methods) reasonably standardizable in broad terms; large catches, high diversity, including tourists; not usable if vegetation wet, so weather-dependent.
Beating	Mainly arthropods on low canopy; cheap; large catches (but escapee component variable); difficult to calibrate as not known what is not dislodged; not usable if vegetation wet, so weather-dependent.
Vegetation clipping and examination	Used for sedentary or low-mobility taxa; laborious and destructive to habitat; can be made highly specific, with little/no bycatch killed; highly selective for plant species.
Chemical knockdown	Animals on vegetation, can provide access to high canopy and other 'difficult-to-sample' habitats; possibility of insecticide drift; can be relatively expensive and labour-intensive, use limited by weather (wind, rain) conditions; large, high-diversity catches.
Hand-collecting	Can target particular taxa, and adjust sampling to suit —use different measures of sampling effort, e.g. time (netting), area (quadrat size) or both (time spent searching defined area).

Vacuum samplers

These, known also as 'suction samplers' are essentially powerful vacuum cleaners, mounted as a backpack or (in the case of larger models) on a conveyer, and used to sample invertebrates living on low vegetation or the ground surface. There are two major patterns: (1) The 'wide hose' type, such as the D-Vac (Dietrich 1961; Fig. 3.8), in which the wide (20 cm or more) opening is held firmly against the ground (substrate) and the vacuum applied uniformly to that defined area, and (2) the 'narrow hose' type in which the hose (ca. 6 cm diameter) is moved systematically over the area defined by a cylinder or quadrat.

The motor power is most commonly from a petrol engine, but hand power or electricity may also be used. For high extraction rates a nozzle wind speed of about 90 miles/hour is needed, and extraction from dry samples can be very high. Efficiency decreases on plants higher than about 15 cm, and the sampler can be used satisfactorily only in dry conditions because the animals

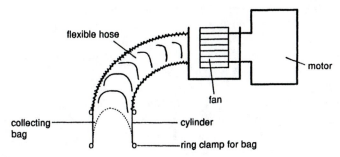

Fig. 3.8 A suction sampler: details of the D-Vac sampler, by which invertebrates are sucked from ground or vegetation into a collecting bag in the end of the flexible hose (after Dietrick 1961).

may otherwise adhere to wet vegetation or wet suction hoses. For large-scale sampling, as for some crop pests, large tractor-mounted suction samplers have been employed. However, small vacuum samplers are portable and easily manipulable. Although they have been assumed commonly to obtain 'total' faunal samples, their efficiency varies greatly on different substrates and vegetation and is very difficult to estimate. One practical drawback is that large amounts of debris are inevitably collected also, so that samples

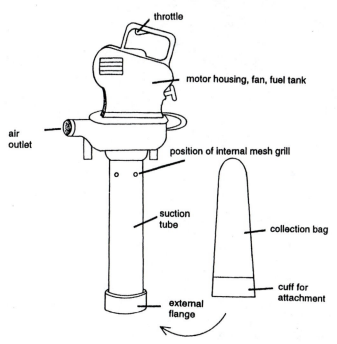

Fig. 3.9 A recent modification of a vacuum sampler for sampling grassland arthropods (Steward and Wright 1995).

tend to be 'dirty' and need considerable sorting effort (p. 137). Another is the cost of large suction machines. A more portable suction apparatus adapted from a lightweight machine designed for collecting garden debris has considerable potential for arthropod sampling (Fig. 3.9; Stewart and Wright 1995), and several similar and relatively cheap adaptations exist, based on similar garden implements.

The samplers are used in surveys of small epigaeic and low vegetation invertebrates, particularly arthropods not strongly attached to vegetation. Samples are cheap to take, and large numbers can be acquired rapidly.

Emergence traps

Many small animals living near the ground are positively phototactic, and can be collected efficiently by placing dark or opaque cones over the vegetation and providing a clear central area to which they move and whence they can be funnelled into a collecting jar (Fig. 3.10). Insects and others can be collected at intervals as they emerge. Large plastic bags or cardboard boxes

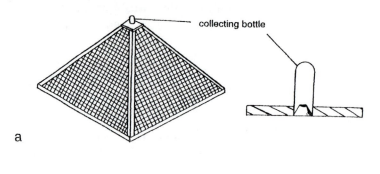

collecting bottle

a

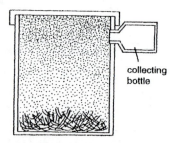

collecting bottle

b

Fig. 3.10 Two patterns of emergence trap: (a) pattern used to cover a defined small area of ground, from which insects are attracted to light and move to a collecting container (shown enlarged); (b) a cardboard box with collecting vial attached, used to recover emerging animals in the laboratory. Litter, debris or foliage is placed in the box.

can be utilized in a similar manner to separate animals from vegetation transported to the laboratory and have been used to collect and concentrate large numbers of parasitoids for biological control work, for example.

Such traps, sometimes termed 'photo-eclectors' are selective but yield predominantly resident taxa. They can thus help in defining the fauna associated with particular habitats, and this is limited only by the ingenuity of the worker. Emergence traps can, for example, be affixed to the trunks of trees to collect bark beetles and their natural enemies as they emerge from the wood. They can thus be used to sample taxa which are usually inconspicuous or immobile (such as parasitoids in insect hosts), and for monitoring their emergence times and seasonal development.

Pitfall traps

As their name implies, pitfall traps are containers sunk into the ground, with the rim level with the ground surface, so that animals wandering on the ground surface fall into them and are captured. Early workers opportunistically used empty cans (Barber traps) and similar containers for collecting in this way, and nowadays disposable plastic cups or dairy food containers are used frequently.

Three patterns are shown in Fig. 3.11. These representatives are designed for long-term use, so that a protective sleeve is employed to prevent the hole from caving in when the trap is removed to retrieve the catch. In Fig. 3.11b, one plastic cup is left *in situ* and supports a second into which the animals fall, and which can be removed and replaced easily. In Fig. 3.11c, the hole is maintained by a plastic drainage pipe 'sleeve' (inserted by hammering a steel spike, Fig. 3.11d, into the ground) which supports a test-tube as the collector.

The first pattern, in various sizes, numbers and configurations, has become almost universal in surveying ground-dwelling arthropods. The second pattern is favoured by some biologists working with thigmotactic animals (such as many myriapods), which may actively enter narrow chambers (as 'burrows') but avoid wider traps. Pitfall traps are used most commonly in transect lines or in grids with regular intervals between them. They may be 'roofed' by lids supported on pegs or long nails, and these can double in being lowered to close the traps if they are to be used only at intervals over a sampling period, and can be provided with bait or liquid preservative. However, such roofs can affect the light intensity near the traps, and may lead to catch bias. Pitfalls can be constructed cheaply from cans, soft drink containers and other household discards.

Unbaited traps containing preservative (such as 80% alcohol with an evaporation retardant such as glycol) have been used extensively in studies of some key groups of ground-active invertebrates such as ants, spiders and carabid beetles; many variations have been noted by Dunn (1989). The traps are conveniently small, cheap, and easy to transport and maintain. They can

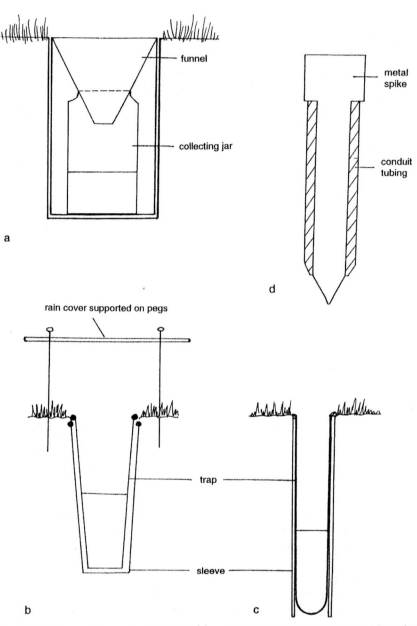

Fig. 3.11 Various patterns of pitfall trap: (a) a jar inside a larger container, with a plastic funnel directing captures to preservative; (b) two plastic cups, the outer one maintaining the shape of the hole, and the inner one being the trap, and removable for emptying. In this model a roof (a disc of plastic or wood) is suspended above the ground on nails to prevent flooding by rain; (c) a test tube suspended in a length of drainage or electrical conduit pipe; (d) a metal spike fits inside the conduit tube (wall thickness exaggerated and hatched) and is driven into the ground to insert the sleeve for test tube pattern traps.

be left in place for up to 2 weeks or so without attention, or opened at intervals over an extended period. After initial placement the traps should be left for several days before commencing trapping, to allow recovery from local disturbance, the 'digging-in effect'. For long periods, undiluted antifreeze can allow for rain dilution and minimize deterioration of specimens (Clark and Blom 1992). However, accurate interpretation of data from pitfall traps is fraught with difficulty, despite apparent amenability to statistical treatments (see review by Spence and Niemaala 1994). Catch size and trapping efficiency is influenced by many factors, including local topography and exposure, temperature, moisture, form of surrounding vegetation, material used in trap construction, the preservative used, number, size, shape and arrangement of traps (Adis 1979). Some of the problems can be overcome in inventory surveys by using many (10–20) traps over long periods or during several intervals, and by mixing traps with different baits, diameters and preservatives, which may all differentially attract or repel animals. For monitoring purposes, and for estimating the relative abundance of species, the trap form should be standardized.

The major use is in sampling surface-active arthropods on the ground, and pitfall traps are used in a wide range of environments. They are most useful in open habitats such as grasslands or arable land, easily replicable and cheap to obtain and use in large numbers. They are most effective for larger organisms, especially beetles, ants and spiders, and have been largely responsible for the broad reference to these groups in conservation assessment. They can also be used, for larger beetles, as adjuncts to mark–release–recapture measurements of population size (Chapter 8).

Soil corers

Samples of soil fauna are obtained most commonly by extracting the animals from soil taken by corers, and several 'split corer' designs (Fig. 3.12) are available to prevent fragmentation and compression of the core as it is extracted. Although simple corers (such as those used to make golf holes or to plant bulbs) can be used, there is some danger of killing animals by undue compression as the soil is removed from the corer, and split corers (in which the two halves are clamped together and can be separated for removal of the core) obviate this, and ensure that the cores can be obtained intact for division into definable horizontal strata.

The animals are then extracted manually or mechanically, as described below (p. 63), with preferred treatment depending on the kind of substrate, the particular animals sought, and the costs. Immobile stages, for example, cannot be separated other than by direct searching or mechanical means, and the same applies to dead animals from cores stored before examination. Likewise, the size of the cores will reflect the size of the prime target animals, but 8–10 cm diameter cores are generally adequate for broad surveys of many

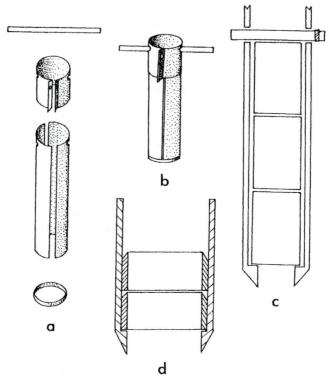

Fig. 3.12 Examples of soil corers used for sampling for invertebrates, (a) a split corer, disassembled to show the various parts which are clamped together for use; (b) the same assembled; (c) a corer with sample tubes already in place; in the model shown, these tubes are 48 mm in diameter and 76 mm long; (d) a similar system in which the cylinders can be transferred directly to an extraction apparatus (re-drawn after Southwood 1978). The inner cylinders are of plastic, and the corers strong metal with a sharpened cutting edge.

small soil invertebrates. The main use is in sampling the numerous relatively inactive taxa rarely sampled by other means, for later extraction or sorting from the substrate.

Direct searching and collecting

'Traditional' collecting techniques, although not always quantified or easily quantifiable, are nevertheless of considerable value in conservation studies in which the aim is to establish the presence of particular taxa, where some form of preliminary appraisal of species richness or diversity is needed as the foundation for more quantitative sampling, or where information is needed on biology or distribution of invertebrates within a habitat. With minimal attention, many such techniques can be applied in reasonably standard ways, so that bases for comparison are either temporal (duration of collecting) or spatial (using quadrats or transects to help define the area sampled) and data of comparative value may be obtained. Many specialists have developed their own techniques for the particular animals they seek, and can become very proficient in their use. Thus, for millipedes in Tasmania, hand-collecting yielded considerably higher returns than pitfall trapping (Mesibov *et al.* 1995).

Aerial netting

Use of the traditional 'butterfly net' to collect or monitor the diversity and numbers of larger insects seen in a fixed time interval or area is an important adjunct in monitoring (p. 174), not least because it may be necessary to net individuals to confirm their identity or to mark them as part of a population study (p. 189). The catches reflect activity (apparency) rather than absolute abundance, and for comparative studies need to be taken at similar times each day and in the same general weather conditions.

Many workers prefer a black or dark green light net mesh to the more usual white net, which seems to be easily detectable by many strongly-flying insects. Netting can also be used to collect aerial insects by randomly 'swishing' through the air. Long handles, up to 10 m or more, are employed by some collectors to net insects flying among trees, but are very ungainly to use, and not amenable to good quantitative work.

Netting in this way is useful for initial surveys of butterflies, dragonflies, and some other insect groups. Sampling effort is difficult to quantify, and prone to collector bias—however inadvertently. Returns can be low, but netting is necessary to confirm identities of species counted on transect or area-based surveys whose identities may otherwise be confused.

Sweep netting

The sweep net is used very extensively for sampling invertebrates from low vegetation, by moving a strongly framed net backward and forward through grass or herbage. The net bags need to be strong to counter tearing but must also allow air-flow, so that heavy canvas is not suitable–animals tend to be 'pushed away' rather than captured. The net bags are usually of synthetic fibre, linen or strong cotton, with a heavier rim to deter fraying along the frame line. Most nets are round but, for quantitative use, a D-shaped frame used vertically can help to define more precisely the area sampled. A detachable screen of coarse mesh can be used to filter out large pieces of plant debris (Noyes 1989). When many samples are to be taken, considerable time can be saved by using detachable zip-off bags which can be closed with their contents and sorted later in the laboratory (Milne 1993).

Sweep netting is valuable in providing a high return for effort, and is simple and cheap to use. However, it can sample only the animals near the top of the vegetation and cannot be used while vegetation is wet. The efficiency of sweep netting is thus influenced strongly by daily or other activity patterns of the animals, weather, and the characteristics of the vegetation. Nevertheless, with adequate care, and samples related to ground area (by sweeping along a belt transect of known width, or by standardizing the number and length of sweep strokes/sample or the sampling period), reasonably replicable samples can be obtained in open vegetation. For example, Janzen (1973) used 800 sweeps of a 38 cm diameter net as a sample in Costa Rica, and similar samples from the USA and UK were compared by Janzen and Pond (1975). Presence of numerous trees or bushes may make standardizing the length of the sweep very difficult, so that a given time spent sweeping may be a more reliable index of sampling effort.

Sweep netting is therefore useful in collecting and surveying insects and other animals exposed on low vegetation. As catches thus reflect activity, in that many insects move up and down vegetation during the day, comparative samples should be taken at around the same time each day, and morning, mid-day and evening samples at the same site may differ substantially in composition.

Beating

Another traditional collector's method involves the use of a beating tray (in its earliest form, simply an umbrella held upside down), a cloth-covered frame held horizontally beneath the branch of a tree which is then struck repeatedly with a stick. Invertebrates are dislodged from the vegetation and collected in the tray when they fall. They can then be collected, aspirated or funnelled into containers. Although strictly a relative method, a sufficiently high proportion of many insects can be sampled to regard it as absolute. Care must be taken not to damage the vegetation unduly, and in some situations it is preferable to shake the vegetation by hand rather than hit it repeatedly. Some workers have recommended using trays with part of the frame made of bungee rubber which can be pressed against tree trunks or other irregular surfaces to reduce escape or droppage of specimens (Upton 1991).

For collecting very small animals some workers prefer to use a tray with raised sides, across which a wire mesh can be placed to act as a sieve and exclude large animals and pieces of vegetation, to facilitate sorting. As with netting, weather and the time of day can influence catches, but some standardization can be obtained by using given numbers of samples, a standard-sized tray (such as 1 m × 1 m square) and standardizing the number of 'hits' (commonly at 10/sample) and the searching time used to retrieve animals from the tray by aspiration or direct individual retrieval. It is important also to clear the tray, by brushing it or inverting it, between samples to avoid carrying specimens over, especially if comparisons are being made across different species of vegetation.

Beating has the same general uses as for sweeping, but for animals on trees and shrubs rather than on herbaceous vegetation.

Vegetation clipping and examination

For detecting sedentary arthropods, such as many scale insects and others which are not dislodged during beating, it is sometimes necessary to cut and bag samples of vegetation for direct examination in the laboratory. In such cases, bases for loose quantification can include volume of foliage or surface area, although many foliage-frequenting organisms tend to have highly contagious distributions. Long-handled pruners are needed for taller vegetation, and it may be advantageous to incorporate a catching net for cut twigs and branches to avoid their loss (or loss of organisms) as they drop. Shooting down samples of foliage may involve either a rifle (Sweney and Jones 1975) or a shotgun (Mazanec 1978). Branches may also be cut by saws on lines established by firing arrows with fine trailer lines used to haul pulleys into the trees (Sweney and Jones 1975). Examination of clipped foliage, especially for small organisms such as mites in domatia, is laborious, but yields taxa not obtainable easily by any other means. In contrast, it is likely to underestimate abundance of large, active and cryptic insects (Majer and Recher 1988).

Leaf-brushing machines have been devised for larger tetranychid mites (Henderson and McBurnie 1943), and grass-frequenting eriophyid mites have been counted by dislodging them by ultrasonic vibration (Gibson 1975). Ryegrass tillers cut into 2–3 cm lengths vibrated in absolute ethanol facilitated removal of 97% of mites from the leaves after 15 s, and the remainder in a further 45 s.

The technique is useful in specific surveys of sedentary or near-sedentary arthropods on vegetation, which are not easily obtained by other methods, and thus augments these in estimating species richness on trees and shrubs, in particular.

Chemical knockdown

The basis of this method is to use non-persistent pesticides to kill or anaesthetize the invertebrates in a unit of habitat, as a means of inventorying the fauna. At its simplest, a commercial household aerosol can of pyrethrin-based insecticide can be used in extracting insects from dense vegetation such as grass tussocks, by spraying the tussock and shaking it over a plastic groundsheet. Similar cans can be mounted on poles to sample from localized areas of low canopy, but most studies have involved commercial 'fogging machines' which can be hoisted into the high canopy. Its particular relevance in conservation studies has been to provide a means to sample the previously inaccessible fauna of forest canopies by misting ('fogging') them with pyrethroid insecticides and collecting the falling insects in funnels or trays suspended near the ground, or on plastic sheets beneath the target trees. The major practical problems are fixing ropes to haul the fogging machine up into the canopy, and sampling in sufficiently calm and dry conditions to ensure that the catch is retrieved (rather than blown away) and uncontaminated by fauna of neighbouring trees, and that pesticide drift is minimized. Setting up an array of standard funnels (to standardize the area of catchment) allows some relationship of the catch to the canopy. With care, and refinements such as radio-triggered fogging machines, the pesticide can be applied reasonably specifically to individual trees or particular aspects of trees. As one example of the regime used, Russell-Smith and Stork (1994) suspended 120 funnelled trays, each of 1 m² area, in forest quadrats in Sulawesi, fogged each quadrat for 5–15 min in early morning, and allowed a 2 h period for the arthropods to drop. Each sample in Britain appraised by Southwood *et al.* (1982) comprised all invertebrates which dropped on to a 1 m² sheet within 1 h of spraying.

Chemical knockdown may severely underestimate sessile insects, which are sampled more reliably by hand-collecting and direct searches of vegetation (Majer and Recher 1988).

The method has been significant in helping to transform knowledge of arthropod species diversity in forest canopy ecosystems (Erwin 1982; Stork 1988), but is reasonably expensive, and the catches are laborious to sort. It is particularly useful for larger insects, and small invertebrates can be considerably under-represented, due to loss as they fall from the trees and failure to dislodge them efficiently.

Hand-collecting

In some habitats, the simplest way to make some preliminary appraisal of the invertebrate fauna is by direct examination based either on area (such as ground quadrats, area of tree bark), number of habitat units or time spent searching. Direct searching is particularly useful in yielding low mobility or cryptic taxa which may not be amenable to many of the methods noted earlier. For small (0.25 m) quadrats, 5 min searching for carabid beetles in Norway gave reliable estimates of absolute abundance (J. Andersen 1995). In contrast, pitfall traps in the same sites yielded more species, but different ordering of relative abundance, so that these two methods were complementary in furnishing a sample of the beetles present.

An important application is for large litter and soil arthropods in which the litter from standard quadrats is sifted or sieved on to a tray and then sorted by hand; animals are taken individually as they are detected.

Even for soil cores, hand searching may be the most effective method of retrieving some groups of animals. For gastropods, Kalinowska (1993) claimed that for 'exact counts' there was no adequate substitute for searching each core by hand, and this has long been recognized as a reliable basic method for earthworms in surveys of soil macrofauna.

Hand-collecting is labour-intensive. Returns depend on the acuity of the individual observer and are often low, simply because many of the target taxa are widely dispersed. Searches for the giant Gippsland earthworm in south-eastern Australia, for example, can necessitate excavation of large amounts of soil to find a single worm (van Praagh 1992). The same caveats apply in other contexts, such as collecting under stones or fallen logs. Such samples are highly patchy but tend to yield characteristic taxa. For many invertebrates, quadrats of 0.5–1.0 m^2 and sampling to a soil depth of 10 cm is adequate, but much deeper samples may be needed at times (Edwards 1991). Adding water to areas can cause some taxa, such as some beetles, to move to the surface, and spraying ground with solutions of formalin, copper sulphate and others has been used widely in the past to sample earthworms and some other soil invertebrates.

Extraction of specimens from soil and litter

Separating the mass of different invertebrates from soil and litter is laborious and, often, difficult. Nevertheless, standardization is important to assure valid comparisons between taxa and samples. Two categories of methods can be used and both have proliferated to provide numerous practical modifications for particular taxa or purposes. The methods are categorized loosely as 'dynamic' (which involve exerting environmental pressures to stimulate the invertebrates to leave the substrate samples actively) and 'physical' (in which

Table 3.3
Recommended methods for extraction of soil arthropods (after Edwards 1991)

| | Soil type/system | | | | | | | | |
| | Peat | | | Clay/Loam | | | Sand | | |
Group	W	P	A	W	P	A	W	P	A
Isopoda	AC	ABC	ABC	AC	ABC	ABC	✔	✔	✔
Pauropoda	ABC	ABC	ABC	ABC	ABC	✔	✔	✔	✔
Symphyla	ABC	ABC	ABC	✔	ABC	✔	✔	✔	✔
Diplopoda	ABC	ABC	ABC	ABC	ABC	✔	✔	✔	✔
Chilopoda	ABC	ABC	ABC	✔	ABC	✔	✔	✔	✔
*Acarina	ABC	ABC	ABC	ABCF	ABCDE	ACD	ABCF	ABC	ABC
Pseudoscorpionida	ABC	ABC	ABC	ABC	ABC	ABC	✔	✔	✔
Araneae	ABC	ABC	ABC	ABC	ABC	ABC	ABC	ABC	✔
*Collembola	ABC	ABC	ABC	✔	ABCD	ABCD	ABCD	ABCD	ABCD
Protura	ABC	ABC	ABC	ABC	✔	✔	✔	✔	✔
Psocoptera	ABC	ABC	ABC	✔	✔	✔	✔	✔	✔
Thysanoptera	ABC	ABC	ABC	DE	DE	✔	✔	✔	✔
Hemiptera	ABC	ABC	ABC	✔	✔	✔	✔	✔	✔
Hymenoptera	ABC	ABC	ABC	✔	✔	✔	✔	✔	✔
Coleoptera	ABC	ABC	ABC	✔	✔	✔	✔	CDEF	CDEF
Diptera	ABC	ABC	ABC	✔	✔	✔	✔	CDEF	CDEF
Eggs/pupae	DEF	DEF	DEF	DEF	DEF	DEF	DEF	DEF	DEF

* Divided into subgroups assessed separately by Edwards. ✔, all methods suitable; A, Tullgren funnel; B, Kempson extractor; C, air-conditioned funnel; D, Salt and Hollick flotation; E, other flotation; F, grease film extractor; W, woodland; P, pasture; A, arable.

the animals are extracted by physical processes, commonly involving preliminary sorting followed by some form of washing or flotation). The latter can obtain inactive stages and dead individuals whereas the former, by definition, applies only to active animals. In general, many of the methods are suitable for a wide range of taxa (Table 3.3). Choice of method may not be particularly critical for a broad survey of larger soil animals. All the 'dynamic' methods can be replicated easily. Dry funnel techniques are the most frequently used, but wet funnels are preferable for the smallest and most delicate taxa.

Dynamic methods

Tullgren and Berlese funnels

The many modifications of dry funnels for extracting invertebrates by using heat and desiccation to stimulate activity are used very widely in studies of soil and litter invertebrates.

The early Berlese funnels consisted of double-walled funnels containing hot water. The substrate was placed on a wire mesh in the funnel and the emerging animals fell into a container beneath this. The Tullgren funnel (Fig. 3.13) is the basis of most modern extraction techniques, and heat from a light bulb suspended over the sample drives the invertebrates downward as the samples dry. The funnels can be used singly or in multiple 'batteries', and can extract from litter spread on a grid above the funnel or from consolidated soil cores which, as Haarlov (1947) showed, should be centred away from the funnel walls to prevent loss of animals from becoming trapped there in condensation.

Edwards (1991) noted some of the more recent refinements of this pattern, designed to maintain steep gradients of humidity and temperature through the samples and to promote efficient extraction. A model noted by Crossley and Blair (1991) can be used in a refrigerated room (15°C) so that small 'Christmas tree lights' can establish a gradient of 20°C and facilitate rapid extraction.

The quantifiable sample for Tullgren funnels can thus be a core of known diameter or volume, or a known volume or ground area cover of litter. Soil cores are usually inverted in the funnels, and only 5–10 cm deep. The intensity of heat supplied (wattage of bulb(s) or heating grid) depends on the size of the funnel, which can be up to a metre or so in diameter, although 20–40 cm is much more common. The extraction time varies with sample size, the moisture and density of the soil, the heat intensity, and the kinds of invertebrates sought. Many small taxa, such as mites, may take up to 2 weeks to leave the substrate while other more active animals may have left in only 12–24 h.

One practical problem is that much soil or litter can also fall through the

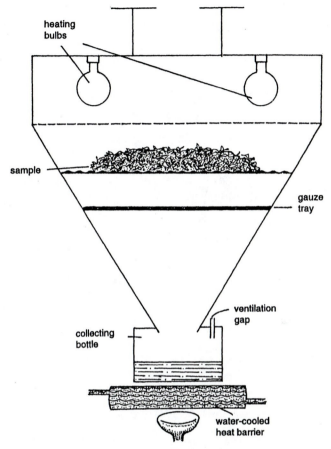

Fig. 3.13 A representative extraction funnel for soil and litter invertebrates. The substrate sample is suspended on a gauze mesh, with a 'trap tray' with card or wooden strips underneath to prevent much of the litter falling into the collecting bottle. Electric bulbs suspended over the sample progressively dry the sample and drive the animals downward. In this model an additional light is present below the sample, as a photo-attractor, and separated from it by a shallow, clear heat-barrier (redrawn after Southwood 1978). In the basic Tullgren funnel, the latter is usually omitted, and only a single heating bulb used.

grid as it becomes dryer, contaminating the samples and increasing the processing costs. Some workers recommend use of a sifter (Fig. 3.14) to concentrate litter before putting it into the funnels. Although general patterns of Tullgren funnel are useful for many kinds of invertebrate animals, many variations have been designed for particular purposes or to favour particular taxonomic groups. For example, Fig. 3.15a shows a pattern suitable for terrestrial Turbellaria (Kolasa 1993), in which a sample of soil is placed on a concave screen of ca. 0.5 mm mesh suspended over a Petri dish containing water, with its lowest point in contact. A low-powered bulb

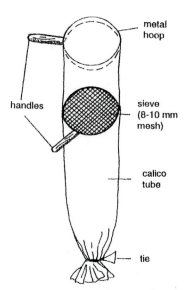

Fig. 3.14 A 'sifter' used to reduce the bulk of litter samples before they are extracted for invertebrates. The litter is placed on a sieve of 10 mm (or so) mesh, and agitated strenuously by turning the two handles repeatedly in opposite directions. Coarser litter is thus filtered out, and the sample for extraction collected in the calico tube below the sieve.

facilitates drying, but care is needed not to overheat the sample and it should not be hot during the first 24 h of extraction. The turbellarians are recovered by hand from the dish.

A related pattern of extractor, by which animals such as molluscs and annelids may be obtained from foliage litter as the water level is lowered gradually, is shown in Fig. 3.15b.

The Kempson extractor

This apparatus (Fig. 3.16), developed by Kempson *et al.* (1963), provides high extraction rates for arthropods and other animals in woodland litter. It comprises a controlled pulsing infra-red lamp protected from surging by a conventional bulb. The extraction bowls, capped with screens to prevent escape of animals, contain preservative (originally aqueous picric acid but now more commonly trisodium orthophosphate), and litter is supported on a cotton net. The advantages of the Kempson extractor over conventional Tullgren funnels are: (1) maintenance of a high humidity on the lower side of the samples so that animals are not lost to desiccation; (2) reduced amounts of debris in the samples; and (3) the facility to increase the amount of heat gradually during extraction by the simmerstat control.

Effective extraction takes about a week. Unlike many Tullgren funnels, however, the Kempson extractor is non-portable, and a large unit which occupies considerable space.

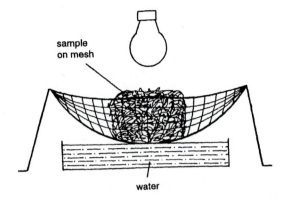

sample
on mesh

water

a

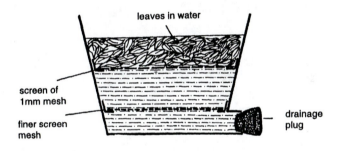

leaves in water

screen of
1mm mesh

finer screen
mesh

drainage
plug

b

Fig. 3.15 Modifications of the wet-funnel technique for extraction of invertebrates from debris: a, a method for extracting terrestrial platyhelminths from litter samples with the bottom of the samples suspended in water; b, extraction for oligochaetes and molluscs from foliage; the water is gradually lowered as animals move down through the foliage.

The Winkler extractor

The Winkler bag extractor (Fig. 3.17) for leaf litter and vegetation debris depends on air drying, via sunlight, of concentrated litter samples placed in net or wire bags suspended inside a canvas outer container with a collecting jar at the bottom of a funnel to catch the animals as they drop. The litter is usually consolidated by sifting (p. 65) to remove larger branches and debris and a series of small samples are combined for simultaneous extraction in the same container.

This apparatus has the advantages of being light, collapsible and easily portable, so it can be used for collecting or sampling in remote areas without access to a power source, simply by suspending the container from a tree branch or a horizontal pole or rope sheltered from rain and excessive wind. Extraction time is typically a few days.

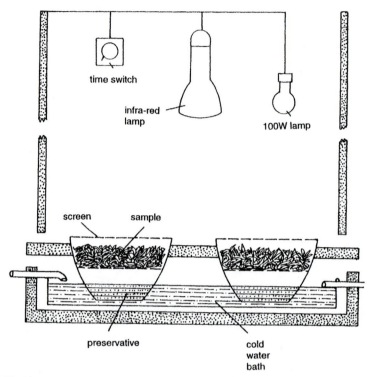

Fig. 3.16 The Kempson bowl extractor. Litter is placed on grids in plastic bowls containing preservative and suspended in cold water bath. The whole apparatus is contained in chamber, and an infra-red lamp (centre) is suspended about 70 cm above the samples. This is operated in pulses, controlled by a time switch (of the kind used for electric cookers), and an ordinary light bulb is employed to protect the system from surging (after Kempson *et al.* 1963).

Wet funnels: Baermann funnels

This method originally comprised a simple glass funnel with a clamped length of rubber tubing sleeved on the stem, in which the sample (either bare or wrapped in muslin) is supported on a metal grid in water, sometimes with an electric light suspended above it (Fig. 3.18) (O'Connor 1962) to heat the water to a maximum of about 40 °C after 3 h.

Many small and delicate soil-frequenting animals are not extracted by dry funnels because they depend on the water films surrounding soil particles for their movement, and are very susceptible to desiccation. In the Baermann funnel and its derivatives, animals move out of the soil in water and collect in the neck of the funnel, from where they can be released into a dish for examination. Heating the samples from above provides a very effective way of extracting nematodes, enchytraeid worms and microarthropods such as tardigrades, which are scarcely extracted by dry funnels. Extraction may take only

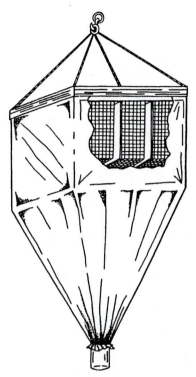

Fig. 3.17 The Winkler bag, for extracting invertebrates from litter when no electric power is available. Samples of litter are placed in mesh (cloth, wire) baskets suspended from a wire frame inside a canvas outer container, which is tied closed across the top; the animals are extracted as the samples dry by being suspended from poles or tree branches in sunlight, and are collected at the bottom of the cone, in a collecting vessel of preservative.

a few hours, but separation of enchytraeids may be more efficient if undertaken without heat over a longer period (Didden *et al*. 1995). The compromise here may be between the number of samples needed for extraction and the space available. Extraction for periods of 2 weeks may not be feasible for large numbers of samples, or if samples are taken at short intervals.

The same principle has been applied to litter, by using a beaker instead of a funnel, and agitating the sample at intervals; this method is particularly rewarding in yielding many microarthropods. A further development (Fig. 3.19) by Nielsen for efficient extraction of Enchytraeidae involves perfusing the sample with saturated air from a warm water bath, so that the worms move upward into cooled sand, from which they can be extracted by simple flotation (p. 71).

Baermann funnels and simple modifications of these are cheap and effective, and can be used on a large scale to survey fauna from many samples of soil. For nematode extractions, soil samples can first be mixed by bulking and

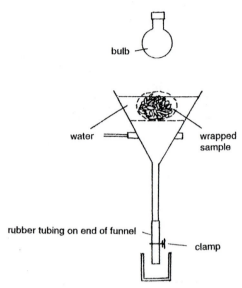

Fig. 3.18 A simple Baermann funnel. Soil is wrapped in muslin and suspended on a grid in a funnel of water heated by a suspended bulb. Nematodes are collected in the neck of the funnel, and can be released into the beaker by loosening the clamp on the lower length of rubber tubing.

subsampling (p. 123), if necessary, and sieved for enclosure of soil in a cloth-covered beaker (Fig. 3.20a) inverted over water. Larger surface area for sample extraction can be obtained by using dishes or trays rather than small funnels. Similar principles can be employed to extract nematodes from plant

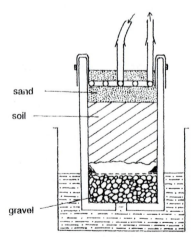

Fig. 3.19 An apparatus for extracting enchytraeid worms from soil. The soil sample is placed on coarse gravel suspended in a warm water bath and overlain by a layer of fine sand cooled by circulating water. Enchytraeids move up into the cooler sand and can be separated by flotation.

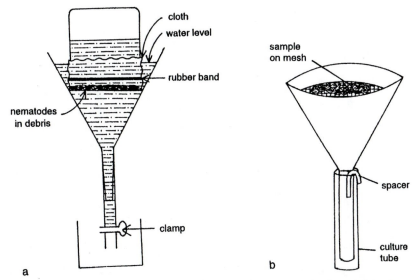

Fig. 3.20 a. The 'inverted beaker' technique for extracting nematodes from debris; the worms move through the fine mesh covering the beaker and are collected in the neck of the funnel; b. Method for incubating plant specimens for nematode extraction: cut pieces of stem, root (etc) placed on grid in funnel, above a culture tube in a humid environment.

material by incubating cut tissues in shallow water so that the worms leave the plants (Fig. 3.20b). Modifications such as mist chambers also facilitate recovery of plant-frequenting nematodes (Dropkin 1980).

Physical methods for terrestrial samples

Soil washing and flotation

These methods may be employed for extracting animals from fresh samples or those preserved and stored in various ways. Often associated with preliminary soil washing (which has the disadvantage of needing use of large volumes of water), flotation relies on the separation of organic and inorganic material released from soil or litter samples. One 'traditional' pattern (Fig. 3.21, after Salt and Hollick 1944) involves hose sieving of soil samples, from which suspended matter is captured on a fine sieve in a 'Ladell' can. This is then subjected to flotation by a solution of magnesium sulphate or other flotation liquid agitated by blowing air through it for 2–3 min. This liberates organic material trapped on the sieve, and the level of the flotation liquid is then raised so that this matter is floated into a collecting tube for direct examination.

The general principle is applicable widely, and a number of similar devices have been described. Direct washing is the most useful way to assess animal

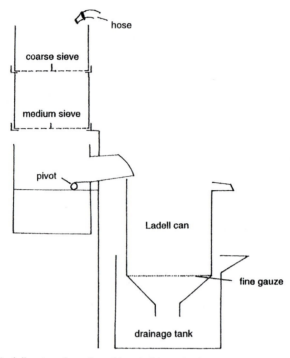

Fig. 3.21 The Ladell system for soil washing. Soil is washed by hosing through a series of sieves, with the elutriate finally tipped from a pivoting container into a Ladell can and allowed to drain through a fine gauze from which the animals are recovered by flotation.

diversity in deeper soils where their density is low and relatively large volumes must be processed (Kethley 1991). Direct flotation in heptane is important in separating arthropods from samples and can also assess eggs and other immobile stages. It relies on characteristics of arthropod cuticle and can thus be used to extract dead specimens from samples which have been stored for some time. One sequence for heptane flotation for soil samples (from Walter *et al.* 1987) is: (1) immersing a soil core in ethanol to kill the invertebrates; (2) placing the sample in a vacuum to evacuate air from plant debris and organic material, then wetting the sample; and (3) placing it into a flask, adding water followed by heptane, and agitating so that arthropods float to the water–heptane interface, whence they can be decanted by sieving (Edwards 1991).

Elutriation

Soil particles have higher specific gravity than soil invertebrates, so sink more rapidly in an upward flow of water. This principle is particularly important in extracting small animals, and has been used extensively for nematodes. Invertebrates are washed out of a soil sample and held in suspension by

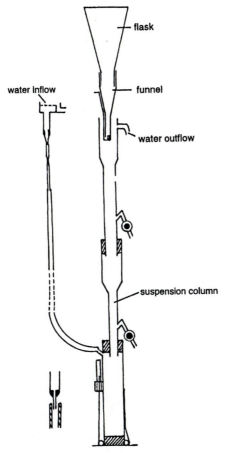

Fig. 3.22 An elutriation technique for extracting invertebrates from soil. (Seinhorst elutriator, effective for nematodes.)

opposing water currents. They are carried thence to an outlet and sieved or concentrated in particular lengths of the column from where they can be removed through stopcocks (Fig. 3.22).

The techniques are reasonably efficient, but the apparatus is quite expensive and the method somewhat cumbersome.

Centrifugation

Small animals can sometimes be separated from soil or litter by centrifuging small samples of the substrate in liquid, and decanting organisms from the centrifuge tubes (Fig. 3.23). This method has also been used extensively for nematodes, but is efficient also for small arthropods such as Acarina and Collembola. Efficiency of extraction depends on the speed and duration of

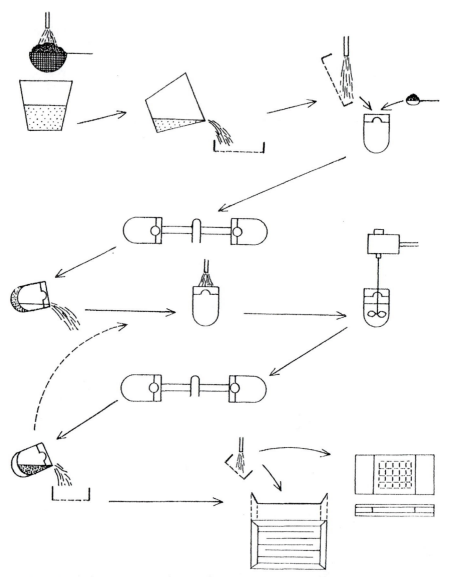

Fig. 3.23 A centrifugation-flotation method for extracting nematodes from soil. Soil is washed through a 1000 μm sieve; the filtrate sieved through a 40-μm cloth; the sieve rinsed into a centrifuge tube with addition of kaolin; the first centrifugation is followed by elimination of supernatant water; sucrose is added and the sample agitated before a second centrifugation (which may be repeated); leading to filtration, collection and counting in trays or grids.

centrifuging, the agent used for extraction, and its density. For soil nematodes from a forest in Cameroon, 1500 g centrifugation for 4 min in Ludox-TM of density 1.15 provided the most efficient extraction of nematodes of all shapes

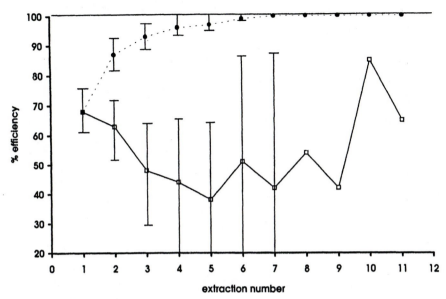

Fig. 3.24 Effect of repeated extractions of the same soil samples on efficiency of extraction of nematodes from Cameroon forests (Bloemers and Hodda 1995) (upper spots, cumulative efficiency; lower squares, efficiency of individual extraction, with approximate 95% confidence limits shown to extraction 7; $n = 16$ sites).

and sizes present (Bloemers and Hodda 1995). Repeated extraction of the same samples (Fig. 3.24) showed 95% efficiency after only three extractions, and the first extraction alone yielded about 70% of the total nematodes. See also p. 96, for application of similar techniques to aquatic samples.

Grease film

Small broken-up soil samples are placed in oblong perspex containers of water lined with greased polystyrene plates. The containers are rotated horizontally for about 15 min, by which time the animals are stuck to the grease (Aucamp and Ryke 1964). The plates can then be removed and examined microscopically. Despite problems of removing specimens for critical examination, this method is efficient for microarthropods and mesoarthropods (Edwards 1991).

Further reading

Curry, J. P. (1994). *Grassland invertebrates*. Chapman & Hall, London.

Dindal, D. L. (ed.) (1990). *Soil biology guide*. Wiley Interscience, New York.

Edwards, C. A. (1991). The assessment of populations of soil-inhabiting invertebrates. *Agriculture, Ecosystems and Environment* **34**, 145–76.

Gorny, M. and Grum, L. (ed.). *Methods in soil zoology*. Elsevier, Amsterdam / Polish Scientific Publishers, Warsaw.

Muirhead-Thomson, R. C. (1991). *Trap responses of flying insects*. Academic Press, London.

Southwood, T. R. E. (1978). *Ecological methods. With particular reference to the study of insect populations*. Chapman & Hall, London.

Steyskal, G. C., Murphy, W. L., and Hoover, E. M. (1986). *Insects and mites: techniques for their collection and preservation*. United States Department of Agriculture, Washington.

Upton, M. S. (1991). *Methods for collecting, preserving and studying insects and allied forms*. Australian Entomological Society, Miscellaneous Publication, No. 3. Brisbane.

4 Sampling invertebrates: aquatic environments

Introduction

This chapter outlines the principles and conditions for use of some of the techniques used to sample invertebrates from aquatic habitats, both freshwater and marine. Many of the principles and apparatus are similar for the two habitats, but there are numerous differences due to scale and ease of access. Many of the marine-based devices used in deeper waters are, in essence, commercial fishing devices and may need to be operated from ships; large dredges and trawls, for example, may also need several kilometres of cable to allow operation in deep water, whereas similar devices for smaller freshwater bodies may need no more than a few metres of rope to permit efficient operation. Rather than towing a net at great depth, it may then be feasible to throw it from a pond bank and haul it back by an attached line. Such marine sampling devices are, in essence, remote and outside the immediate control of the operator. From the ecologist's point of view, they provide only minimal data sets with little idea of sampling efficiency or representativeness, because the performance of the devices cannot be monitored adequately at great depths.

Successful sampling in the deep sea, using apparatus suspended on (perhaps) several kilometres of wire or cable poses particular problems for standardization and assuming satisfactory performance. From the conservationist's viewpoint, use of such techniques is opportunistic, usually prohibitively expensive, and of little relevance to practical management.

Techniques such as deep-water trawls demonstrate the refinements possible when collecting commercial taxa, when funding is readily available to explore methods to increase sampling efficiency and thereby increase profits, and is atypical of many direct conservation exercises. It does, though, demonstrate the need for opportunism in studying invertebrates, and much useful information on species incidence and diversity can be accrued from such operations if samples can be rescued for scientific appraisal.

Deep-water marine benthic invertebrates have only rarely been involved in conservation argument or proposals, as most practical concerns over marine invertebrates relate to littoral or shallow water taxa for which the effects of habitat disturbance or commercial harvesting, respectively, are often obvious. These systems are much more amenable to reliable sampling. However, the recent and accelerating debate on marine organism diversity has relied heavily on the information derived from oceanic benthic samples. Poore and Wilson (1992), for example, summarized data from such samples in many parts of the world in attempting to assess diversity in different areas. Sampling techniques for deep-water fauna may well assume increased conservation relevance in the next few years, as the needs for such diversity estimates as templates for patterns paralleling those used in terrestrial environments for setting conservation priorities, and for additional comparative studies and mapping of diversity become greater. As Gourbalt and Warwick (1994) noted, 'misconceptions concerning global patterns of biodiversity may have arisen in the past because of lack of standardization of sampling and analytical protocols'.

As with terrestrial systems, major differences in approach are related to the habitat being assessed—in this case the major differentiation is the substrate below the water, and the water body itself. The two habitat categories support distinct, but overlapping, cohorts of animals. Changes in benthic populations are of particular value in studies involving monitoring of environmental effects, because most of the organisms have short life cycles and respond rapidly to habitat change. Many of the organisms are also relatively sedentary, so that plot-based sampling is reasonably reliable. Parts of Chapter 8 (p. 174) link strongly with the techniques noted here. In many aquatic surveys, monitoring incorporates both inspection of plots and the gathering of samples for detailed analysis.

Substrate samplers

The major division of techniques reflects the texture of substrates, whether hard or soft. Corers, grabs and dredges are used predominantly for soft substrates, whereas Surber samplers, nets and enclosed samplers are useful for hard substrates which would not be penetrated by the other devices.

Surber sampler

The Surber sampler (Fig. 4.1) is used widely in sampling the benthos (both epibenthos and infauna) of shallow running waters, such as streams and rivers. A net, with or without a collecting vial attached at its apex, is attached to a hinged metal frame which folds flat for ease of transport. The other part of the frame is lowered to define an area, commonly a square of side 30 or 50 cm, and the substrate in this area is agitated by hand, brush, or other tool so that the organisms present to a given depth, or on stones or vegetation there, are swept into the downstream net.

Because some stones or habitat components will often lie across the

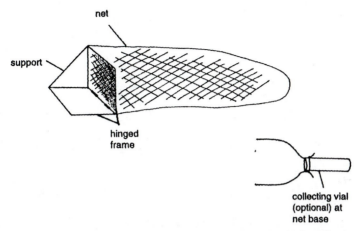

Fig. 4.1 A Surber sampler for collecting benthic invertebrates in shallow flowing water. A hinged frame describes an area of substrate which is agitated by hand or mechanical tool in a standard manner so that animals are carried into the net bag downstream. The bag can be fitted with a collecting vial (inset), if required.

boundary of the defined quadrat, care must be taken to treat these consistently across a series of sample units. The method is not generally suitable for soft-bottomed streams, and only larger organisms are collected reliably.

Grabs

Grabs (and dredges, below, although the terms are sometimes used synonymously for grab) occur in many different patterns and are used to sample the soft or fine grain substrates of freshwater or marine bodies. Two common patterns, both of them in use for several decades, are the Ekman 'dredge' (Fig. 4.2) and the Petersen grab (Fig. 4.3), and these models illustrate two methods by which such apparatus is operated. They, and numerous others, are lowered with the jaws locked/held open until they reach the bottom. With the Ekman dredge, a heavy metal 'messenger' attached to the line is then released, and strikes a spring mechanism to release the jaws; the substrate sample is thereby enclosed for hauling to the surface. This sampler relies largely on its own weight for successful operation, and is used most efficiently on soft muddy bottoms. Large pieces of vegetation or other obstructions may prevent the jaws from closing fully, and invalidate the sample.

The Petersen grab can work effectively in some heavier substrates such as gravel. When it reaches the bottom on lowering, the holding bar is freed so that the weighted jaws start to close; closure is completed as hoisting starts, by the weight of the grab itself.

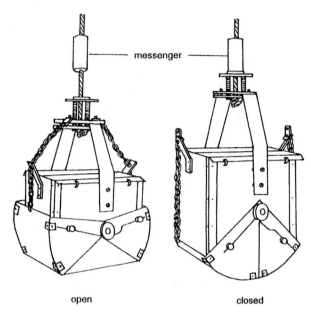

Fig. 4.2 The Ekman dredge: (left), open position, for lowering; (right), closed for hauling.

A slight modification often adopted involves using grabs with a counter-poised weight instead of a messenger. Several kinds of freshwater benthic grabs were compared by Elliott and Drake (1981a: p. 116), who noted that about 60 kinds had already been developed. They have continued to proliferate. Larger grabs, mainly for marine use, can be very heavy (up to about 750 kg) and require a large boat with a powered winch to operate them, and lighter ones are commonly in the range of 10–20 kg. Most may suffer from incomplete closure due to blockage or oblique hauling resulting from boat drift, and lever-operated models (such as the Petersen) may be triggered accidentally during descent.

Most grabs take only surface, or near-surface, benthic samples (Eleftheriou

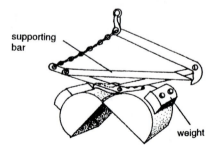

Fig. 4.3 The Petersen grab: open for lowering. The jaws are held open by a supporting bar which is dislodged when the substrate is reached.

and Holme 1984) and are thus not suitable for deeper fauna, which may necessitate use of a suction sampler (p. 84) or other device for recovery. The many patterns of large marine grab used for marine macrofauna are noted by these authors. The smaller models needed for studies of the meiofauna include some which can be opened from the top, allowing for taking cores without overly disturbing the layers of sediment. The Bacescu sampler is particularly suitable for this as it incorporates a core tube in the grab.

Dredges

Elliott and Drake (1981*b*) regarded dredges as the 'deep-water equivalent of the pond net' for quantitative sampling of invertebrates. They are samplers which are dragged across, and dig into, the bottom to gather a sample. Freshwater dredges are usually much lighter than their marine counterparts, and they can be used from small boats or from the bank. The Naturalists' dredge, similar to the dredge shown in Fig. 4.4, is used widely, and other patterns have the mouth triangular (the Irish dredge) or circular (the Fast dredge). Of these, the Irish dredge has the net protected by metal strips, and the Fast dredge has the net shielded in an open metal cylinder.

Comparative studies on these models (Elliott and Drake 1981b) showed that the Naturalists' dredge (two sizes tested) was more consistent than the others in the estimation of the relative abundance of major taxa, and more efficient in terms of estimating the total richness at each site. Large differences between models in sampling intervals for equivalent returns were evident—at the extreme, a small, lightweight Irish dredge would need to be

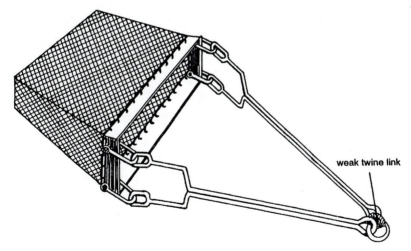

weak twine link

Fig. 4.4 The Naturalists' dredge.

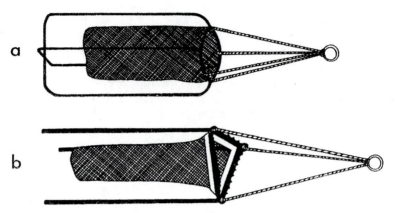

Fig. 4.5 Two patterns of simple tow-dredge: a, a tow net on runners; b, a triangular net designed to lie flat on the bottom, bag protected by metal rods.

used about 150 times to take a sample comparable with five times for the large version of the Naturalists' dredge!

Two patterns of such dredge (or 'tow nets') are shown in Fig. 4.5, and exemplify the general principle of protecting the delicate net inside a heavy iron frame. The round-framed net will always operate horizontally, with the four frame spars acting as 'sled runners' for towing. The triangular dredge (Irish dredge) shown can have mouth frame toothed so that it digs into the bottom while the net is towed; the catch thereby contains the animals from the uppermost layers of the substrate. Any such net can also have an external, coarse (5–6 cm mesh) net bag to protect the internal net.

Dendy sampler

The Dendy inverting sampler (Fig. 4.6) is useful for soft sediments, as well as those containing gravel or some vegetation. It is suitable for use in water up to 2–3 m deep, and is a brass cylinder (the standard length of which determines the depth of operation) and a rod by which the open end of the cylinder is driven vertically into the substrate. A cord is then pulled to invert the cylinder and the sample, other than that which drains through the gauze bottom, is retrieved. One disadvantage is that the usually organism-rich surface layer of the substrate is disturbed. The Dendy sampler is easily handled in shallow water, and samples can be taken rapidly.

Corers

Vertical cores of the substrate are also used widely as bottom samplers, although the large corers used in marine macrofaunal surveys are cumbersome and difficult to operate, in addition to being very expensive (Eleftheriou and Holme 1984). For meiofauna, though, corers are used for standard

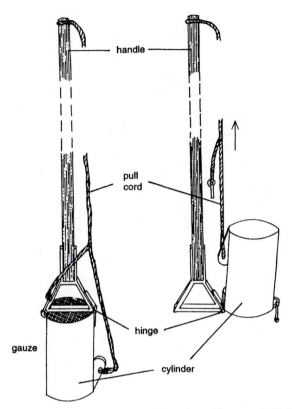

Fig. 4.6 The Dendy inverting sampler: a, position when driven vertically into the mud; b, inverted ready to lift (re-drawn after Southwood 1978).

sampling in intertidal and sublittoral zones, and small diameter samples are adequate for this. Even corers as small as 1 cm diameter can yield good samples in fauna-rich estuarine muds, and 2–4 cm diameter for searching intertidal zones. Such samplers collect all species non-selectively within a sand column (Gourbalt and Warwick 1994).

At its simplest, a corer consists of a smooth bore tube (commonly of transparent plastic, so that the sample can be seen) pushed or tapped into the substrate before the top is plugged and the corer withdrawn to produce core samples, commonly of length 30–50 cm.

As for soil corers (p. 57), split corer designs can be useful to safeguard the material obtained. Heavier corers are used commonly in the sublittoral zones and others involve tubes designed to fall vertically and penetrate by their own weight. For some of these, retrieving the samples is difficult, as discussed by McIntyre and Warwick (1984).

The length of the core needed must be determined by investigation. In general short (ca. 10 cm) cores may be adequate for muds, as most animals

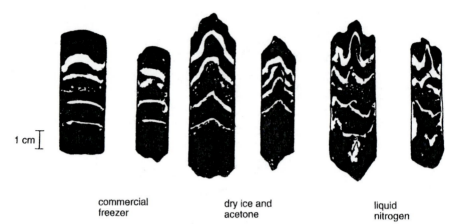

1 cm

| commercial | dry ice and | liquid |
| freezer | acetone | nitrogen |

Fig. 4.7 Effect of different methods of freezing on benthic substrate cores. The white bands were horizontal in fresh samples and resulted as shown (Rutledge and Fleeger 1988).

occur in the uppermost 6–8 cm, but interstitial animals may still be common at depths of 50 cm or more in sands, and the deeper species may be different from those near the surface. Cores are not retained adequately if the medium contains a high proportion of water.

On rocky or stony bottoms in fresh water where coring is difficult without causing massive disturbance to the animals and the substrate, it may be feasible to freeze the core *in situ*, and retrieve it intact to determine the distribution of the benthic fauna (Marchant and Lillywhite 1989). However, such operations are expensive and difficult, not least because of need for several people to handle the apparatus and samples adequately. Freezing cores *in situ* has been recommended for studies on the microdistribution of animals in sediments (Blomqvist 1991). However, sediment layers can be vertically distorted when core samples are frozen, so that care may be needed in assessing the distribution of meiobenthic animals (Fig. 4.7; Rutledge and Fleeger 1988), when such fine-scale information is needed.

Suction samplers

Various patterns of metal cylinders and boxes have been used in freshwater benthic sampling to delineate areas of substrate prior to its removal by various means. Airlift samplers (Fig. 4.8) and suction devices are both employed commonly, and elaborate powered suction devices mounted on sleds or operated by SCUBA divers are used in some marine macrofaunal surveys.

A hand-operated suction sampler designed for a wide range of shallow (to 50 cm deep water) freshwater environments (Boulton 1985; Fig. 4.9) overcomes the problems of many airlift samplers which cannot sample adequately for stones larger than about 32 mm modal particle size (Drake

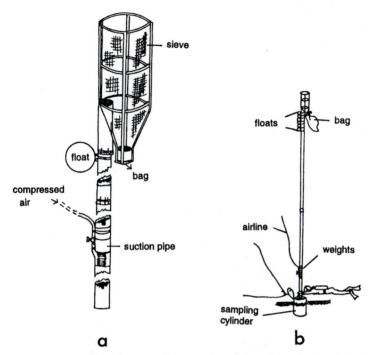

Fig. 4.8 An air-lift suction sampler: a, details of upper sieve and attachment of compressed air line; b, in operation, with diver manipulating the sampling cylinder.

and Elliott 1982). Boulton's sampler consists of a floorless galvanized iron box with a rim of thick sponge rubber to provide a good seal with the substrate and which encloses 0.05 m² of substrate. The contents of the box can be agitated by hand, through a sleeve net, while the water and its contents are removed by a hand-operated bilge pump to a net with a collecting bottle attached. The substrate can be disturbed to a standard depth, and the entrance to the flexible ('swimming pool') hose can be barred to prevent ingress of large objects which might block the hose or valves. As the device does not rely on any water current to wash animals into a container, it can be used equally well in still and running water, and eliminates problems of sampling variability due to differential scouring, or backwash from clogged nets.

Not all pumps need be complex. Simple 'bait pumps' used by anglers can provide worthwhile samples of interstitial fauna from fine sediments or sand in shallow waters.

Trawls and sledges

The epibenthos, and animals in the surface layers of the substrate, can often be collected by some form of trawl or sledge, particularly in large bodies of water. Many models require boats for their operation, and much commercial

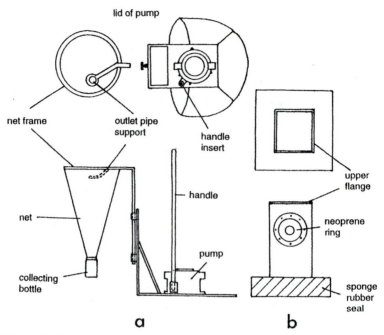

Fig. 4.9 The Boulton sampler, for sampling benthos in shallow still or running water: top and side views of (a) pump frame and (b) sampling box (after Boulton 1985).

fisheries gear (ranging from moderate-sized trawls to large hydraulic dredges) can provide qualitative samples of epifauna. Beam trawls are used commercially for crustaceans, and hydraulic dredges for some molluscs, for example, but the large mesh of some commercial trawls deliberately allows for retention of only large individuals.

Bottom sledges range from simple plankton nets supported on runners to those with tickler chains or similar devices to disturb animals resting on the bottom. Many have the net protected by a heavy frame (cf. p. 82) and many need to be operated in remote or unseen conditions.

The 'small biology trawl' shown in Fig. 4.10 has the net held extended in a frame so that it does not become entangled around the mouth of the trawl while it is lowered. The simple dredge shown in Fig. 4.4 represents a pattern used on stony or rocky substrates, being based on a heavy metal frame which can break off protruding rocks. Many models have one of the arms linked to the towing ring with weak twine which will break if the sledge becomes impeded or caught in the substrate, thus facilitating its retrieval. Likewise, weighted drags can also be made to break away rather than lose the whole apparatus. Large dredges and trawls can provide useful comparative data if tow distances can be standardized adequately and performance measured reasonably accurately.

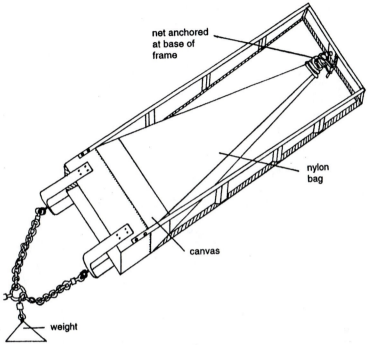

net anchored
at base of
frame

nylon
bag

canvas

weight

Fig. 4.10 The Small Biology Trawl, with the bag suspended inside a strong (3 m length) metal frame.

Bait traps

Bait traps, including commercial crab pots and lobster pots, can be useful for estimating presence and size of populations of some decapod crustaceans, as can simple retreats such as clay pots for octopus. Their use depends on sufficient knowledge and understanding of the behaviour of the target species. The variables (Fig. 4.11; Krouse 1989) include: (1) the type of bait, amount of bait, its age and whether it is easily accessible, and (2) the trap design in relation to interference between animals before entering, and escape ports for undersized animals. Many bait traps appear to be very inefficient for general studies.

Direct searching and collecting

As in terrestrial habitats, various direct examination techniques, without rigid quantification, provide valuable preliminary information on many aquatic invertebrate groups. Many of the methods can form the basis of more systematic surveys.

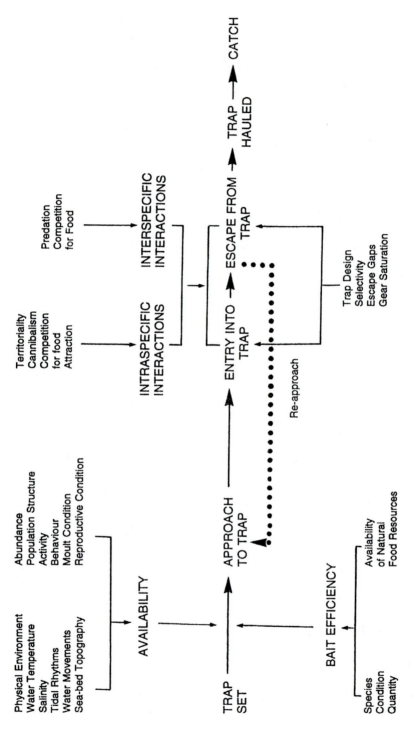

Fig. 4.11 Factors influencing capture efficiency of baited traps for marine crustaceans (after Krouse 1989).

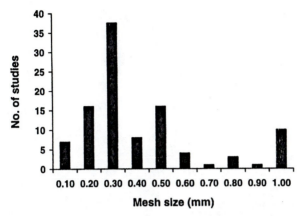

Fig. 4.12 Mesh size of nets used in a series of studies on freshwater invertebrates (after Winterbourn 1985).

Dip netting

A simple circular dip net, with or without a collecting tube at the apex, as well as being used in open water, can be used to disturb the substrate and search among debris or vegetation. A mesh sieve can be used in like manner to retrieve animals from similar habitats. Direct search of vegetation and substrate samples in white trays with shallow water is laborious but often very rewarding. Mesh size of sieves or nets varies considerably in different studies (Fig. 4.12), although standard mesh sizes are now recommended in many protocols.

Kick samples

The simplest approach to collecting benthic invertebrates, feasible only in shallow water, involves taking 'kick samples', using a similar principle to the Surber sampler (p. 79). A net is held so that water flows through it, and the substrate upstream is disturbed or 'kicked' so that the released benthos are swept into the net. This technique can be standardized on a catch/effort basis by standardizing the number of kicks or the time interval employed, but is essentially non-quantitative. Most animals in rapidly flowing streams occur under stones, and a high proportion can be collected by this method. Individual stones can be brushed or scrubbed in front of the net. Kick sampling is one of very few techniques available for rivers with a rough substrate and where water levels vary considerably (Winterbourn 1985).

Beach sampling

Shallow water or firm sandy bottoms on shores can be sampled using a sliding 'push net' (Fig. 4.13), also useful for capturing nekton associated with seagrass beds and similar vegetation.

angled wooden/steel bar

Fig. 4.13 A 'push net' for collecting invertebrates on sandy substrates.

Exposed intertidal zones can be studied either by examining quadrats or more extensive extractive sampling. Corers (p. 82) can be used to sample meiofauna, and direct digging (for polychaete worms: Brown 1993) or raking (for sandy beach molluscs, such as cockles and clams) can also reveal many other animals. Both area and depth can be standardized, and raking, by formalizing spacing of tines, can also incorporate some estimations of individual size of particular macroinvertebrates. On rocky shores, direct counts, with or without removal of sedentary or near-sedentary animals, can be made in quadrats, and photographs are often used to verify the counts. For monitoring (p. 182) permanent quadrats can be established, as occurs in deeper water for regular inspection by SCUBA divers.

Artificial substrates

Various forms of artificial substrate, such as multiplate samplers (Hester-Dendy samplers), wooden blocks with holes drilled in them, net bags, or wire mesh trays filled with stones (basket samplers), can be used to detect mobile benthic animals through colonization, if time permits. Usually, at least several weeks, often much longer, are needed. Placing a box or tray in a pond or stream substrate and filling it with cleaned mud or stones to match (or allowing it to fill naturally with sediment) can lead to very accurate samples of the bottom fauna in due course. Artificial substrates can provide suitable habitats of uniform composition and area, and can facilitate comparison of fauna at different sites irrespective of the natural substrate conditions (Davenport 1985). They can thus play an important role in standardizing samples in monitoring programmes, and are particularly valuable for use in areas which cannot be sampled adequately by other means. Their major uses in monitoring therefore include:

(1)   short-term intensive studies in large rivers;

(2)   monitoring of discharge in small streams; and

(3)   augmenting information gained from other techniques.

Multiplate samplers consist of a series of 7.5 cm square board or ceramic plates held together on a central bolt and separated by 'spacers' of various depths. They can be suspended in water or anchored on the substrate and may yield taxa only rarely captured by netting. As well as being cheap to construct, multiplate samplers can reduce sample processing time because they are disassembled easily and animals dislodged with minimal damage. Large numbers of samples can be examined in a short time.

Basket samplers can be useful in distinguishing differences in invertebrate community composition attributable to the effects of discharges (Davenport 1985). They can be simple baskets, or more elaborate boxes which can be sealed with plastic slides before they are extracted, so that disturbance or escape of animals is minimized.

Meiobenthic samplers

Meiobenthic fauna of sandy beaches can be sampled by digging holes and filtering the water which seeps into them through a 40 μm mesh. Agitation of the water can detach organisms from sand grains, and the technique is referred to as the Karaman/Chappuis (or KC) method.

Individual stone sampling

In rocky streams where samplers cannot be used easily, sampling from individual stones can be carried out by rolling and brushing them in front of a net, as noted above. The number of stones and estimates of their surface area can be used as expressions of sampling intensity. As for Surber samplers and others, escape of organisms can be thwarted by enclosing the samples—such as by use of the enclosing stone-lifter described by Doeg and Lake (1981). Quantitative sampling of the infauna of rocks is extremely difficult; some organisms can be induced to leave their retreats by leaving the rocks in 'stale' water for a period, but many must be collected by laborious search.

Examination of vegetation

Netting and benthic sampling can easily mix up and confuse interpretation of the animals living on vegetation and on the substrate. Because submerged vegetation may be the specific habitat of many invertebrates, direct examination may be needed to characterize the fauna fully, and methods for this generally involve cutting the plants, enclosing them, and sorting and sieving them in white trays. Gerking (1957) reviewed many early studies, and designed a sampler which encloses an area of vegetation which can then be clipped off close to the substrate and retrieved for examination. Such techniques are most convenient for use in shallow (to ca. 1 m deep) water.

Open water samplers

Sampling of invertebrates in open water is often very difficult, especially in marine systems, because of lack of knowledge of their movement patterns in the water column. A quotation used by Fraser (1979), referring particularly to plankton sampling 'Problems associated with variation of time and space among pelagic organisms are already difficult enough to evaluate without imposing additional complexity through the inadequate understanding of the sampling tools' (Aron *et al.* 1965) remains true, despite valiant attempts to advance the science and to standardize methods more fully. Most methods involve netting, filtering invertebrates from the water body through a mesh. Various difficulties are associated with the size of mesh, the filtration efficiency, drag, clogging, towing speed and avoidance by target taxa (Heron 1979; Vannucci 1979). Again from Fraser (1979): '...organisms smaller than a given mesh size go through the meshes in an unknown and variable quantity dependent on their shape, protuberances, activity, elasticity, and the amount of clogging. How much easier it would be to sample plankton if it consisted only of smooth spherical balls'!

The impetus for development and refinement of the two major categories of method used to sample animals in free water masses, plankton netting and mid-water trawling, has come predominantly from marine fisheries. As two examples, from among many:

1. Quantitative sampling of commercial decapod crustacea larvae to estimate stock size for exploitation involves quantitative sampling of larvae, estimates of effective fecundity and adult sex ratios (Nicholls and Thompson 1988). The planktonic larvae undergo diurnal vertical movements in the water column. Their expected density varies with sampler size and duration of tow, and their ability to escape capture will also be influenced by the speed of sampling. Without knowledge of distribution it is necessary to sample the whole water column, and Nicholls and Thompson recommended using high-speed sampling using a double oblique tow from the surface to the seabed and return, using a sampler with a 20–40 cm opening towed at 25 m/s, so that about 200 s are spent in each 10 m depth layer.

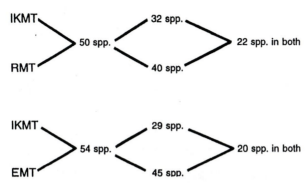

Fig. 4.14 Variations in catches of cephalopods between three patterns of mid-water trawl (IKMT-Isaacs-Kidd mid-water trawl, RMT—rectangular mid-water trawl, EMT—Engel trawl) (Roper 1977).

2. Three patterns of mid-water trawls gave considerable differences in their catches of pelagic cephalopod molluscs in the North Atlantic, although each was effective singly (Roper 1977). The Isaacs-Kidd 3 m closing mid-water trawl (IKMT), the rectangular mid-water trawl (8 m² opening, closing) and the Engel trawl (small, 1400 mesh, non-closing) each caught a range of species, but in comparative trials the level of species overlap between methods was reasonably low (Fig. 4.14).

Recommended standards for plankton nets (e.g. UNESCO 1979) and trawls exist and such considerations are also relevant to sampling in freshwater bodies; despite the usual difference in scale, the problems of sampling efficiency are generally similar. In general, the standards differ for organisms in different size classes, and expert advice should be sought when designing a sampling programme. However, some radical recent changes in plankton sampling technology, such as the Moored, Automated, Serial Zooplankton Pump (MASZP: National Research Council 1995) coupled with immunological markers for planktonic larvae of various benthic invertebrates indicate moves toward increasing capability to assess assemblages of small invertebrates which are likely to become very important as they become more generally available.

Plankton nets

Plankton nets have been the standard device for sampling the smaller animals in water columns, and have varied from simple conical tow nets (Fig. 4.15), and nets which can be closed before raising from particular depths, to more elaborate samplers equipped with flow-meters and/or paravanes to aid quantification of sampling volume and consistency of performance. Mesh size and characteristics are critical (Fraser 1979), and the smallest plankton (largely outside the scope of this work) are sampled better by closing bottles

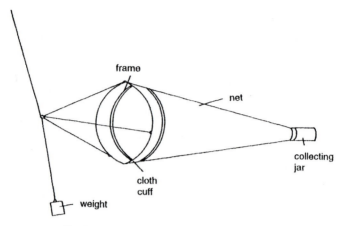

Fig. 4.15 A plankton net, suspended for towing.

which provide water samples from given depths or positions in the column. More active plankton are captured by relatively faster tows using enclosed nets, such as the Clarke-Bumpus sampler (Fig. 4.16), which has a closing device and has been described as 'the transition from conventional nets to rapid tow industry'. Such samplers usually incorporate a flow meter, and have been used extensively for studying the vertical distribution of organisms in the water column. The smallest settled animals, such as rotifers, may be sampled by using a phytoplankton net cast from the bank of a pond and dragged back through any macrophyte patches present (Langley *et al.* 1995).

Continuous sampling of plankton (Colebrook 1979, for summary of development) has involved towing at a standard depth (commonly, 10 m), and

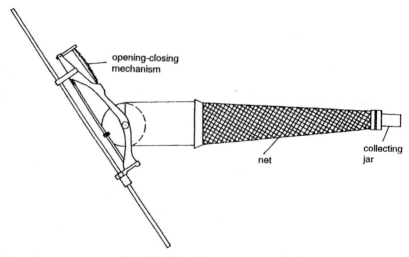

Fig. 4.16 The Clarke-Bumpus sampler.

admitting water through a small aperture (12.5 mm^2), filtering the plankton through a slowly scrolling band of bolting silk which is spooled with another band to sandwich the plankton in preservative.

Mid-water trawls

Again, a variety of patterns exist, but much attention has been paid, particularly, to the IKMT. Its advantages have been tabulated by UNESCO (1979), with emphasis on the need for adopting a standard pattern for sampling use, and for catching larger plankton and smaller nekton in the 2–10 cm body length range. The main advantages of IKMT include a large mouth free of obstructions such as bridles, that it is self-depressing, is versatile and easier to use than conical nets with a similar mouth area, and can be towed at great depths and at high speed. The major disadvantage is the lack of measure of volume of water filtered, so that it is semiquantitative rather than fully quantifiable. Nevertheless, the IKMT has been the most widely used device in this category.

Electrofishing

This method, used widely for sampling fish populations in ponds and shallow lakes and rivers, can also be used for populations of some larger invertebrates, such as shrimps. With care, the stunned shrimps can be collected from the water surface by netting and later released, so that the method may be adapted for broad surveys of such species. Early trials (Elliott and Bagenal 1972) showed that electrofishing may cause epibenthic taxa to be dislodged from the substrate and become temporarily amenable to drift net sampling. Populations of shrimps in small streams can be assessed by this technique (Penczak and Rodriguez 1990).

In addition to the methods noted here, there is some potential for 'opportunistic documentation' of aquatic, particularly marine, invertebrates through analysis of fisheries bycatch, although the practicalities can be complex. Even for many commercially harvested species, information on population dynamics, biology and distribution is very incomplete, despite its relevance to stock assessment and optimizing harvest levels (Caddy 1989b). Many fisheries now include elaborate attempts to reduce bycatch, be it vertebrate or invertebrate. The brown shrimp (*Crangon crangon*) fishery off the Netherlands, for example, uses selective trawls which allow escape of all fish while retaining shrimp by diverting them into a cod-end (Boddeke 1989). Fisheries target taxa may themselves be difficult to study because of the need for rapid processing. Little is known of many cephalopods, for example, which may be fished by freezer trawlers and processed on capture (de Laguna 1989).

Little ecological information relevant to conservation is available for some whole groups of fished invertebrates, such as echinoderms (Conand and Sloan 1989). Sampling of commercial catches, particularly crustaceans or molluscs, can entail inspection of the catches themselves, or of documents such as purchase slips. Data obtainable in port may aid interpretation of size and frequency of different classes of animals, such as changes in the sex ratio of lobsters (Parsons *et al.* 1983) and data from the catching vessels can provide biological information through interpretation of methods, location, catching depth, and other factors.

Extraction of specimens from substrate samples

As for soil and litter samples in terrestrial studies (p. 63), the extraction of benthic macroinvertebrates from substrate samples can be accomplished in several different ways, including direct searching and sorting by hand, and the optimal method will differ with the texture of the sediments, whether the material sought is live or dead, and for different taxonomic groups and size categories. For large samples, such as those obtained by large marine grabs or trawls, the important initial task is to reduce the amount of material to a more transportable volume. At sea, grab samples are commonly deposited on to a sieving table or hopper, where the contents can be washed through a sieve (or a series of sieves) with a hose, or (for more delicate animals) mechanically shaken for sieving, perhaps after initial hand-picking of larger animals. Sieve sizes may be critical and, in studies where coarse deposits necessitate using wide-meshed sieves, small samples can be sieved through a finer mesh to indicate what losses may be occurring.

Subsequent sorting will depend on the taxa selected. Hand sorting may be entirely adequate if particular large or conspicuous species and larger individuals only are needed, but more complex treatment is necessary for smaller organisms and the principles used for terrestrial fauna (p. 71) can be applied. Flotation and elutriation are thus both used commonly for benthic macrofauna. In flotation extraction of marine taxa, some chemicals commonly used are unsatisfactory with mud and silts without careful adjustment of the specific gravity, because organic debris also floats (Eleftheriou and Holme 1984).

For meiofauna (McIntyre and Warwick 1984), which are examined only relatively infrequently in conservation assessments, extraction methods differ according to: (1) the kind of sediment; (2) whether the samples are fresh or preserved; and (3) whether extraction is to be quantitative or qualitative. If information is needed on vertical distribution of fauna, the samples should be divided into the strata as soon as possible after collecting.

Coarse sediments—live material

Live material can be extracted by simple decantation, and efficiency is

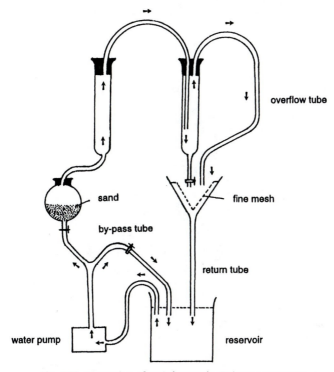

Fig. 4.17 Extraction of meiofauna: the Boisseau apparatus.

improved markedly if the whole sample is treated with an anaesthetic (such as isotonic magnesium chloride) to cause many animals to release their grip on sand grains without adverse effects. Elutriation involves such techniques as the Boisseau apparatus (Fig. 4.17), a closed system involving the use of a small water pump with a by-pass and collecting the fauna washed from the sand on a fine sieve, from where they can be washed, into a Petri dish of seawater.

Behavioural treatments are exemplified by the Uhlig technique (Fig. 4.18), in which crushed seawater ice gradually melts and induces the animals to move downward to a collecting dish. Although good for meiofauna, some groups of macrofauna do not respond to this method and must later be elutriated from the sample. The method is suitable for sandy sediments and, although much lower for some groups, extraction efficiency can be as high as 75% (Hulings and Gray 1971).

Fine sediments—live material

Extracting live material from fine muds and silts is difficult other than by centrifugation and decanting the resuspended supernatant through a fine

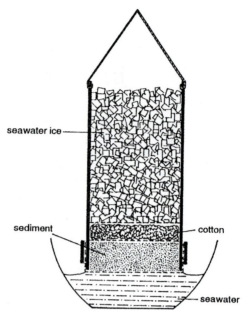

seawater ice

sediment

cotton

seawater

Fig. 4.18 Apparatus for separating interstitial fauna from sand by sea-water ice (Uhlig technique).

mesh (McIntyre and Warwick 1984). However, the Swedmark technique (Fig. 4.19) can be used for sand and mud; the sediment, in seawater, is suspended by a large silicone-coated pipette and sieved by gently rocking the sieve(s) in seawater so that the filtrate is returned to the original sample. Microscopic examination of the sieve in seawater then allows further analysis of the samples.

Coarse sediments—dead material

This most commonly involves extraction from samples preserved in formalin for transport or storage. The general techniques of decantation and elutriation are also effective for preserved material, and can sometimes be more efficient than for living animals. It may be useful to stain the samples to facilitate finding the specimens, and a solution of Rose Bengal (1 g in 1 litre of water, formalin or alcohol; immerse the sample for several hours) is often recommended; its use may shorten direct sorting time very substantially.

Fine sediments—dead material

This combination is difficult to treat, because of presence of lumps of clay or other masses, and some pretreatment of samples—such as by ultrasonic

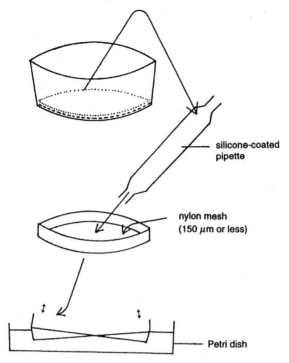

silicone-coated pipette

nylon mesh (150 μm or less)

Petri dish

Fig. 4.19 Extraction of meiofauna: the Swedmark technique.

vibration or freezing followed by thawing is often used to break down the samples. The sediment sample can then be suspended in 'Ludox-TM' (*care: toxic!*) and combining this with centrifugation and addition of kaolin powder before centrifugation has proved very successful (McIntyre and Warwick 1984). After spinning the screened sediment at 6000 r.p.m. for 7 min, the kaolin settles last and prevents the sediment from being disturbed as the water is poured off. Ludox-TM is added and the sediment resuspended by agitating, if necessary breaking the kaolin plug. Re-centrifuging (using the same regime as before) and pouring the supernatant into a fine sieve, then washing it thoroughly with tap water before transferring to a sorting dish, is followed three times for each sample and separates all but very few animals in clean solution. These can then be sorted as needed.

Further reading

Burd, B. J., Nemec, A., and Brinkhurst, R. O. (1990). The development and application of analytical methods in benthic marine infaunal studies. *Advances in Marine Biology* **26**, 169–247.

Holme, N. A. and McIntyre, A. D. (ed.) (1984). *Methods for the study of marine benthos*. Blackwell Scientific, Oxford.

Hulings, N. C. and Gray, J. S. (1971). *A manual for the study of meiofauna*. Smithsonian Contributions to Zoology No. 78.

Hynes, H. B. N. (1960). *The biology of polluted waters*. Liverpool University Press, Liverpool.

Rosenberg, D. M. and Resh, V. H. (ed.) (1993). *Freshwater monitoring and benthic macroinvertebrates*. Chapman & Hall, New York.

Schlieper, C. (ed.) (1972). *Research methods in marine biology* (trans. by E. Drucker). University of Washington Press, Seattle.

5 Assessing use of sampling methods

Introduction

The methods described, or alluded to, in the previous chapters exemplify the great variety of active or passive techniques available to extract invertebrates from natural habitats, and many of the difficulties of quantification or of relying on any single method to provide definitive information. Most groups of invertebrates can thus be collected or sampled more formally by several different methods, and a broad summary (Table 5.1) can act as an initial guide in selecting those of use for a given target group. The innumerable modifications of the methods are eloquent testimony to the difficulties involved, and to the problems of trying to make adequate comparison between different surveys or habitats even when similar methods are used throughout. The methods discussed, used with care, do not destroy the habitats in which they sample, although there are occasional exceptions. Heavy trawls, for example, may cause damage to seabeds. Destructive sampling methods (such as the extensive stripping of tree bark or breaking up rotting wood to collect saproxylic taxa, or draining of whole small water bodies) have little place in conservation-orientated assessment, and this may become important in documenting rare species or the fauna of very restricted habitats. 'Codes' for collecting by hobbyists and others counsel strongly the need to leave habitat undisturbed or, at least, in fit condition for their characteristic inhabitants to continue to thrive there. One such code is summarized in Table 5.2 (JCCBI 1976), and its recommendations are widely applicable. Especial care is needed not to remove more than the minimum necessary number of known rare or vulnerable taxa, or to disturb small habitat patches unnecessarily.

Most methods are biased in efficiency towards particular taxa, size classes, behavioural categories, or other subsets of the total invertebrate fauna, and uncritical comparisons between surveys based on different techniques may commonly be spurious. Even using the same methods, uncritical comparison between sites may disregard significant factors affecting invertebrate diversity and abundance, even if these are sufficiently well understood to incorporate into analyses. Likewise, it is necessary to specify very clearly *any* departure from standard sampling regimes and, even, to note apparently small peculiarities in trap construction or design which may influence either 'total catchability' or the relative abundance of different taxonomic or functional groups.

Table 5.1
Recommended sampling methods for major groups of invertebrates

Taxon	Collecting/sampling methods
Porifera (sponges)	Hand-collecting; raking; dredging and trawling.
Coelenterata (sea anemones, hydroids, corals, jellyfish	Hand-collecting from vegetation (freshwater), rock pools (littoral marine forms), or directly in shallow water or with aid of SCUBA; dredging and trawling (deep water); dip netting or tow netting (pelagic forms).
Platyhelminthes Turbellaria (flatworms)	Hand-collecting or direct searching (terrestrial flatworms under logs, in rotting wood, among mosses, etc.; freshwater forms under stones or among vegetation); sweeping aquatic vegetation with fine-meshed net; wet funnel extraction of litter, gentle dry funnel extractions sometimes useful, but care is needed to avoid desiccation; dredging (deeper water).
Parasitic forms (flukes, tapeworms)	Direct examination of hosts; most species are site-specific parasites, either on gills of fish (Monogenea) or internally; collecting depends on adequate examination, which must be undertaken as soon as possible after host capture or death. Gut contents should be examined directly and by sedimentation, in addition to other parts of the body, including linings of cavities. Gut wall scraping or stripping needed for smaller specimens, which are easily obscured in folds. If in cysts or tumours, cut out and preserve with surrounding tissues.
Nemertinea (ribbon worms)	As for flatworms. Most are marine and can be found under stones: fewer are freshwater or occur in moist soils.
Nematoda (roundworms)	
Free-living forms	Most are small: wet (Baermann) funnel extraction of soil or plant material; centrifugation; elutriation. Washing of vegetation, followed by elutriation.
Parasitic forms	Direct examination of hosts; sedimentation and centrifugation of gut contents, as for parasitic platyhelminths.
Rotifera (rotifers)	Pelagic forms: plankton-type tow nets or fine dipnets. Non-pelagic forms: collect aquatic vegetation and cover with water in jars, illumination from one side will usually attract rotifers to that side in a few hours: collect directly: collect scrapings from dried up pool margins: rotifers likely to emerge when mud is wetted.
Brachiopoda (lamp-shells)	Dredging, trawling; mainly from deeper waters.
Ectoprocta	Found mainly as incrustations or colonies on hard substrates, such as rocks, shells, timber or boat bottoms. Hand collecting, and examination of substrate samples and scrapings.
Echinodermata (starfish, sea urchins and their allies)	Direct searching on littoral or reef zones, and among seaweeds; dredging and trawling for deeper water forms; digging for burrowing forms along lower reaches of shores.

Table 5.1 (*Continued*)

Taxon	Collecting/sampling methods
Annelida (segmented worms)	
Polychaeta (bristleworms)	Mainly marine. Direct searching; digging in mud/sand and sifting these; under stones, fissures in rocks and corals (may need to split these to extract worms); collect containers of seaweed and examine by hand; trawling, dredging, benthic grabs, netting: examine surfaces of shells, rocks and other objects retrieved; sheltering worms will emerge after a few hours of submersion in seawater; tow-netting and dip-netting for pelagic forms.
Oligochaeta (earthworms)	Terrestrial: direct collecting by digging and sieving surface layers of soil, and among rotting vegetation, and searching under stones and in/under fallen wood; funnel extractions from soil or humus, but not usually as efficient as hand-sorting. For enchytraeids, core samples are used for wet funnel extraction, or use of a Nielsen sampler or similar device. Some oligochaetes collectable from the ground surface after rain or flooding with a chemical such as weak formalin (25 ml of 37% formalin to 5 l water for area of 0.5 m^2, and collect all worms surfacing over 10 min). Aquatic: cores and dredging from mud and sand can be used for tubificids; benthic grabs generally less effective than for many other taxa, but these and dredges useful for deep water forms.
Hirudinea (leeches)	Direct searching of stones, mud, vegetation (aquatic forms) or low vegetation (wet terrestrial environments); most commonly found attached to hosts: inspect possible hosts routinely on capture.
Mollusca	Shells alone may be useful indicators of diversity or of presence and distribution of particular species. Terrestrial: slugs and snails usually collected by direct searching in litter, on and among vegetation, under stones, in/under rotting wood (etc.); many are most active in wet weather or at night, and are more cryptic in dry conditions. Funnel extraction/sieving of leafmould and litter may be useful for smaller forms. Freshwater: direct examination and sifting of submerged vegetation (obtained by netting, direct collection or grappling), mud, stones; netting; dredging and trawling for deep water forms. Marine: direct collection on shores, using transects or quadrats as sampling base, or more casually; raking on sandy shores for selected taxa; netting and trawling, more rarely bait-lining, for pelagic cephalopods.

(*Continued*)

Table 5.1 (*Continued*)

Taxon	Collecting/sampling methods
Arthropoda	Numerous techniques used for sampling this massive group; the following are examples, only, of the approaches used.
Pycnogonida (seaspiders)	Direct searching, especially among seaweeds; dredging for deeper water forms.
Onychophora (velvetworms)	Direct searching in damp terrestrial habitats such as leaf litter, under rotting wood, in caves; more rarely found by funnel extractions from litter samples, but their low density usually makes this unreliable for detection.
Tardigrada (water bears)	Aquatic: sandy bottoms—stir in water, decant immediately after sand settles, sieve through fine mesh (pores ca. 44 μm), and transfer specimens from screen into storage jar. Terrestrial (vegetation, soil): similar approach used; samples of vegetation (bryophytes, in particular), soil or litter in small paper bag until processing, then place in water for several hours, decant excess water and sieve. Supernatant filtering, as for nematodes, after centrifugation.
Arachnida (spiders, mites, scorpions and their relatives)	Aquatic: watermites collected by tow-netting (as for small crustaceans), sweeping submerged vegetation with fine dip net, and sorting catches in white tray; direct searches of submergent vegetation, mosses and other substrates, and extraction from these. Terrestrial: beating and sweeping of vegetation for many spiders, opilionids and mites; vacuum samplers in low vegetation; direct searches of vegetation, litter, under bark and stones; sifting of vegetation debris; small forms (many mites) closely associated with vegetation and may need direct microscopical examination or flotation. Dry funnel extractions from litter and soil: Tullgren funnels used commonly, but flotation techniques useful for small forms and particularly useful for samples concentrated by sifting; slow extraction (2–4 days) by funnels often recommended, and high gradient extractors for relatively small cores good for some mites. Pitfall traps commonly used for epigaeic spiders. Larger spiders and scorpions, collected individually, may be dangerous: use long-handled forceps for handling. Parasitic mites and ticks collected directly from hosts, with small mites often difficult to detect.
Myriapoda (centipedes, millipedes)	Most common in terrestrial habitats, on/close to ground. Direct searching of litter, under bark, and sieving vegetation; night collections useful, as many species nocturnal; dry funnel extraction of litter and soil; pitfall traps (narrow traps sometimes preferred); sweeping vegetation. Few aquatic millipedes: searches of waterside banks and vegetation. Symphyla often deeper in soil: as deep soil samples not extracted well by dry funnels, collect by hand crumbling soil in water, then wet sieving and flotation for individual retrieval of specimens.

Table 5.1 (*Continued*)

Taxon	Collecting/sampling methods
Crustacea	Aquatic: many small forms (larvae of marine taxa, copepods, cladocerans and others) collected by plankton nets or dip-netting; sweeping nets through submerged vegetation (especially for freshwater), and direct examination of vegetation after sorting in white tray. Benthic samplers, and searches on/under rocks (amphipods). Many crustaceans are bottom-dwellers, so that samples of mud/sand, even if dried, can yield large numbers if allowed to stand in water. Bait traps for larger forms (some decapods), and trawls also used. Direct searches of submerged and inter-tidal rock and wooden surfaces for barnacles. Terrestrial: direct searches, mainly in wet environments (especially amphipods), leaf litter, moss beds, under stones and logs, under bark; funnel extraction and flotation of litter samples. Pitfall trapping sometimes used for isopods, as is vegetable baiting.
Insecta (true insects)	(Numerous). Winged adults: range of aerial methods used. Malaise traps; flight intercept traps; light traps; suction traps; water traps used widely in open country; individual netting of some taxa common. Terrestrial. Soil/litter: dry funnel extraction; direct searching in trays after sifting litter samples or breaking up soil; direct searching under rocks, fallen wood, among decaying vegetation and debris; pitfall traps; emergence traps for selected forms; various specialized techniques may be employed for particular groups, such as breaking up dead wood for saproxylic taxa such as termites and many beetle larvae. Low vegetation: direct searching, particularly for sedentary taxa such as scale insects; collection of galls or leaf mines for later adult emergence; insecticide fogging of tree trunks or dense vegetation such as tussocks; sorting of cut vegetation on trays; sweeping and vacuum sampling. Higher vegetation: beating of accessible branches; cutting for direct examination; insecticide fogging. Aquatic. Adults of many insects with aquatic larvae are amenable to capture by many of the above methods, such as netting, sweeping and beating of waterside vegetation, or nearby light trapping. Benthic larvae and others: Surber samples or kick samples in running water; dredges, grabs, corers; sieving mud and sand preceding direct collecting; direct searches of stones and submerged vegetation; dip-netting among vegetation and in free water; emergence traps can sometimes be moored on the water surface to trap emerging Diptera and others. Parasitic forms. Direct searches of hosts for fleas and lice; extraction of host habitats, such as nest or burrow contents, in dry funnels.
Other Hexapoda	As for insects, above

Table 5.2
A code for insect collecting—selected points, modified from the code prepared
by the Joint Committee for the Conservation of British Insects (JCCBI 1976).
The advice was designed particularly for hobbyist collectors, but is applicable
much more widely in conservation

1.	No more specimens than are strictly required for any purpose should be killed. Where possible, insects should be examined without killing them, and released.
2.	Specimens of 'listed' species should be collected with restraint, with those species in greatest danger not collected at all.
3.	Previously unknown localities for rare species should be notified to any controlling body.
4.	Collectors should attempt to 'break new ground' rather than simply continuing to exploit local or rare species from the same locality or localities.
5.	The catch at a light-trap should not be killed casually for subsequent examination.
6.	If a trap used for scientific purposes is found to be catching rare or local species unnecessarily, its use should be curtailed, or the trap re-sited.
7.	Always seek permission to collect on reserves or private land, comply with any conditions of access laid down in granting permission, and supply lists of taxa collected to any appropriate authority.
8.	Do as little damage to the environment as possible. As examples: • replace overturned logs and stones in their original position • do not 'exhaust' limited habitats such as bark or dead wood—leave some undisturbed • replace water weed and moss in the appropriate habitat • do not break branches and foliage unnecessarily by beating or deliberate removal
9.	Collect only as many larvae or other livestock as can be housed and fed properly. Release unwanted reared material in the original locality. Seek advice before undertaking any releases into areas outside the species' normal range.

The two major general problems are:

(1) assessing the efficiency of any given trap design/method in capturing the fauna present, and

(2) comparing the catches from different trap designs, even when they appear to be very similar.

Even more generally, pending more comparative studies of trap efficiency, it is important to ensure that suites of traps used in comparative studies are identical in construction, as well as standardizing duration and periodicity of the times they are operated, as urged in many recent accounts. Replication of sampling effort is sometimes very difficult, because variations of catch occur as results of slight differences in aspect or position, even if the traps themselves are identical and used over similar periods. Cross-trap differences can be confused easily with cross-site differences.

Sampling sets

Despite the attractions of cost and simplicity it is also unwise to rely on any single trapping method for inventory work where complete (or reasonably complete) information on species richness is sought. 'No single survey method or sampling technique can be used for future inventories of rare and endangered invertebrates' (Scudder 1996). Disney (1986), among others, has advocated the use of 'sampling sets', in which several different methods are employed together to help compensate for the bias of any individual method. As he emphasized, any particular collecting method is selective and even some common species may not be collected easily—or at all. Initial selection of methods will reflect the predominant target taxa but the greater the range of taxa to be incorporated into a survey, the greater the array of techniques which must be used simultaneously and, in most cases, the greater the cost of the trapping programme and subsequent analysis (Chapter 6). Low-cost simple combinations of sampling methods may be needed particularly in the tropics (Stork 1994), where funding may be especially limited. Examples of such sampling sets from selected surveys of terrestrial arthropods are shown in Table 5.3.

As well as providing a more complete array of the taxa of a site through complementarity of their catches, sampling sets can help to overcome some of the practical difficulties by allowing for combining results of individual traps, and trap types, into a single data set (such as a species list) for a site. Disney (1986) suggested that a sample unit for terrestrial arthropods might include a white water trap, a yellow water trap, and a set of 10 pitfall traps, each trap of standard size and pattern. This whole unit can then be replicated 10 times in each site being sampled. The number of replicates represents a compromise between adequate data for valid statistical analysis, allowances for accidents to some units, and not overly increasing the effort needed to achieve valid results.

In cases where monitoring of a number of identified key groups is advo-cated rather than seeking the broadest possible range of captures, combina-tions of sampling method will be dictated by the optimal ones for those groups. Thus, for assessing arthropod groups in old growth forests in the northwestern United States, Lattin (1993) identified several key groups and sampling regimes for each to provide estimates of trends in a range of trophic groups (Table 5.4). In their studies on Tasmanian rain forest invertebrates, Coy et al. (1993) used nine methods to obtain, collectively, samples from the various habitats in this complex system. More generally (Marshall et al. 1994), a protocol for sampling terrestrial arthropods to assess regional diversity could include, at the least, Malaise traps, flight intercept traps and pan traps as well as some form of behavioural extractor for litter invertebrates, but the complexity of any such regime will also depend on funding available for subsequent analysis. For use of eight methods as a representative sampling

Table 5.3
Sampling sets for terrestrial arthropods: some examples

Authors	Methods	Regime
Disney (1986)	1 18 × 18 cm white water trap 1 23 cm diameter yellow water trap 10 5 cm diameter pitfall traps	Replicate set 10 times/site
Coy et al. (1993)	9 main methods, grouped, directed to soil, litter, moss denizens; four methods reasonably quantitative Sweep/beat, litter (funnel extraction), moss (funnel extractor), soil cores, hand collection, vacuum sampling, yellow pans, pitfall traps, knockdown.	Used in various combinations over variety of sites in Tasmania: usually at least 6 methods/site
Marshall et al. (1994)	2 Malaise traps	1–7 days, oriented at 90°, spaced 25 m apart
	2 Flight intercept traps	1–7 days, oriented at 90°, spaced 25 m apart
	4 Pan traps (15 × 17 cm)	1 day–1 month spaced 10 m apart
	4 Pitfall traps (450 ml)	1 day–1 month spaced 10 m apart
	Behavioural extractor (funnels)	4/year, 10 samples/period
Hammond (1991)	3 Malaise traps—44 weeks	Together with litter sampling and use of a small canopy Malaise trap part of the time, these constituted a 'core sampling regime' for lowland forest plots (February–May)
	4 × 5 unbaited pitfall traps, 7.5 cm diameter	
	3 flight interception traps—13 or 15 weeks 10 yellow pan traps, on plastic sheet	
Gadagker et al. (1990)	1 Light trap sweeping	In centre of plot: 7 h. 6, 10 × 10 m quadrats, and swept between 100 and 1200 h.
	5 pitfall traps, 9 cm diameter	1 in each of 5 10 × 10 m quadrats, overnight sample, ca. 18 h.
	5 scented traps (sugar, yeast, methyl parathion, pineapple essence)	1 in each of 5 10 × 10 m quadrats, 1 m from ground, ca. 18 h.
Canaday (1987)	2 patterns of yellow dish pan traps, suspended	Intensity of sampling varied over period July–August 1984
	1 window trap, suspended 1 light trap sticky trap sweep netting	

Table 5.4
An example of how arthoropod taxa may be used for monitoring: functional roles and sampling methods in old-growth Pacific-Northwest forests (after Lattin 1993)

Group	Functional role	Sampling methods
Acarina Oribatid mites	Fungal, litter feeders, predators	High-gradient litter and soil extractors
Diplopoda Millipedes	Litter breakdown	Pitfall traps
Collembola	Litter/soil organic	Berlese funnels, high-gradient extractors
Insecta Hemiptera:		

Heteroptera
  Lygaeidae
  Miridae
	Seed feeders on ground
	Foliage feeders, predators
		Pitfall traps
		Beating foliage

Coleoptera
  Carabidae
  Scolytidae
	Predators, seed feeders
	Xylophagous
		Pitfall traps
		Pheromone, intercept traps

Hymenoptera Symphyta	Foliage feeders	Malaise traps

Lepidoptera
  Caterpillars
  Adults
	Foliage feeders
	Nectar feeders
		Beating, branch clipping
		Blacklight traps

set in British Columbia, the minimum costs per monthly sample (using biology undergraduate students rather than specialists, costed at $10/h), needed to cover 344 h/month per site for sorting and processing alone. Identification to family levels adds another 340 h/month per site—assuming that sufficient expertise can be hired for this rate. Scudder (1996) suggested that the costs could easily triple if higher levels of expertise were needed.

The complementarity of catches from different traps is shown well by Basset's (1988) combination of a small Malaise trap and an interception trap in tree canopy. Over a year, five such combinations amassed nearly 25 000 insects, with the composition by major groups differing considerably (Table 5.5), although with much of the ranking of groups by abundance little changed. Pitfall trapping may provide a considerably different suite of carabid beetles from direct searches of grassland in the same habitats (J. Andersen 1995). Inferences on energy flow and other ecological processes may be biased considerably without knowledge of catches from different methods: for example, large carabids may be over-represented in pitfall traps relative to small species. And, in a study of carabid beetles captured in Alberta, Canada, the numbers caught differed considerably between pitfall traps which were left undisturbed over the trapping period, moved slightly (about 30 cm) when

Table 5.5

Arthropod catches in interception traps (Malaise trap and window trap subunits) in Queensland rain forest canopy (five traps; results from 1 year of continuous trapping in crowns of *Argyrodendron actinophyllum*; given as percentage mean and SE) (extracted from Basset 1988)

Group	Total	Malaise trap	(Rank)	Window trap	(Rank)
Total	24758	14597		10161	
Araneae	3.67 ± 0.39	4.15 ± 0.71	5	3.44 ± 0.42	5
Blattodea	2.32 ± 0.49	2.90 ± 0.70	7	1.70 ± 0.31	8
Homoptera	13.50 ± 1.74	19.49 ± 1.60	2	5.86 ± 1.27	3
Psocoptera	2.03 ± 0.45	1.56 ± 0.44	8	2.53 ± 0.50	7
Coleoptera	29.82 ± 3.62	10.26 ± 2.04	3	54.36 ± 4.33	1
Diptera					
Nematocera	28.06 ± 2.11	43.63 ± 2.42	1	8.06 ± 1.08	2
Brachycera	4.96 ± 0.91	4.18 ± 0.27	4	5.59 ± 0.96	4
Lepidoptera	3.36 ± 0.35	3.69 ± 0.40	6	3.01 ± 0.43	6
Others	2.70	2.06		3.79	

emptied, or moved to a new position each week (Digweed *et al.* 1995). In that study both depletion (removal of beetles) and disturbance (trap resiting) affected beetle catches in forest environments.

In the tropical rain forests of Sulawesi, Hammond (1991) employed different techniques to facilitate comparison with previous results and to ensure the suitability and robustness of the collecting methods for making direct comparisons of insect species composition in the samples. Noyes (1989) compared five methods of catching Hymenoptera in the same system and found some clear differences (Table 5.6). In terms of sampling effort, Noyes

Table 5.6

Samples of Hymenoptera taken in Sulawesi rain forest by five different methods: composition by major groups (data at 220 m, forest, standardized as number of individuals for 10 Malaise trap days, 100 yellow pan trap days and 60 min sweeping) (information extracted from tables 2 and 3 of Noyes 1989)

Superfamily	No. families	Sampling method				
		MT	YPT	SW	FIT	FOG
Ichneumonoidea	(2)	199 (60)	46 (17)	223 (34)	87 (15)	68 (14)
Evanioidea	(1)	8	2	—	18	—
Proctotrupoidea	(3)	451 (26)	64 (10)	187 (16)	393 (21)	10 (6)
Ceraphronoidea	(1)	22 (11)	13 (10)	7 (5)	98 (14)	14 (11)
Cynipoidea	(1)	31 (25)	2 (6)	47 (14)	51 (10)	—
Chalcidoidea	(11)	246 (81)	58 (52)	141 (104)	93 (24)	981 (61)
Chrysidoidea	(3)	16 ⎫	6 ⎫	8 ⎫	60 ⎫	—
Apoidea	(2)	27 ⎬ (27)	12 ⎬ (9)	5 ⎬ (12)	5 ⎬ (12)	—
Vespoidea	(4)	25 ⎭	9 ⎭	4 ⎭	8 ⎭	—

MT, Malaise trap; YPT, yellow pan traps; SW, sweeping; FIT, flight intercept traps; FOG, canopy fog; figure in parentheses is α for major groups.

found that a sample of 1000 Hymenoptera would be collected from 8.8 Malaise trap days, 95.5 yellow pan trap days, 17 flight intercept days, 109 m^2 of canopy fogged, or 67 min of sweeping. However, each of the methods yielded a different taxon composition of wasps. Likewise, a combination of chemical knockdown and direct examination of branch clippings of *Eucalyptus* in Western Australia provided complementary data in estimating arboreal invertebrate diversity (Majer and Recher 1988).

Sampling sets for freshwater benthic invertebrates include using Surber samplers with different mesh sizes, hand-collecting and hand-netting for Ephemeroptera, Plecoptera, Trichoptera in streams, and combinations of sweep-netting (one to five samples) in littoral areas with 10 traps for mobile taxa, three grab samples and three nocturnal vertical tow samples in lakes (Kelso 1987). Combination of kick net or Surber samples, grab samples, timed hand collections and artificial substrate collections occur in several published Rapid Biodiversity Assessment (RBA) protocols (Lenat 1988; Resh and Jackson 1991). In such contexts, minimal sampling sets are useful in reducing costs, if sampling quality can be maintained.

Sampling bias: comparative studies

For between-site comparisons, relatively small differences in vegetation structure or water quality may need to be considered, either in relation to environmental gradients or more mosaic variations within a site or patch of habitat. In the former context, for example, different species of tree usually harbour different suites of consumers and their associated natural enemies; the degree of 'open-ness' may affect accessibility of traps, such as Malaise traps by flying insects—for which an example from Costa Rica is shown in Fig. 5.1 (Buskirk and Buskirk 1976); and height and density of ground flora may influence the efficiency of ground traps such as water traps and pitfalls through their relative concealment or exposure. Likewise, benthic samples in streams can be influenced by substrate type, the extent and composition of vegetation and detritus, and the speed of water flow. Marine littoral samples are affected by degree of exposure, wave direction, insolation—and so on. In short, the degree of sampling replication must be sufficient to counter the considerable degree of heterogeneity 'recognized' by invertebrates, which influences their distribution within a habitat. Netting efficiency of a small beam trawl for prawns can vary between adjacent areas of the same seagrass beds on consecutive nights (Loneragan *et al.* 1995). Estimates of capture efficiency between different sampling devices have generally been developed from absolute differences between them (Long and Wang 1994). Long and Wang used the representation of the seven most abundant taxa of marine benthos (collectively comprising 81% of 15 047 individuals) to compare capture efficiency of a grab and an airlift corer on the Great Barrier Reef by

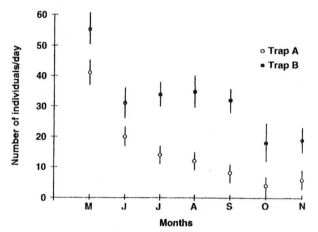

Fig. 5.1 Catches of Malaise traps. Daily capture rate in two Malaise traps, in Costa Rica (Buskirk and Buskirk 1976). Trap B (solid circles) was in dense 1 m herbaceous growth in forest; trap A (open circles) was in sparse understorey under 25 m dense canopy; mean ± s.d. for each month shown.

comparing the signal–noise (mean–standard deviation) ratio of the catches. This approach incorporates consideration of the variance, rather than absolute catches alone.

Unsuspected variability in habitat or resources may be important in interpreting sample composition and, even for particular species, abundance can vary locally in many ways (p. 34). The periphery of fields tends to support more terrestrial gastropods than the central areas (Godan 1983), and many molluscs, arthropods and others decrease rapidly away from particular plants. The field slug *Agriolimax reticulatus* may be more common near *Dactylis glomerata* than near other grasses on a lawn (South 1965); nematodes may be distributed very patchily over a field and usually occur in clusters (Dropkin 1980); and many other examples parallel these. Heterogeneity among habitats is commonly reflected in increased variance in trap catches at a site. However, variations and differences in trap catches can be extraordinarily difficult to interpret even by experts in the taxa involved, and surveys need to address clearly either:

(1) incorporating a suite of different methods to approach a relatively useful species list, while realizing that obtaining a complete inventory of the species present at a site may only rarely be possible, or

(2) using one method, but with sound justification through realizing the limitations imposed, its efficiency and biases, in providing adequate return of information for the effort involved.

As Disney *et al.* (1982) stated, for terrestrial insects 'it is axiomatic that any particular method for collecting insects will be selective with regard to the

Table 5.7
An example of differential catches of insects by different kinds of trap:
Diptera in Yorkshire (from Disney *et al.* 1982)

			Trap type			
	Total	Pitfall	3 Yellow water traps	3 White water traps	Malaise trap 1*	Malaise trap 2*
Agromyzidae						
Individuals	92	1	61	13	2	15
Species	16	1	12	7	1	5
Phoridae						
Individuals	144	2	20	106	1	15
Species	15	1	8	9	1	7

*Malaise trap 1 with collecting bottle a little below the highest point; Malaise trap 2 with
collecting bottle fitted at highest point of trap, otherwise similar to no. 1.
Results based on 24 h catch on a lawn.

species present in a particular habitat', but the extent of such selectivity is
usually entirely unknown and undocumented.

Comparisons of different methods used together to survey insects, such as
Diptera in northern England (Disney *et al.* 1982), tropical insects in India
(Gadagkar *et al.* 1990), Hymenoptera in Sulawesi (Noyes 1989) or forest
insects in California (Canaday 1987) exemplify many of the problems
and biases present at the two scales of single site surveys (Malham Tarn,
Yorkshire: Disney) and in different sites using the same set of methods
at each.

Disney's Yorkshire Diptera data (Table 5.7) show major biases in
overall level of family diversity between different methods, as well as some
considerable differences in species richness within some families. Thus, for
Agromyzidae, 12 species were caught in yellow water traps, seven in white
water traps and only one each in pitfalls and one of the Malaise trap designs.
Preference for white or yellow traps by Phoridae (scuttle flies) was seen at the
species level, and presence of common species with a preference of this
nature dictates the need for very careful interpretation. The relative effectiveness of Malaise traps and pan traps was assessed for Phoridae in Costa
Rica (Brown and Feener 1995). Malaise traps were clearly superior, indicating that Disney *et al.*'s data may not be universally applicable and, in general,
local trials are needed in any such studies rather than simple acceptance of
implications and inferences made far away or on other groups of animals.

Different orders of insects were predominant constituents of catches made
by different methods in Gadagkar *et al.*'s (1990) survey (Fig 5.2): Coleoptera
in light traps, Hymenoptera in sweep samples and pitfall traps, and Diptera in
scent (i.e. bait) traps. Lepidoptera were represented poorly in all their
methods, and Gadagkar's samples cannot be placed firmly in the template of
a comprehensive survey (Stork 1994). One important emphasis of their

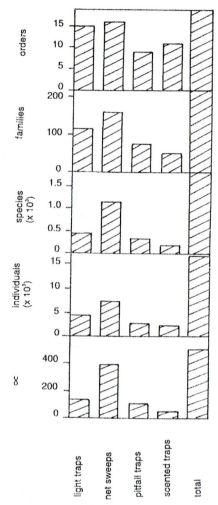

Fig. 5.2 Numbers of (top to bottom) orders, families, species, individuals and α diversity of insects trapped by different methods (Gadagker *et al.* 1990).

regime is the logistical one induced by sampling at low intensity, but over a substantial number of higher taxa. Rather than having to discard a high proportion of catches (as may occur, for example, with large light trap catches when focusing on particular taxa), all taxa collected could be investigated. Gadagkar and his colleagues suggested that concentrating on single groups may not help in detecting community level changes in the insect fauna.

Noyes' (1989) conclusions from his extensive Hymenoptera data (Table 5.6) indicated the kinds of biases for this group of insects which may well be paralleled in other studies.

trap type

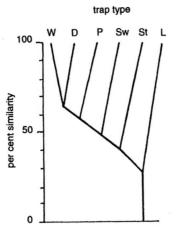

Fig. 5.3 Percentage similarity of insects caught by various trap types in North American forests (Canaday 1987). (D, dish pan trap; L, light trap; P, pan trap; Sw, sweeping; St, sticky trap; W, window trap).

Canaday's (1987) survey of insects on Douglas fir (*Pseudotsuga menziesi*) in California forests stressed the selection of traps which were suitable for remote field conditions in that they could be left unattended for long periods, were inexpensive, simple to operate, and could capture a broad array of insect taxa. These methods were all giving 'relative measures' of the fauna rather than absolute densities, and sets of five different traps (light trap, window trap, two kinds of pan trap, sticky traps) and sweep-netting were compared across five locations. Considerably different catches resulted from each method and confirm that use of different methods with 'complementary catchability' may be needed for inventory or diversity studies. Thus, as the percentage similarity of catches of light trap and dishpan trap was low, these two may be a worthwhile combination in yielding higher numbers of taxa/sampling effort than (say) water and dishpan traps, whose catches were much more similar (Fig. 5.3). Such quantification is still rather unusual, but gives a rationale for selection of sampling sets, rather than relying on 'operator intuition' or 'hearsay evidence'.

Influence of trap design on efficiency has been alluded to previously for Malaise traps. Similar caveats apply to virtually all methods, and bear re-emphasis here. As another pertinent example, Taylor and Brown (1972) attempted to standardize light trap catches of moths, and compared various patterns of 'Rothamsted-type' traps and 'Muguga-type' traps. The ways in which moths respond to light are complex (Muirhead-Thomson 1991), and observations of moth flight tracks by television cameras in Britain revealed considerable disorientation and changes in speed and direction of flight as they approached a light source (Gaydecki 1984). Differences of various sorts were related to light intensity and wavelength, but in the East African trials

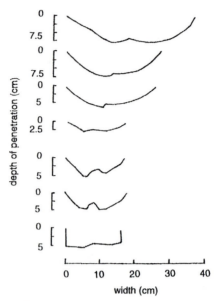

Fig. 5.4 Grab profiles in fine gravel of seven kinds of grab used in sampling fresh-water benthic invertebrates (Elliot and Drake 1981a). Types of grab, from top of diagram are Van-Veen, weighted Ponar, Ponar, Freidinger, Dietz-Lagond, Birge-Ekman, Allan.

noted above the standard Muguga mercury vapour light trap captured about 50 times as many moths as the Rothamsted tungsten trap. Clearly, knowledge of any such massive differences in catchability is important in quantitative sampling attempts, and the degree of error or poor inference in interpretation resulting from ignorance or simply ignoring such biases is indeed high. As emphasized earlier, the assumptions made about a particular sampling or collecting method may be very difficult to quantify and justify. The substantial biases noted for various sampling techniques in Chapter 4 are compounded by comparisons made at different times and/or in different places using only slightly differing trap designs or regimes, which often require critical appraisal if they are to be taken as even reasonably valid.

Direct comparative studies are still relatively rare. Elliott and Drake (1981a) compared the performance of seven patterns of benthic grab operated from a small boat. These grabs had different capture profiles and depths of penetration into the substrate (Fig. 5.4), and their efficiency was affected by the kind of substrate. Christie (1975) also noted that the volume of sediment sampled by a grab varied with the kind of sediment. Some models failed to operate on muddy bottoms, or jammed commonly in fine gravel. If '50%' is regarded as the 'minimum acceptable efficiency', only three of the seven patterns were adequate for use in fine gravel, and no grab was capable of sampling substrates of stones > 16 mm in diameter. The mean number of taxa and individual relative densities varied considerably across different grabs and on different substrates. Most earlier comparative work on benthic grabs (see Elliott and Tullett 1978) was restricted to only two or three grab patterns, and more extensive rigid comparisons are rare, as for most other sampling methods for invertebrates. More are needed, and must take into account the aims of surveys in which the techniques are used, and the limitations of the technique. Elliott and Drake's studies on benthic macro-invertebrate sampling in deep rivers incorporated grabs (Elliott and Drake 1981a), dredges (Elliott and Drake 1981b) and airlift samplers (Drake and Elliott 1982). Only one of the 14 devices sampled benthos effectively from small (16–32 mm diameter) stones, and none sampled adequately from larger stones. Five different patterns of the popular Ekman grab, compared through direct SCUBA diver observations and photography (Blomqvist 1990) (an approach which has great potential to clarify the performance of many kinds of underwater samplers), all frequently produced inadequate samples because of faults in operation. These included tilting (which may result in redistribution of the enclosed material, contamination from outside, and escape of active fauna), brimming (so that sediment enters from the top of the trap), as well as failure of the tripping mechanism. Tilting was a particular problem in the taller trap models. A supporting four-legged stand to stabilize such grabs might lead to substantially enhanced performance. Similarly, a stable four-footed 'tom-tom corer' in which each foot takes a separate core of soft sediment, may overcome many of the problems of more conventional corers (Chandler et al. 1988). This can be lowered slowly to reduce disturbance from a bow wave effect, and be weighted for additional stability. Sampling tools for marine benthos have been compared extensively under three main criteria, with many studies summarized by Eleftheriou and Holme (1984):

1. The digging characteristics of the sampler, including depth of penetration, volume of sediment captured and extent of disturbance.

2. The efficiency of capture, in relation to giving a realistic picture of the fauna.

3. Technical characteristics, such as ease of manipulation and access, and reliability. Some can be operated only from large vessels, for example.

Choice of a sampler is usually a compromise involving survey needs, opportunity, availability or affordability of gear, and working conditions.

Comparison of a range of sampling methods for soil arthropods (Edwards and Fletcher 1971) classified by order or family in three major categories of soil (peat, clay or loam, sand) indicated the apparent selectivity of some methods over others, but most of the methods were suitable for many arthropod groups (Table 3.3, p. 63). Wet and dry extraction techniques were compared for peat arthropods in Canada by McElligott and Lewis (1995). Wet extraction yielded about three times as many invertebrates as dry extraction for a given volume of substrate, but several groups of invertebrates were extracted more efficiently by one or other method. Thus, oligochaetes, larval Chironomidae, and sphaeriid clams were obtained more efficiently by wet extraction, and larvae of several families of Diptera (Tabanidae, Tipulidae, Empididae, Dolichopodidae) by dry extraction.

As well as variations in catchability due to differences in trap design, many sampling methods are influenced heavily by environmental conditions such as weather or water flow. Light traps, for example, are highly sensitive to changes in behaviour of flying insects due to humidity, moonlight, temperature, wind and many other variables. Many stream invertebrate samplers which depend upon water currents to wash invertebrates into a net are influenced by variable flows. Resh (1979) showed that yields may be diminished by low flows or by backwash from high velocity currents. As noted above, the performance of grabs is influenced substantially by substrate characteristics, and various limitations of given collecting apparatus have been addressed specifically in some recent and innovative designs. Grizzle and Stegner (1985) designed a benthic 'quantitative grab' which overcame any of the limitations of earlier models by having a more even 'bite profile', overcoming the problems of irregular sample size (McIntyre 1971) and, hence, of sample contents (Christie 1975); and Boulton's (1988) sampler (p. 86) eliminates variables due to water currents and can be used both in running and still waters.

However, despite the great array of sampling techniques and devices now available, some invertebrates are very difficult to sample comprehensively and their incidence in catches has a strong element of chance. This applies not only to rare taxa (Chapter 8), whose incidence parallels problems in other groups of organisms, but also reflects the difficulties of obtaining samples sufficiently large to be representative of complex and diverse assemblages—for example, by benthic grabs in very deep water, or knockdown samples from tall forest canopy. Larger or active invertebrates may easily evade capture, or grabs may not penetrate sufficiently deep to retrieve infauna effectively.

Sampling protocols

Melding a mass of confusing and sometimes contradictory information into coherent 'recipes' for surveys of numerous disparate taxa is not easy, and any attempts to do so are likely to have shortcomings. The great variety of techniques and sampling regimes, many of them not fully standardized, itself tends to reflect the frustrations of practitioners over what has gone before. The sampling sets discussed above (see Tables 5.2 and 5.3) exemplify the kinds of approach which have eventuated to encompass the needs of broad surveys. Development of replicable protocols for biodiversity assessment mirrors the survey needs noted in Table 2.1 (p. 13), and the following points augment these.

1. All relevant habitats and habitat subunits likely to be occupied by a target group at a site should be sampled concurrently, in ways which will maximize accurate comparison between them. The sampling methods must provide representative collections of taxa from each habitat or unit appraised. If only a subset from the total available habitats is examined, this must be made clear. Thus, Tullgren funnels and sweep-netting in a terrestrial system each sample from important habitat subsets, with little overlap in coverage, but neither method primarily appraises the fauna of trees in the area. Valid comparisons can thus be made only with samples taken by the same means elsewhere, or at different times, but even small differences in sampling technique may invalidate these.

For many RBA procedures, one short cut is to deliberately restrict the number of habitats sampled: for example, to the more accessible littoral regions in freshwater bodies.

2. Repeated samples over the duration of a survey should extend over a period sufficient to reveal/reflect changes in abundance and species composition due to seasonal variations, unless 'spot' samples taken at the same time(s) each year are used for inter-site or inter-year comparisons, as in monitoring. The actual sampling period will depend on latitude and climate, as determinants of the 'active period' of particular focal groups.

If assessing the effects of a particular environmental disturbance, sampling of the affected site should extend well beyond the disturbance, with parallel samples from undamaged 'control' sites wherever possible. Ideally, control sites should be close to the disturbed site(s), and similar in topography.

3. Ensure that the sites sampled are sufficiently typical to provide representative samples of the area being investigated: this may entail preliminary appraisal of transects and/or quadrats over a larger area. If the samples are biased in relation to a site (such as by beating or sweeping only some plant species in a mixed stand, or surveying the benthos of stony patches on a generally muddy substrate), limitations must be specified and either countered by changed sampling effort or restricting any comparisons accordingly. Vegetation type (terrestrial) and substrate texture (aquatic) are among the important determinants of invertebrate distributions, and must be characterized adequately for survey interpretation.

4. Combinations of sampling methods will almost always yield more taxa than use of any single method alone. For an inventory survey, it follows that employing combinations of different methods will furnish more comprehensive results. For particular target groups, methods can often be selected to provide good returns but, in general, as costs increase with proliferation of

sampling, passive techniques should be incorporated wherever feasible. It may be possible to store some of the samples unsorted, pending analysis of others, but in practice this option is restricted by deadlines for reporting and completion of analysis.

Numerous published accounts rely most heavily on the techniques noted below for the various habitats sampled individually. Their limitations and functioning can be reasonably well standardized, at least within the confines of an individual exercise.

Habitat categorization which has fostered the diversity of sampling methods for invertebrates grossly parallels the classification promoted by Elton and Miller (1954). Complementarity of methods in a survey will normally account for the sequence of 'vertical layers' of interest. Thus, for terrestrial invertebrates, a full combination of methods should assess the fauna of upper soil horizons, ground surface and litter, low vegetation (with possible subdivision according to taxon, height or growth form), higher vegetation, and air (for winged insects, or colonization processes). Aquatic surveys also need different methods to sample from the substrate, through substrate surface, water body (with likely division into shallow and profundal zones, and vegetated/non-vegetated areas), submerged and emergent vegetation, and air over the water. Running and still water may necessitate some differences in approach.

Superimposed on these divisions are possible needs to sample along habitat gradients, such as along shorelines, at altitudinal intervals on a hillside or reef, or across successional stages of vegetation. Sampling of 'special' habitats, such as caves, largely draws on the general methods developed for broader use.

The following combinations of method may be considered for inventory surveys, with additional combinations of terrestrial and aquatic sampling needed for wetlands or broader regional studies.

Terrestrial habitats

1. Soil and litter. Dry funnels are the most usual technique and are particularly suitable for use with peat or clay soils. Flotation is preferred for sandy soils. Replicated samples extracted by Tullgren funnels can be augmented by wet funnel extractions to obtain nematodes, enchytraeids and other 'more delicate' fauna.

The basis for sampling can be either soil cores or gravimetric/area-based litter samples, both of which are needed in a comprehensive study. If funnels are not available, the simplest form of assessing macroinvertebrates such as earthworms, molluscs and many arthropods, is to mark out an area (quadrat, circle) of soil or litter in the field and remove it progressively to spread on a plastic sheet for direct searching by gradually breaking into smaller fragments, collecting the animals individually as they are found. For soil fauna, quadrats of 0.5–1 m^2 sorted to a depth of 10 cm are adequate (Edwards 1991).

2. Epigaeic fauna are most commonly obtained by extractions as above, or active forms (such as beetles, spiders and ants) by pitfall traps. These are used commonly in grids of 10, 20 or 25 traps, with regular (1–5 m) spacing between traps, lines of traps along transects, or by spacing traps randomly in a plot. Once set, and left to counter the digging-in effect (p. 57), they are inspected at defined intervals of up to a fortnight, provided that the catch is preserved satisfactorily over that period. Common long-term regimes involve either continuous interval trapping, using traps for part of each month (2–14 days), or once every 2–3 months to give spot samples of seasonal incidence. For such purposes, they can be left *in situ* and closed when not required.

Water traps are used in similar conformations as pitfall traps, and vacuum samplers tend to combine the spectrum of organisms captured by these methods, although without such clear implication of the animals' activity or dispersal playing a part in the capture process. Whereas water traps are particularly suitable for small winged insects, vacuum samplers are used extensively to collect apterous arthropods such as springtails (Collembola) and mites (Acarina). They can be used directly on the ground surface or vegetation, or to sweep across low vegetation such as grasses. Emergence traps on the ground also indicate resident fauna, but do not provide any form of comprehensive sample of the taxa present. They can be used effectively to appraise the fauna which colonize dung, carrion, fungi and similar discrete restricted habitats.

3. Low vegetation fauna, from a few centimetres above ground to that on shrubs and lower branches of trees can be appraised by standardized beating (trees, shrubs) or sweep-netting (especially when the foliage is not too dense, so that the sweeping action is not impeded by wood or other obstructions). Specialized groups such as flower visitors or groups of larger insects sometimes useful as indicators (hoverflies, butterflies, aculeate Hymenoptera) assessed by timed direct searches or netting under suitable conditions and at similar times each sampling occasion provide useful comparative information. As with any method, sampling effort should be quantified—here as the 'number of sweeps of known [stated] length', 'time spent sampling' or similar index. Direct examination of foliage (known number of leaves or foliage area) is needed for sedentary taxa not dislodged by more active techniques.

4. Sampling options for high vegetation are clearly limited. The tree canopy is often neglected in surveys, and insecticide fogging for chemical knockdown is the only worthwhile practical option for most practitioners.

5. Aerial insects tend to be sampled by whatever method is most easily available. Malaise, suction and intercept traps all function throughout the time they are set, whereas light traps are obviously of nocturnal application. Each of these methods can provide information not necessarily obtained by the other techniques.

Aquatic habitats

Most practical surveys related to conservation are confined to the more accessible shallow waters, shorelines, reefs, and small water bodies, without the heavy gear which can be operated only from large vessels and under remote conditions.

1. Substrate. Corers, grabs and dredges are used variously for sampling substrates, with the texture of the substrate being the most important influence on choice of method. Several different substrates in the same water body may need sampling by different methods. The Dendy sampler or some form of suction sampler is useful for soft sediments, but effective sampling of the benthos associated with rocks or boulders is difficult: smaller rocks can be removed for direct brushing or examination in a tray of water, but loss of specimens when the rocks are lifted is difficult to estimate. In flowing shallow water the Surber sampler (quadrat-based) or equivalent kick-sampling is a nearly universal approach. Hand collecting is a common adjunct to this.

2. Aquatic vegetation. Submerged vegetation can be sampled by two complementary methods. A net can be swept among the plants *in situ*, and plant material can be gathered, preferably bagged or put into some closable container under water, and sorted by hand in a white, sided tray of water, with timed searches used to calibrate sampling effort.

3. The water column is sampled directly by netting, using a simple dip net (often with a collecting tube whose contents can be preserved directly or sorted in a tray, as above), or more specialized gear such as a towed plankton net or mid-water or vertical trawl in larger lakes.

Many surveys emphasize the need to obtain particular taxonomic groups. Again, rigid general protocols for most invertebrate groups have not been defined. One exception is for soil nematodes, for which the Society of Nematologists has listed recommendations for the number and kind of

Table 5.8
Recommendations for a general sampling protocol for soil nematodes
(after Barker 1978)

---

a. Number and dimensions of cores
   1. A 2 cm sampling tube should be used to minimum depth of 20 cm, so that each core provides ca. 62 cm³ of soil.
   2. Minimum number of cores to be collected for one soil sample:
      - small plots (1–5 m²) 10 cores
      - medium plots (5–100 m²) 20 or more cores
      - large plots (>100 m²) 30 or more cores
      - for trees, 5 cores near plant and 5 cores near drip line

b. Sampling frequency for community analysis. Samples at least monthly for a year, but with a minimum of three times a year.

c. Treatment.
   - place samples in plastic bags and keep cool to avoid mortality of particular taxa and subsequent biased interpretation
   - if cannot process entire sample, screen and mix thoroughly to bulk
   - extract (Baermann funnel for 3 days, collecting nematodes at 24 h intervals

---

samples needed to provide an adequately representative sample (Barker 1978); these emphasize the more general need to consider the sampling environment carefully, and include details of subsequent treatment of the samples (Table 5.8).

Subsampling

One major logistic problem allied closely with the sampling regime employed is the sheer bulk of invertebrates which may be accumulated during even a moderately complete survey. The cost of processing the samples often precludes total appraisal of all the samples gathered, and necessitates some form of subsampling from the catches, so that analysis and interpretation is based on only a subset of the accumulated specimens. Thus light traps are a popular (indeed, almost universal) tool for sampling night-flying Lepidoptera, but can provide vast numbers of individuals for examination. In Kenya, Taylor *et al.* (1979) reported one trap catching more than 6.7 kg of moths in a single night; Williams (1945) recorded 113 256 moths taken over a year of sampling in Kansas, and there are many similar figures from other surveys. The large catches are often claimed to be a major advantage in providing representative samples of nocturnal moth fauna. On the one hand, such numbers render surveys extremely useful through providing solid information for analysis of diversity and species incidence: Holloway's (1977 and later) light trap surveys of moths in the western Pacific have been instrumental in clarifying local and regional diversity patterns of this insect group. On the other, they may be an effective deterrent to adequate analysis without subsampling.

Wide differences in sample size between similar traps in an area are common and, whereas the size of the catch may be important in itself, catches of vastly different sizes may be difficult to compare meaningfully. In their Kenyan light trap studies noted above, Taylor *et al.* (1979) were comparing the spectrum of moth size categories caught in traps at ground level and at 24.5 m above the ground. In situations where the low level trap caught enormous numbers of moths, the moths in the upper level trap were counted and weighed, and an equivalent weight (only) of the larger catch was appraised so that comparative analysis involved similar-sized samples.

Another approach, adopted by Thomas and Thomas (1994) in the forests of New Brunswick, Canada, also recognized the need to reduce sample size to: (1) reduce the processing costs for the data obtained, and (2) diminish the possible adverse effects of removal trapping on the moth populations, by restricting the trapping period. No single-night sample estimated accurately the log. series and index of diversity generated from the total catch over 29 nights, and some sampling effort was needed each night. However, a single hour capture each night had no effect on the overall pattern of species abundance, and the value for alpha was the same as that derived from trapping for 8 h each night. This restricted trapping regime greatly reduced the catch size (from 6088 to 971 moths) and also the number of species (255 to 161) so, whereas it was a valuable strategy for comparing species diversity between different sites when data are collected in a similar way, it is of very limited use in studies from which more complete inventories are anticipated. The principle of restricting trapping intensity, especially in cases where the catch is 'automatically' killed, is important in assessing the fauna of restricted or isolated sites, especially if knowingly rare species or species of particular conservation significance are involved. In some small sites, continued series of removal samples has some potential to change the structure of the community.

Light trap catches (to pursue the same context further) exemplify catches where size varies many-fold and often unpredictably on sequences of trapping occasions (nights), and where subsampling of some sort is often necessary. During a survey of caddis flies (Trichoptera) in Canada, catches ranged from zero to 0.5 million insects/night, and exceeded 10 000/night on more than 32% of occasions (Corbet 1966). A versatile subsampling system was needed to analyse the catches reliably. The insects were collected in fluid, and the initial step was to remove manually large irregularly shaped 'contaminant' insects such as some larger moths and beetles. The catch was then stirred and strained, and measured out in 25 ml units so that the total catch was recorded volumetrically to the nearest quarter of a unit. Subsequent procedure depended on the overall volume of the catch, as follows:

1. Catch of three or more than three units. Three units selected at random are each placed in an annular dish divided radially into sixteenths. The

insects are covered in alcohol, distributed evenly, and two opposite sectors enumerated as the subsample.

2. Catch of >1–<3 units. One-eighth of each complete dishful is examined in the above manner.

3. Catch of >1/4–<1 unit. One-eighth of the total catch is examined.

4. Catch of <1/4 unit. The whole catch is examined. Errors can arise from disturbing the insects in the dish before sector sampling, and on deciding the inclusivity of insects overlapping sector boundaries. In Corbet's trials, insects overlapping one side of the boundary of each sector were included.

Scales of abundance, of the form 0–10 with defined numerical ranges for each category, are often useful for determining the frequencies of abundant organisms. Codes such as these can be used to record large amounts of data but also to record data in a comparative standard format. For marine invertebrates, Eleftheriou and Holme (1984) recommended the scheme used by Heath and Scott (1977). This includes two '1–9' scale sets, one for quantity (present to abundant) and relating this to a second scale reflecting substrate area or sampling effort, as summarized in Table 5.9.

Quantitative problems of comparison become severe if we work from the premise exemplified by Dropkin's (1980) statement, writing on plant parasitic nematodes, that 'Every laboratory develops its own techniques for collecting nematodes from soil and plants' (echoed by McSorley, 1987 as 'Proliferation of extraction methods over the past 35 years has produced a nematological 'Tower of Babel' in which comparison of results between laboratories is difficult' and for other invertebrates, such as Cummins, 1962 'The number of aquatic insect sampling devices roughly reflects the number of researchers').

Table 5.9
Table of abundance codes, as a basis for standardizing species abundance in samples (after Heath and Scott 1977). One category is taken from each of the two scales, as applied to benthic macrofauna. Each scale (quantity, unit) is a 1–9 division

	Quantity		Unit
1.	Present (no numerical data)	1.	$/cm^2$
2.	<1	2.	$/m^2$
3.	1–10	3.	$/cm^3$
4.	11–100	4.	$/m^3$
5.	101–1000	5.	per trawl haul
6.	1001–10 000	6.	per dredge haul
7.	>10 000	7.	per 15 min search (foot or diving)
8.	Absent (none found during careful search of suitable habitat)	8.	per 30 min search (foot or diving)
9.	Other	9.	Other

As noted earlier, any 'standard' sampling device is open to innumerable variations, many of which are not calibrated or considered for standardization or comparison, and have never been compared objectively by the same workers or under similar conditions. Some such vagaries, together with those which result from unknown distribution of the taxa, can be overcome in part by pooling series of samples, and then subsampling. Procedures at all stages of sampling need to be defined accurately, and in as standard a manner as possible. Thus, some variations in distribution of soil nematodes can be countered by combining different soil cores and mixing these thoroughly before taking a representative volume (commonly 100 cm^3) for extraction. The extraction parameters then need to be defined clearly and any sub-sampling (for example by counting on representative areas of a counting dish or slide) detailed in order to furnish relevant data for quantitative comparison with other studies, and for replication of the sampling protocol by other workers. Thus, for nematodes, McSorley (1987) suggested that, although no one method is suitable for all situations, it may be feasible to standardize several methods sufficiently to reduce the 'confusing numbers of modifications and variations' that are available. Determining extraction efficiencies was regarded as critical in facilitating standardization.

Subsampling (or 'two-stage sampling': Elliott 1977) is the only reasonable way to deal with large samples for which total examination either is impossible or is unlikely to yield additional information concomitant with the additional costs involved, It may be necessary, or warranted, to appraise samples fully if the target taxa are rare or elusive and could be overlooked in subsamples, for example, or where high-quality inventories are needed, as subsampling inevitably leads to 'loss' of taxa in relation to the total sample. But in many comparative studies no such impediment arises, because the aim is likely to be to establish relative figures of incidence, species richness, or abundance based on a given sampling effort. However, it will usually be necessary to assess the consistency of series of subsamples in relation to the data provided by each, and allow for sufficient replication to counter marked variations. Subsampling is also valuable in single species studies (Chapter 8) for which it may be necessary to enumerate the relative abundance of different instars or growth stages.

Subsamples can be taken randomly (such as after mixing a fluid-preserved collection or sample thoroughly and allowing it to settle in a divided container such as that designed by Elmgren (1973; Fig. 5.5), or in a more stratified manner—as by extracting soil animals from different depths in a series of corer samples. As in other aspects of invertebrate sampling, sufficient detail should be documented to facilitate replication and appraisal by other workers. The subsample can then comprise a unit of habitat (such as the volume of soil noted above) or a definable number of animals (Langley *et al.* 1995 used 100 rotifers from each sample from ponds).

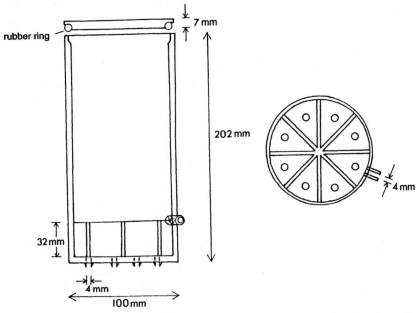

Fig. 5.5 A sample divider, in which specimens of small animals suspended in liquid are allowed to settle into a divided container, only some units of which may be processed further (after Elmgren 1973).

Another approach to effective subsampling is to adjust the sample processing method(s) so that only particular size categories are available for sorting. For marine benthic samples, the time needed to sort samples is determined largely by the mesh size of the sieves used to screen the sediments in the early stages of processing the samples, and this can be adjusted without loss of significant information in some cases. If comprehensive inventories are indeed needed this approach is not valid, but in many pollution or monitoring studies it may be wholly satisfactory to appraise only a limited range of size classes (McIntyre *et al.* 1984), or to analyse samples above the species level (James *et al.* 1995; see Chapter 6). A coarse sieve (1 or 2 mm mesh) may then be entirely suitable, in leading to greatly reduced work and sampling costs, if it retains sufficient numbers of the key taxa. Whereas a finer sieve (of, say, 0.5 mm mesh) will retain many more small species and immature stages of larger ones, which may be more sensitive to habitat changes, this information can be gathered only at considerably greater expense so that, yet again, the needs/outcome should be specified clearly in the sampling design. Mesh size, in this context, is a critical aspect of processing benthic fauna samples and can determine the incidence of larger taxonomic groups in samples. Thus, a sieve mesh of 0.85 mm was very suitable for molluscs in macrofaunal samples and retained about 95% of individuals from grab samples, but a much finer mesh would be needed for equivalent proportions of crustaceans (0.27 mm) or nematodes (0.15 mm). Overall, a 0.27 mm mesh collected about 95% of all individuals but, if only biomass estimates were needed, more than 90% was retained on a 1.4 mm mesh sieve (Reisch 1959; Eleftheriou and Holme 1984). Details will differ in different surveys, but Reisch's study is important in indicating the need to specify the aims clearly in determining the balance between idealism and expediency in sampling invertebrates. The mesh size needed may not always reflect the size of the organisms being collected. Many polychaetes from marine benthos may fragment into pieces smaller than 1 mm during shipboard processing, so that a 0.5 mm sieve may be needed (Rees 1984). Seasonal samples with the aim of interpreting changes in community patterns or size changes of particular taxa could be misleading if based on the coarse mesh alone.

An important formal caveat is to ensure that 'subsamples' are not equated with 'replicate samples' (Eberhardt and Thomas 1991) in increasing the number of samples for statistical analysis. As in other ecological work, replication for conservation assessment is commonly not undertaken, either because of logistic constraints or because of small site investigations where larger numbers of samples might harm critical habitat or vulnerable populations. Nevertheless, comparative designs need acceptable numbers of replicates. As Hurlbert (1984) noted, replication is often impossible—for example,

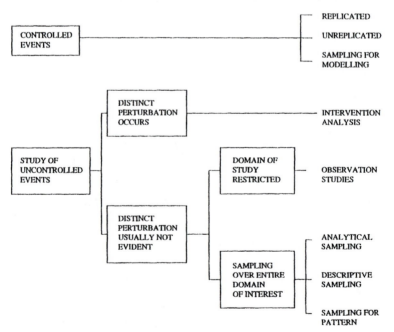

Fig. 5.6 Categories of ecological studies and sampling regimes (after Eberhard and Thomas 1991).

when large-scale systems are studied—but false statistical inference may be very common. In a survey of 537 papers on manipulative experiments in ecology, Hurlbert found that 62 (12%) involved pseudoreplication and 191 clearly designed studies still involved 50 (28%) with pseudoreplication. Problems of statistical inference occur abundantly: Hurlbert cited a survey by Underwood (1981) in which he showed that 78% of 143 papers in marine biology included statistical errors of one form or another. Adequate experimental design and analysis is clearly necessary in ecological work on invertebrates and conservation assessment, not least to maintain credibility. Assuring the quality of data from a sampling programme necessitates sound measurement techniques and an understanding of sampling theory (Norris and Georges 1991).

In sampling for invertebrates and other organisms, the two major approaches may be thought of as 'descriptive' and 'analytical' (Cochran 1977). The first aims to gather information about the taxa or particular trends, such as their numbers, age structure or distribution, and is typified by many conservation surveys involving species. The second implies comparison between different subgroups to investigate hypotheses about reasons for the differences, such as the effects of disturbance. The options are set out clearly by Eberhardt and Thomas (1991), who recognized eight categories of method, with the initial dichotomy of observing some uncontrolled process (descriptive) or conducting a controlled experiment (analytical) (Fig. 5.6).

How much sampling is enough?

The critical question in any survey such as those noted above relates to the extent and duration of sampling needed to produce valid results. In many cases, the amount of sampling is dictated by access (benthic samples in deep marine systems reflect the costs of shipboard time), opportunity (remote sites in all systems may be far from a normal operational base, and it may not be feasible to transport all gear conventionally used, or to stay for long periods), and many other factors—such as the costs of sample processing, as reflected in the number of taxonomic groups analysed (Chapter 6). Pragmatically, estimates such as Scudder's (1996) CAN$50 000/site per year to process and identify invertebrate samples to family level in a reasonably adequate sampling set (p. 107) are not generally likely to be fulfilled.

Nevertheless, even when sampling effort is quantifiable, and apparently sufficient, it may be difficult to appraise the results because of lack of solid background information on the fauna, or to compare them with other sites subject to different sampling intensity. If such comparisons are to be made, some assurance of 'sampling quality' is needed. In essence, if little can be gained by further sampling it would be a waste of time and funds, but if many characteristic species remain to be discovered, more effort is clearly needed

(Colwell and Coddington 1994). In one of the few attempts to define 'enough sampling', Brown and Feener (1995) assumed that for an intensive survey, 95% of the fauna should be identified, and that 10 years sampling at a single site would be a reasonable maximum period. Different data sets from their limited Malaise trap catches of Diptera gave different estimates of the sampling effort needed to achieve 95% of the estimated species diversity, but it seemed likely that trapping for only 1 year might be generally sufficient to do so. Similar trials on other groups and with other trapping methods would be valuable in guiding planning of future surveys. At the least, some estimate of the 'reliability' of short-term surveys in relation to the likely results from long-term studies may be of critical importance in planning management. However, the results or implications from surveys may be discouraging: a rough estimate of 20 worker-years for complete analysis of all insects on a 1 ha plot in West Africa was regarded by Eggleton and Bignell (1995) as 'probably an underestimate'!

Sample size may have profound ramifications on conclusions drawn about species richness, abundance or biomass, and on the underlying processes integrating the community. Most surveys on sandy beach macroinvertebrates have been based on sampling areas smaller than 4.5 m² (Jaramillo *et al.* 1995). Sampling areas of 1 m² and 2 m² resulted in underestimations averaging about 40% and 20%, respectively, of the species, but the sample size needs consideration also in relation to the state of the beach. The most dissipative beaches support the highest numbers of species, compared with low numbers on reflective beaches, and must be sampled more extensively to yield these.

With greater species richness, more sampling is needed to collect most of

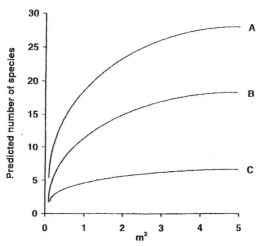

Fig. 5.7 Predicted number of species in relation to increase in sampling area on beaches (modified after more comprehensive appraisal by Jaramillo *et al.* 1995). A, most dissipative; C, most reflective beach.

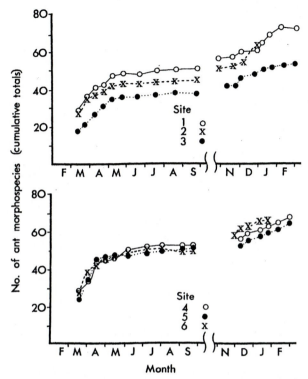

Fig. 5.8 Species accumulation curves; cumulative numbers of morphospecies of ants from pitfall traps at Mount Piper, Victoria—note apparent asymptotes (implying saturation sampling) after initial sampling period, and resumption of new species discovery once sampling resumed (after Hinkley and New 1997).

the species (Fig. 5.7). Many workers have plotted 'species accumulation curves', as in Fig. 5.8, in relation to increasing sampling effort or a time series of successive samples, with the implication that sampling is sufficient once the number of new taxa yielded does not increase, or increases only slightly. However, the period of a survey may be important in avoiding spurious results. Figure 5.8 shows morphospecies accumulation curves for ants in pitfall traps on six plots in Victoria, Australia (Hinkley and New 1997). All sites reached a convincing species asymptote over an initial sampling period. However, this reflected, in part, decreasing ant activity at the onset of cooler winter weather. Resumption of sampling later revealed the curves to be spurious in relation to the total ant fauna present, and the later totals for each plot were considerably higher than initially implied. Many surveys have been too short to reveal such trends, and the limitations of short-term samples are often difficult to define without placing them in a larger context of seasonal variation. One important approach to assessing sampling validity involves simulation of increased sampling effort from data obtained by 'real' trapping. Thus, for spiders captured in pitfall traps in orchards in Hungary,

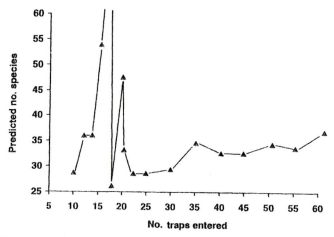

Fig. 5.9 Changes in predicted number of spider species in pitfall traps as function of number of traps included in initial data set (after Samu and Lövei 1995).

the resulting species accumulation curves were described by an asymptotic function to estimate total species number corresponding to a sampling effort which would have covered the whole area at that time (Samu and Lovei 1995). Actual and predicted species numbers for a given sampling effort (in this case, number of pitfall traps) can be compared and the minimum valid sampling effort thus defined. In Samu and Lovei's study, use of fewer than 30 traps in the initial simulation caused extrapolations to vary widely (Fig. 5.9).

Addition of a different sampling method may reveal numerous fresh taxa because of different trapping biases, as noted earlier. Thus, Finnamore (1994) found that addition of a Malaise trap to his sequence of 13 pan traps yielded more than 500 'new' species of Hymenoptera, whereas addition of more pans provided little additional diversity (Fig. 5.10). Using a range of sampling methods is probably of general importance in producing even reasonably

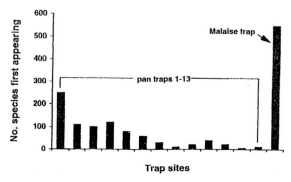

Fig. 5.10 Effect of adding another trap method (Malaise trap) on apparent richness of Hymenoptera in Canada (Finnamore 1994).

valid inventories (Hammond 1994), just as addition of different sites may yield additional species resulting from habitat heterogeneity at a larger spatial scale.

Although the biases of each common trapping method for invertebrates are gradually coming to be understood better, there are still many anomalies and rigid assessment of the catches of a variety of sampling methods is still needed. Estimation of 'biodiversity' from local sampling is still a complex exercise. Methods of attempting this for local richness estimates (reviewed by Colwell and Coddington 1994) can be based on:

1. extrapolating species accumulation curves;

2. fitting parametric distributions of relative abundance; or

3. using non-parametric techniques based on distribution of individuals among species or species among samples.

Further reading

Colwell, R. K. and Coddington, J. A. (1994). Estimating terrestrial biodiversity through extrapolation. *Philosophical Transactions of the Royal Society of London B* **345**, 101–18.

Dindal, D. L. (ed.) (1990). *Soil biology guide*. Wiley-Interscience, New York.

Eberhardt, L. L. and Thomas, J. M. (1991). Designing environmental field studies. *Ecological Monographs* **61**, 53–73.

Eleftheriou, A. and Holme, N. A. (1984). Macrofauna techniques. In *Methods for the study of marine benthos* (ed. N.A. Holme and A.D. McIntyre), pp. 140–216. Blackwell Scientific, Oxford.

Elliott, J. M. (1977). *Some methods for the statistical analysis of samples of benthic invertebrates*. Freshwater Biological Association, Scientific Publication No. 25. Ambleside.

Hurlbert, S. H. (1984). Pseudoreplication and the design of ecological field experiments. *Ecological Monographs* **54**, 187–211.

6 Processing and interpreting invertebrate samples

Introduction

Gaining consistent and reliable samples of invertebrates is the first stage in the process of detecting the presence of particular taxa or of interpreting the diversity and ecology of invertebrate assemblages, and many of the subsequent stages pose even greater problems, both in ensuring reliability and in the costs involved. Indeed, simply gaining the samples commonly may be among the cheaper phases of an invertebrate survey. However, some sampling exercises, such as offshore benthic sampling involving ship time over extended periods and utilizing expensive gear, tend to have much higher costs than others (Kingston and Riddle 1984). But, for any field surveys, the costs are clearly wasted unless the material is interpreted and used effectively.

Preparing and processing the accumulated material is a complex logistic sequence involving: (1) preservation; (2) sorting to taxonomic groups or other consistently-recognizable categories; (3) mounting or otherwise preparing specimens for identification; (4) obtaining reliable identification; (5) integrating the identifications, commonly through use of databases; (6) providing for analysis and recovery of the accumulated information; and (7) ensuring that the information is disseminated adequately, and providing for deposition of voucher material and collections as archival material (Fig. 6.1, Table 2.1). The costs of following this sequence, which reflect the amount of material to be processed and the expertise needed, depend also on the number of target invertebrate groups in a survey, and the level of identification and analysis needed. These considerations are, or should be, just as important as those already raised in designing a sampling programme, and the associated costs budgeted realistically in the planning phase of a survey. Published details of costings are scarce and prior budgeting is difficult, but it is virtually certain that the real costs will be much higher than anticipated, perhaps several-fold more than preliminary estimates. As long ago as 1976, Saila *et al.* noted that the costs of sorting a marine benthic grab sample were about 12 times those of collecting it. The ratio of sampling cost to processing cost for terrestrial arthropod samples can be as low as 1 : 40, as another guide (Marshall *et al.* 1994), with considerable variation between individual methods (based on minimum time for sample processing and limited sorting, based on a standard hourly rate: Table 6.1).

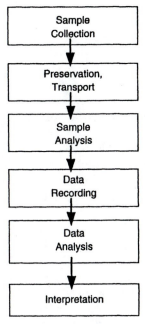

Fig. 6.1 The practical steps in an ecological survey for invertebrates.

Sample sorting and preparation should be planned carefully in relation to needs for identification.

Preservation and sorting in the field

Many of the passive collecting techniques noted earlier present material already dead and in preservative. In such instances the main urgent needs are

Table 6.1
Estimates of minimum time (h) to process samples from one site for recommended sampling protocols. (Based on use of experienced sorter, sorting specimens to family level only; inexperienced sorters initially take much longer) (from Marshall *et al.* 1994)

	Time required/sample				Total time	
Method	Sort	Prepare	Identity	Total	No. samples/month	Total
Malaise trap	1.5	3.5	5	10	8	80
Flight intercept trap	3	5	8	16	8	128
Pan trap	1.5	3.5	5	10	16	160
Pitfall trap	0.5	1	2	3.5	16	56
Behavioural extractor	3	5	8	16	5	80
Total	9.5	18	28	55.5	—	504

to ensure that the invertebrates are adequately preserved (such as by placing them in fresh liquid preservative in standard evaporation-retarding containers for longer-term storage, or replenishing preservative in the trapping containers), and that the samples are documented and labelled clearly before any sorting or amalgamation takes place. Some other methods provide samples of living animals either alone (insects in light traps) or in a sample of their physical habitat (benthic grabs, soil cores) from which they must be extracted and sorted. Living animals may either be killed and preserved in the field, or transported alive to the laboratory; in some cases it may be feasible to release them *in situ* (after counting easily recognizable moths in a light trap, or crustaceans in a trap pot), but this is relatively rare. Even liberation may need considerable care: nocturnal moths liberated in the daytime may be unusually · susceptible to predation by birds, or aquatic crustaceans to fish, for example. Living animals must be transported in a manner which ensures their safe arrival, with the organisms undamaged and amenable to processing. As McSorley (1987) commented 'the handling of samples between sampling and evaluation cannot be ignored, since careless handling or storage can nullify laborious sampling efforts'.

Preliminary field sorting may be needed if mixed samples contain taxa which must be treated in different ways and which might not be needed and, if detected in time, could be released. Marine benthic dredges and trawls, for example, can collect large volumes of material indiscriminately. The 'bycatch' (p. 95) in catches of focal species can be very high, sometimes many-fold that of the desired taxa, and much can be returned to the ocean with some chance of survival. For mixed benthic samples it may be necessary to:

1. Isolate specimens which need to be retained alive and treat these with special care.

2. Preserve others in different ways, such as:

    (i) narcotizing taxa which might contract or autotomize if killed too abruptly (this applies to many soft-bodied taxa);

    (ii) directly preserving others in alcohol, formalin or any special fixative needed for histological or anatomical examination.

Common recommendations for transporting living invertebrates include avoiding high temperatures and rough handling, and storing samples for the shortest time possible before extracting their contents. With nematodes, population changes in soil can occur during storage, and the practical need is for the shortest possible storage interval at temperatures low enough to minimize such changes (McSorley 1987). Soil samples can be packed in the field simply into sealable plastic bags, but for extraction techniques where intact soil cores are needed, cylindrical containers approximating the core diameter are needed. Plastic 'drainpipes' are useful; metal containers can be used, but metal toxicity may cause some mortality in the samples and this may need to be tested for specific target taxa.

Benthic samples may be transported wet in waterproof containers, as desiccation can be damaging. Samples of vegetation (such as plant roots for nematode extractions, foliage, blossom or fruit for insects) are usually transported in paper or plastic bags. The former prevent 'sweating' but, conversely, the contents must not be allowed to dry out.

Transportation on land is most effective in ice cooler boxes or car fridges but if these are not available care must be taken to keep the samples as cool as possible and avoid direct insolation. Spillproof jars, such as preserver jars with liquid-tight seals, are often useful, as are large thermos flasks for animals in water, sediment or vegetation. Containers for marine invertebrates, particularly, must be checked carefully in case they are attacked chemically by seawater or preservative, or release toxic substances into the water inside. Duration and regime of such temporary storage and transport can be critical. As two examples of the problems which may arise:

1. Washing of soil samples should normally be undertaken within 24 h of collecting the samples. Kethley (1991) found an inverse correlation between the time before washing and the numbers of microarthropods collected.

2. Marine invertebrate samples, especially from great depths, undergo considerable shock and change of regimes as they are brought from cold deep to warmer surface conditions. Refrigeration may be vital if these are to be kept alive, as they may reach the ship adequately buffered in sediment. Many such animals may need to be anaesthetized carefully before they are preserved.

The expectation and, often untested, assumption is that the samples of invertebrates which reach the laboratory—either dead or alive—will represent the field assemblages or populations adequately. If preserved, the material must also be in suitable condition for further treatment and examination of taxonomic features, and living material can be extracted and preserved in optimal fashion.

Laboratory sorting and identification of specimens

Analysis of mixed invertebrate samples usually commences with sorting and separation to higher taxonomic category. In general, sorting to major groups (phyla or orders) is undertaken by non-specialists under some more experienced guidance, or from reference texts, but such sorting can have several different bases.

The most common basis in conservation work is the 'survey count', where all the individuals in the various samples (or subsamples) are recorded as totals for each taxon, and the grand total is reiterated as 'individuals/unit of habitat' or 'individuals/sample'. Volumetric estimates are employed for some large samples, such as benthos or light trap catches (p. 123), and involve measuring the catch volume in some graduated container such as a measuring cylinder, under standard conditions. This kind of index can also be related commonly to sampling unit or some measure of sampling effort, and is also applicable to gravimetric analyses of production or biomass. However, even simple counting can be a complicated and laborious process, because of the large numbers involved. In benthic grab and dredge samples, some taxa such as tubificid worms fragment easily, and it may be necessary to approximate their numbers by counting all fragments and dividing by two (Welch 1948). Alternatively, tubificids may aggregate to form tight masses which are difficult to separate and enumerate. Many mud-frequenting invertebrates are translucent and easily overlooked unless they are stained (p. 98).

Great care is needed to avoid major errors in sorting. Sorting the same samples twice increased the number of species in Coleman's (1980) three-replicate trial on marine invertebrates by about 13%, most of the additions being polychaete worms and crustaceans—groups whose quantification is important in determining marine benthic diversity (p. 143). Repeated extractions of litter and soil may reveal that initial treatment yields only a small proportion of the organisms present.

Even simple changes in sorting procedures, such as using a low power stereo microscope rather than relying solely on naked eye sorting, can produce dramatic differences in interpretation. In a comparative exercise on marine benthos (Barnett 1979), this step replicated on the same set of samples increased the number of nematodes recorded from one to 482 (12 samples), and the presence of nematodes in a set of 105 samples rose from 16 to 64 samples. Even experienced technicians failed to find many animals unless a microscope was used. Such sorting errors clearly have major implications in interpreting samples in terms of diversity and frequency of occurrence of taxa. Coleman (1980) suggested that errors result also from changes in a worker's sorting efficiency as sorting time increases (reflecting tedium and boredom) and that the pressures associated with the need to sort samples reasonably rapidly (cost limitations) would also lead to inefficiencies as accuracy may be sacrificed for speed. Sources of sorting error can be grouped under several major causes.

1. Sample size and physical characteristics.

2. Differences in sorting efficiency between different workers, and variations in the same worker over time.

3. The kind of animal—size, conspicuousness, ease of recognition.

4. The degree of precision needed in the sorting, and consideration of the effects of incomplete sorting on the interpretation of the samples.

The routine activity of sorting can also lead to other confusions, and laboratory discipline is important. Thus, only one trap sample at a time should be investigated, so that possible cross-contamination or mislabelling of samples is avoided (Danks 1996).

Taxonomic need

Whereas recognition of major groups of invertebrates is usually, although not always, straightforward, sorting to finer taxonomic levels can become a complex and demanding operation involving costly preparations of material, and may need specialist participation. In practice, the compromise is usually between the increased information gained from more precise identifications to genus or species level (rather than relying on family or order identifications alone) and the costs involved in achieving this. The process may involve buying the time of experienced taxonomists if they are available to participate. If sorting to these levels is undertaken by non-specialists, it may be necessary or advisable to have voucher material (p. 157) checked by specialists as part of the continuous quality control needed in most invertebrate surveys. Differing taxonomic levels of interpretation reflect different survey purposes, and that invertebrates may respond to environmental changes at higher or lower taxonomic levels. At any level, it is practically useful to accumulate progressively a 'reference collection' of different taxa as they are distinguished, to form the basis for comparison as sorting and identification proceeds.

In many analyses published from invertebrate surveys, differences in levels of taxonomic analysis tend to reflect the diversity and 'importance' of different invertebrate groups, and the availability of relevant taxonomic expertise—in other words, on a combination of utility and feasibility. Analysis may also depend on the system under study. Reviewing studies of freshwater benthic invertebrates, Resh and McElravy (1993) found that insect groups were usually ($n = 90$ studies) identified to genus level (most commonly) or species, whereas nematodes, annelids and water mites were identified only to family level or above. Despite the widespread recognition of needs for species-level identifications in many freshwater monitoring surveys, many authors have accepted the validity of using higher taxa because of the difficulties of proceeding further rather than on any more scientifically defensible grounds. Species-level identifications are often of critical importance for understanding ecological interactions in an assemblage, and Danks (1996) emphasized that individual (species-level) specializations render grouping of insects by family level generally inappropriate, despite the taxonomic difficulties of proceeding further.

Writing on soil fauna, Moldenke *et al.* (1991) commented that workers' interest 'often wanes when they are faced with the investment in time and effort required to obtain the taxonomic skills necessary to expand their research progress...(they) frequently view learning the taxonomy of soil fauna as an insurmountable task'. Advocates for species-level identifications recognize the formidable difficulties and ambiguities involved, but adopt three major categories of reasoning (after Resh and McElravy 1993).

1. Recognition that 'the species' is a basic biological unit, with the greatest information content emanating from this level of analysis. Amalgamating these at higher levels may result in loss of important information and decreased sensitivity of interpretation. Important but subtle changes may be missed in monitoring programmes.

2. Identification above the species level may lead to misleading estimates in diversity indices and other biological measurements that rely on accurate fine-level separations.

3. Analysis may suffer. Species data is the level usually employed in multi-variate analyses, for example. Comparison of assemblages solely in terms of the families or orders present may be meaningless, because many are widespread and diverse.

However, the stance of using only levels above the species can indeed be justified in particular contexts. Resh and McElravy (1993) listed the following as scenarios where this could apply for benthic invertebrates.

1. To detect incidence of gross pollution which has dramatic effects on the benthos.

2. To provide early warning of changes indicating the need for more detailed study.

3. When indices which are relatively insensitive to information loss are used to simplify presentation of results.

4. When taxa in a higher taxonomic group are reasonably consistent in their response to a given environmental change. This may be very difficult to determine.

Good taxonomy plays an integral and critical part in invertebrate conservation and survey programmes, irrespective of the level at which it is applied, and simple sorting is a critical exercise in which mistakes must be avoided if the integrity and value of the work is to be upheld. Many errors are the consequence of inexperience and lack of specialist advice. In one common context, overestimation of diversity can arise for three main reasons (Beattie *et al.* 1993).

1. When juvenile stages do not resemble the corresponding adults but co-occur with them.

2. When the two sexes are dissimilar as adults.

3. Where there is polymorphism so that the different morphs may be sorted as equivalent to different taxa.

The information needed to obviate these, and other, pitfalls may not be available readily.

Levels of identification

However, 'identification' has two levels in practical analysis: separation to consistently recognizable units (which are given terms such as 'morphospecies', 'recognizable taxonomic units' [RTUs], or 'operational taxonomic units' [OTUs]), sorted on morphological grounds, which also in many cases represent or approximate 'real' species, and formal allocation of generic and specific names to the units recognized. The 'RTU level' is valuable in RBA surveys (p. 28), because recognition is a rigorous, consistent process that provides comparable data from different samples and sites, which can form the basis for operational analyses. With responsible deposition of voucher material (p. 153), the data have archival value just as if 'real names' were available.

The conditions for such analyses are twofold (Beattie *et al.* 1993). The first is that in any given group RTUs and species have a reasonably constant ratio. This can be established by comparing the sorting results by non-specialists and specialists in the relevant group to determine the non-specialists' error rate in allocating specimens to categories. Second, it is necessary to establish and maintain a system to ensure the uniqueness and consistent recognition of each RTU. Logistically, it is far harder to sort organisms to named species than to RTUs, because needs for critical comparison with specimens and literature descriptions add to the work. Many groups need critical revision to ensure that the available names are applied correctly (Eggleton and Bignell 1995), an intent usually far from the mind of a field surveyor.

One major advantage of the morphospecies approach is that specimen sorting for some invertebrate groups may be undertaken effectively after only limited training. Tests by Oliver and Beattie (1993) showed high correspondence between RTUs and species for ants and spiders, but lower correspondence for littoral polychaete worms. For approximately 300 species of beetles sorted sporadically by volunteers and students from 600 bulked invertebrate samples, specialist checking revealed fewer than 10 mistakes (Yen 1993), but the taxonomic groups amenable to this approach need careful selection, together with defining the level of accuracy needed. For their studies on terrestrial invertebrates from pitfall traps, Oliver and Beattie (1996) generated three inventories: (1) morphospecies categorized with little specialist input and likely to be subject to severe revision with more critical examination; (2) corrected morphospecies based on specialist examination of the voucher specimens and subsequent manipulation of the earlier data to adjust for splitting and lumping; and (3) species, the initial data set corrected completely for splitting and lumping. The three inventories represented an increasing cost structure and increasing accuracy of identification. Results of site comparisons were largely constant regardless of the level of analysis, suggesting that careful use of morphospecies may indeed be warranted in such studies.

There are few, if any, hard-and-fast rules for the level of identification needed in a given invertebrate survey, but feasibility and need must be appraised carefully. It is indeed important to balance the considerations that: (1) obtaining invertebrate inventory data of the quality taken for granted by workers on mammals, birds and some other well known groups in many parts of the world is often impracticable, and (2) even for the invertebrate taxa which can be named reliably to species level, biological information pertinent to that level is likely to be fragmentary or (most often) non-existent. Pragmatically, fine-level identification is likely to be costly and slow, coarse-level identification (e.g. to family) much cheaper and more rapid. Linked intricately with taxonomic interpretation for diversity assessment is understanding the biases and scope of the sampling methods employed to collect the material interpreted. Thus, for sandy beach fauna, nematode species composition in samples can change with sampling method even though nematode diversity may not do so (Gourbalt and Warwick 1994).

Most environmental questions could probably be answered more precisely with the aid of fine-level taxonomy because, as Jones (1993) emphasized, much of the background information on ecological change and conservation has been expressed at the species level. He cited the following as examples.

1. Studies on diversity, intermediate disturbance, predation and habitat diversity.

2. General biology and ecology studies.

3. Extinction and status evaluation studies.

4. Geographical information systems.

5. Strategies for conserving biodiversity.

6. Legislation and legal requirements, such as protective legislation for rare species.

In contrast, Warwick (1993), and others, have emphasized that coarser taxonomy (even at the phylum level) may be sufficient for some baseline studies associated with impacts such as marine pollution, but such ideas need to be tested critically. Also for benthic fauna, Long and Lewis (1987) found family level identification sufficient for broad community characterization based on abundance. The rapidly increasing need for Environmental Impact Statements and the like dictates that coarse taxonomy is needed wherever valid, simply to cope with the demand for analysis of invertebrate assemblages; however, this approach is not always optimal or used sufficiently self-critically.

Ellis (1985) used the term 'taxonomic sufficiency' to emphasize that in any project the organisms must be identified to a level which balances the need to indicate biology (including diversity) of the organisms with accuracy in making the identifications. 'Accuracy' reflects placing individuals to the correct taxon, and 'precision' is consistency in placing all conspecific individuals to the same taxon—so that precision may occur without accuracy, and if both are poor the values of diversity calculated may be very misleading. Diversity measurements on different levels of sufficiency in trial samples of marine invertebrates led to different ranking of diversity across three sites at the different levels. An earlier set of inter-laboratory comparisons on species identifications (Ellis and Cross 1981) emphasized the importance of taxonomic quality control. Fewer than half of the nine laboratories produced 100% accuracy in the identification of six species for which they claimed expertise—and one provided correct identification of only one species! Such results render the need for voucher material for later checking of names embarrassingly obvious.

In some cases, available published information can dictate the particular taxonomic level that must be used, or which can be used most expeditiously. For meiofauna, Herman and Heip (1988) noted that family level identifications of copepods avoided the laborious dissections needed to proceed to finer levels, and availability of a pictorial key to nematode genera (Platt and Warwick 1983) rendered identification to genus level in many groups more straightforward than recognizing families formally. In other cases, pragmatism is important: the general appearance of an onychophoran (velvetworm) is unmistakable and, whereas the finer taxonomy of this group is poor with many (perhaps, most) of the species undescribed and difficult to differentiate, the simple presence of any species in a sample from some habitats may be sufficient to render that habitat or site worthy of conservation attention.

Warwick (1993) summarized earlier studies on deciding the level of taxonomic sufficiency by aggregating species-level data into successively higher levels (genera, families, phyla) and analysing the data in various ways. For soft bottom macrobenthos from marine samples, disturbance can often be detected at the highest taxonomic levels. Indeed, responses to pollution can sometimes be even more clear than at species level, reflecting a degree of coherence among species in higher taxa in regard to their responses to disturbance. Herman and Heip (1988) drew similar inferences from marine invertebrates in Norway. Warwick (1993) suggested that the response of organisms to contaminants is more likely to represent (or be a function of) the 'integrated physiology' for a given type of systematic organization such as 'a crustacean' or 'a polychaete' rather than any natural ecological group to which that organism might belong. For macrobenthos, there may be strong correspondence between taxonomic grouping and ecological role. Whether this generalization is more widely valid is open to question, but it merits careful investigation in its relevance to survey logistics.

Herman and Heip's (1988) study in Norway led them to conclude that identification of harpacticoid copepods and nematodes to genus or family was probably sufficient for the practical purpose of comparing stations, and that information contained in species abundance data was preserved even when the taxa were grouped randomly!

Obviating the need for specialized taxonomic knowledge has been suggested for many groups by various forms of approximation. Thus, for marine meiobenthic nematodes Cairns et al. (1968) suggested estimating diversity in samples by arranging individuals into a random sequence and recording the number of 'runs', where a run is a maximal sequence of consecutive specimens of the same species. Specimen 1 is compared with specimen 2, then specimen 2 with specimen 3, and so on. This approach could enable otherwise intractable nematode assemblages to be utilized in pollution studies, and could contribute to a protocol for monitoring benthic communities (Moore et al. 1987), but should be checked for each site by examining the extent of error in diversity estimates. Underestimation is likely to be most obvious in groups with many superficially similar taxa, or many congeneric forms. Counting may also take the form of identifying a fixed number of specimens taken sequentially or randomly from a preserved sample: thus, Langley et al. (1995) examined 100 rotifers from 5 ml of each formalin-preserved sample to assemble species lists for each of a series of ponds. Inevitably, it becomes tempting to transfer any potential short cut which has worked successfully in one context to more broader use. This can be dangerous without further critical testing to confirm its validity in the new context.

Whatever level of taxonomic resolution is decided upon, sorting, preparing and identifying/recognizing specimens are the most costly phases of many invertebrate surveys. It follows that any economies, including lowered taxonomic resolution, may be highly desirable. However, it is important to dispel the widespread notion that the formal naming of organisms with a latinized binomial is a prerequisite to invertebrate biodiversity studies. Consistent recognition and coding of RTUs essentially serves the same function as formal names in allowing for retrieval and use of data relevant to that 'species' (Cranston 1993). Either epithet is a summary diagnosis for the suite of features which characterize that entity. Although 'a name' is a critical key to the published information which exists on that species, any misapplication of that name will result in confusion.

Sample processing: who does what?

The major sequence of sample processing therefore may take the following form.

1. Preservation and 'cleaning' of the samples, to separate the organisms needed from other matter such as soil, sediment, vegetation or general debris.

2. Sorting to taxonomic group, preparing specimens and undertaking coarse-level taxonomic assessment.

3. Extending this to finer taxonomic levels when necessary.

4. Ensuring that allocation to name or category is consistent throughout the sample or series of samples.

The participation of non-specialist sorters is becoming an important part of this sequence. Such 'parataxonomists' or 'biological diversity technicians' are vital in a world where support for professional taxonomists is declining rapidly, despite strong advocacy for the importance of systematics as a discipline underpinning the study of biological diversity (SA2000 1994). Especially in the tropics, even relatively superficial surveys produce myriad invertebrate taxa which have not been named, and many of these are unrepresented in major institutional collections. As Gaston and May (1992) emphasized, the distribution of global taxonomic expertise does not correspond with that of species richness or of need for fundamental knowledge of invertebrate faunas, as it is concentrated largely in some of the temperate regions of the world. The existence of vast numbers of invertebrate species which are undescribed or are recognizable by only a few experienced systematists is a major problem for those seeking to interpret invertebrate assemblages from any major habitat in most parts of the world.

The proposal for using parataxonomists stems, in part, from the undertaking by Costa Rica's Instituto Nacional de Biodiversidad (INBio) to prepare a species inventory for the country. Because of the impossibilities of training numerous local professional taxonomists, and limitations on the availability of taxonomists elsewhere, INBio decided to utilize local people to collaborate with biology graduates and the international taxonomist community (Janzen et al. 1993). Parataxonomists are selected there among country people, usually having only primary school education. Six months training is given in the collection and preparation of specimens, and in taxonomy, and the employees then spend 17 days/month in the field, at biodiversity offices throughout the country, and 7 days/month at INBio headquarters. For the later week they are able to liaise with more experienced taxonomists and to further their skills by the advice received. In Costa Rica the taxonomists themselves mainly lack research degrees and are generalists, rather than specialists in particular taxonomic groups. Their role is to liaise between parataxonomists and the international community of systematists for identification and description of new taxa (Alberch 1993). Inevitably, there are substantial gaps in promoting such cooperation. Emphasis on the training of parataxonomists in Costa Rica has been to enable them to work independently and to understand the philosophy which underpins their work. The early training courses therefore addressed a wide range of questions on biodiversity, collection use, sampling effort, taxonomy, use and construction of field guides, and conservation responsibility (details in Janzen *et al.* 1993; Heywood 1995). This broad emphasis differs considerably from simply employing technicians as 'pairs of hands', without them appreciating the likely outcomes of their work.

There have been few attempts specifically to quantify the performance of parataxonomists and thus to provide quality control of their activities, but Cranston and Hillman (1992) investigated and compared results from sorting freshwater invertebrate samples by non-specialists and specialists. Taxonomic accuracy was best for taxa differentiated mostly at the higher taxonomic levels, diminished if different immature instars of the same species showed consistent morphological differences, and produced serious underestimates if specific-level characters were minor or microscopic. In short, greater experience, equating with greater expertise, is needed for finer level work, and the needed skills are acquired best in direct consultation with specialists in the particular invertebrate groups under study. Kitching (1993) used volunteer labour trained 'on the spot' to sort arboreal arthropods to order level in the field. Selected orders were then separated to family and morphospecies by professional, non-taxonomist, technicians and the categories checked in collaboration with specialists.

While initiating sorting, specialist advice may be very relevant in helping to determine the most important diagnostic features of the animals and the main problems that inexperienced workers may encounter. As emphasized earlier, this is simply an aspect of quality control. Ellis (1988) commented that, without it, there is substantial risk that comparisons over time and between places will be invalid (or 'statistically noisy') and that expensively-gathered specimens may, in essence, be wasted together with the mass of environmental data accompanying them. Ellis showed convincingly that quality control undertaken by initially non-experienced taxonomy students under competent supervision could provide new information of considerable value in refining environmental assessment from a copper mine through interpreting invertebrates in benthos influenced by mine tailings. Incorporating such exercises in the practical teaching of taxonomy, using a variety of modern techniques, could become much more widespread and might help to counter the generally poor image of taxonomy among many biology students, and overcome the lack of funding by seeking sponsorship from proprietors with interests in the practical outcomes.

In practice, the decline in the number and interests of professional taxonomists has serious ramifications in obtaining the kind of help needed to interpret invertebrate samples adequately, and the costs estimated to describe even relatively well known faunas completely are high. For North American insects and arachnids alone, Kostarab and Shaefer (1990) estimated that at least 525 scientists and 525 illustrators would require 10 years to produce the needed new descriptions and illustrations (including early stages) and, at an average salary of US$40 000, this work would cost at least US$42 million annually, neglecting increases in salary and overheads which would inevitably occur. Similar figures have been projected for other exercises of this nature. In the same essay Kosztarab and Shaefer noted the substantial reduction of the USDA Systematic Entomology Laboratory staff to 23 research and two service scientists, with the likelihood of further reductions within a few years. Similar reductions are becoming commonplace in many countries which have traditionally been leaders in fostering taxonomic expertise and in probing the characteristics of invertebrate faunas throughout the world.

All too often, the level of identification achieved for invertebrate samples is determined by logistic capability rather than defined scientific need. As Cranston (1989) noted, this is a rather arbitrary criterion and its value for assessing and comparing communities is usually unknown. Pragmatically, species-level identifications tend to be made reliably only if specialist advice is not needed (for example, because of availability of excellent, well-illustrated, recent published accounts, or of comprehensive reference collections so that many ambiguities can be avoided) or is available readily and cheaply. Other levels of identification are also made according to the accessibility and usefulness (which is often not appraised critically) of identification keys (Cranston 1989). At the present time, many broad-based environmental consultants are seeking to establish themselves as reputable authorities, and many of them have little expertise with invertebrate identifications. Some form of recognized accreditation or acknowledgment of proficiency in this field may become a more widespread need.

A further factor that influences which groups of invertebrates may be appraised is the small size of many taxa. Jones (1993) offered the suggestion of using a sieve with a coarse (>1 mm) mesh to exclude small specimens from marine benthic samples on the grounds that they are disproportionately time-consuming (that is, costly) to extract and process and were often numerous, if RBA is pursued. Yen (1993) noted that, although microinvertebrates may be more important ecologically than the larger forms in the same environments, they are indeed often ignored, and new methods to incorporate them effectively need to be developed.

The limitation of specialist taxonomic input restricts the scope and utility of many invertebrate surveys, and funding applications need to incorporate realistic budgets to provide for this, if needed. Choice of focal groups, estimates of the level and extent of taxonomic advice and separations, and prior approaches to relevant specialists are therefore important. The options noted for identifications of terrestrial arthropods by Marshall *et al.* (1994) apply equally to other groups of invertebrates.

1. Taxa are sorted consistently to morphospecies and assigned a consistent code number.

2. Taxa are sorted to some level above species, with the caveats noted earlier (p. 141).

3. Only the taxonomic groups which can be identified readily are appraised.

4. Resources are sought to resolve problems of recognition and naming the taxa involved through original taxonomic revision.

Brinkhurst (1993) found that, in the long run, it was cheaper to employ the best available taxonomists directly to determine benthic fauna, rather than simply use them to verify identifications made by relatively unskilled staff. However, such expertise may not be available and 'All Taxon Biological Inventory' surveys (ATBIs) are usually not feasible.

Preparing specimens for identification

The costs of necessary processing of specimens, and of identifying them, are increasing steadily. The International Institute of Entomology has recently (Annual Report 1994) instigated a charge of £100/specimen for identifying insects, as a real reflection of the costs of maintaining a well-resourced taxonomic workforce, and institutions are increasingly being committed to recovering costs for such services as their budgets diminish. The potential users of identifications and other collection-based data need to understand that taxonomy is a dynamic science, and that those services may be costly to obtain (Danks 1991). Several recent authors (such as Miller 1991; Danks 1991) have summarized the problems of maintaining and safeguarding major institutional collections, and the ever-increasing need to so as their unique value in studies of biodiversity comes to be appreciated and their roles diversify (Danks 1991). Collections which are not curated properly deteriorate. Precise costs for processing specimens are difficult to obtain (Nielsen and West 1994), but are usually far greater than anticipated by field biologists collecting vast numbers of specimens for which they anticipate formal taxonomic resolution!

Two principles are involved in preparing specimens for identification, or transmittal to specialists.

1. Optimal treatment of specimens, to render them well-preserved and housed or mounted in identifiable condition.

2. Tracking specimens unambiguously once they have been separated from the sample in which they were collected.

Specimen treatment

Preparation of specimens varies considerably with the group of invertebrates involved. In many cases, clean specimens in a general liquid preservative such as ethyl alcohol or formalin are adequate, but even this may not occur. Martin's (1977) comment, for insects, that 'the standard methods of mounting and preserving various kinds... are so widely known that it is difficult to attribute the high proportion of badly mounted or incorrectly preserved specimens in many collections to anything but carelessness' applies much more widely, and has not diminished in significance in recent times. Few things can alienate specialist taxonomists approached for help more than extremely poor or carelessly presented material submitted for examination, both as a reflection of the collector's attitude and because of the practical difficulties and increased work which are caused. Consider, as example, the following (true) scenarios.

1. Moths collected in alcohol and subsequently shaken so that the scales, all-important in many species diagnoses, are washed off.

2. Small beetles and other insects from the same samples dried, but covered in moth scales so that many of their taxonomic features are obscured. These were also posted loose in vials, with minimal packing, so that most were badly broken on reception. Loose dry insects which can 'rattle' are decidedly fragile, and one loose specimen in a box can function like a dentist's pulverizing mill and reduce others to rubble.

3. Small arthropods preserved in alcohol but enveloped in spider silk, with loss of limbs and some partially eaten. This situation can arise easily when these animals are collected by beating or sweeping and kept in the same container before killing.

4. Arthropods covered in mucus from gastropods kept in the same containers.

Any practising taxonomist will have many similar anecdotes. Each of the above, and many similar cases, could be obviated with little prior effort, and the two pertinent steps are: (1) to use standard recommended preparation techniques, readily available from manuals such as BMNH (1954, 1961) and many texts on various invertebrate groups, and (2) to seek advice from collaborating specialists on how they would prefer the material to be prepared and presented. In many cases, such practical advice is readily forthcoming. Table 6.2 summarizes some of the recommended preservation and preparation methods for various groups.

Cleaning of contaminated specimens may be as simple as washing in water or ammonia and brushing with a fine soft paintbrush. An ultrasonic cleaner is useful for hard or dry specimens (although should be used with care to avoid damage to delicate specimens by turbulence), but much contamination can be avoided easily with care in collecting. For example, insect killing bottles used for Lepidoptera will inevitably contain large numbers of scales, and should not be used for other insects which these might contaminate. Drying and mounting of insects stored in alcohol may also require considerable care to avoid distortion: it is common to critical-point dry small parasitic Hymenoptera to counter collapse and shrinkage, for instance.

It is also implicit, unless prior arrangement has been made to the contrary, that specimens sent to a specialist will have been sorted to, at least, major group (perhaps including, separately, any 'doubtful' taxa) rather than be included in the general unsorted mass of the sample. Most taxonomists have received (and, unless circumstances are highly unusual, rejected) unsolicited requests along the lines of 'We have 200 jars of unsorted soil invertebrates/benthic fauna/insect sweep samples which we need identified. Will you identify the nematodes/molluscs/worms/beetles in these?'

Many specialists will appreciate an offer to retain any specimens of particular interest for their own research: the likelihood of seeing something unusual is a notable 'carrot' in seeking taxonomic help.

Specimen tracking

It is vital to ensure that the information afforded by specimens once they have been sorted and separated from the sample can be regained for synthesis and interpretation. At its simplest, this entails providing each specimen with a data label relating it unambiguously to its sampling content before it is dispersed, and maintaining a register of specimens sent elsewhere so that their whereabouts are traceable and known. Once the specimens are identified formally, to whatever level is needed, the information can be incorporated into databases which can be augmented progressively to describe the sample.

Labels must adhere to the standards of permanence and legibility needed for museum specimens, a fact which is often overlooked by inexperienced workers who may confine details to those needed for their own work without regard to the wider importance of specimens as archival material. Thus,

Table 6.2

Recommended methods for preservation/preparation for major groups of invertebrates (partly after BMNH 1954; Upton 1991). (**NB**: *Formalin is regarded as a dangerous chemical: consult local health and safety regulations before use: alcohol may usually be substituted as a preservative*)

Taxon	Preparation/preservation methods
Porifera	Preserve in strong (70–90%) alcohol: change after 24 h. Large specimens may be dried, but small pieces detached for spirit preservation.
Coelenterata	Preserve in 10% formalin buffered with hexamine. (Except Ctenophora, which disintegrate: drop into chromosmic acid mixture [100 ml of 1% chromic acid and 2 ml 1% osmic acid] for 15–60 min, then grade to 70% alcohol). Hydroids, gorgonians, antipatharians and corals can be preserved dry if necessary, but samples should be preserved also in formalin, as above, or strong alcohol (taxa with calcareous skeletons, such as many Anthozoa).
Platyhelminthes	
Turbellaria	Extend in water; fix in 3–5% formalin; store in 70–90% alcohol. Other good killing and fixing agents include Steinman's fluid [1 part distilled water, 1 part concentrated nitric acid, 1 part 5% sodium chloride in saturated mercuric chloride]. Large species can be killed directed in boiling water.
Cestoda Trematoda	Fix in 5–10% formalin; store in fresh 3–5% formalin; may be necessary to fix for histological examination. Shake in 1% salt solution, add 10% formalin; store in fresh 3–5% formalin; fix for histological examination if necessary, and store in 70–90% alcohol.
Nemertinea	Anaesthetize with chloral hydrate in water (6–12 h), then kill in 10% formalin or 30–50% alcohol, storing respectively in 3–5% formalin or 70–90% alcohol.
Nematoda	Narcotize (e.g. by heating to 50–60° in water. Kill in 3–5% formalin or hot 70–90% alcohol; store in fresh preserving fluid. Can use heat or chemical fixation, or combination of these.

(Continued)

Table 6.2 (*Continued*)

Taxon	Preparation/preservation methods
Rotifera	Narcotize then fix with osmic acid and store in weak (5–10%) formalin after repeated washing in water.
Brachiopoda	Narcotize by adding alcohol to seawater (up to 10% by volume); preserve in 70–90% alcohol.
Bryozoa (Ectoprocta)	Preserve in 70–90% alcohol; change after several h. Large marine colonies can be dried but sample detached for spirit presentation. Non-calcareous forms can be preserved in 5% formalin. Freshwater taxa can be narcotized before preservation.
Echinodermata	Hard specimens: 70% alcohol; soft specimens: narcotize with Epsom salts or menthol in seawater, add alcohol slowly; preserve in 70–75% alcohol (industrial methyl alcohol the best preservative for soft holothurians, etc.). May be necessary to open body (drill holes in sea urchins) or inject to preserve well. Large specimens can be sun-dried after a few hours in freshwater. **NB**: *Formalin should never be used as a permanent preservative, as it dissolves the spicules and other calcareous structures.*
Annelida	Polychaetes: anaesthetize to deter fragmentation, by adding small amounts of alcohol to worms in water; or add menthol to crystals to the seawater. After straightening, add 70% alcohol; store in 70–90% alcohol, not in formalin for long-term storage. Oligochaetes: can preserve directly in 70–90% alcohol; better to anaesthetize as above, transfer to 10% formalin overnight, then to alcohol. Some workers recommend storage in 5% formalin, and initial formalin fixation necessary for good histological/anatomical studies for accurate taxonomy. Hirudinea: anaesthetize by adding Epsom salts (magnesium sulphate) to water; fix in 3–5% formalin; store after 12–24 h in 70–90% alcohol or 3–5% formalin.
Mollusca	Shells stored dry in individual vials or trays. Narcotize by asphyxiation, such as by drowning in water with small amount of menthol, or adding a small piece of tobacco (nicotine); kill in 5% formalin when extended; (short term: unsuitable for storage unless neutral); preserve and store in 70–90% alcohol.

Table 6.2 (Continued)

Taxon	Preparation/preservation methods
Arthropoda	
Pycnogonida	Kill and store in 70–90% alcohol.
Onychophora	Kill in hot water (can also use an entomological killing bottle); preserve and store in 70–90% alcohol.
Tardigrada	Fix in small amounts of boiling water or (80%) alcohol; necessary to slide-mount (Hoyer's medium used commonly) for detailed study.
Arachnida	Kill and preserve in 70–90% alcohol.
(Acari)	Kill and store in 70% alcohol; slide-mounting usual for storage and examination.
Myriapoda	Kill and store in 70–90% alcohol; isopropyl alcohol best for permanent storage. Some workers recommend fixing for 12 h in 70% alcohol and 1–3% glacial acetic acid, followed by storage as above.
Crustacea	(Small): narcotize; kill in 5% neutralized formalin; store in 70–90% alcohol.
	(Large): narcotize; kill and store in 70–90% alcohol. All: if killed in formalin, wash thoroughly in water before transfer to alcohol; note that some specialists may advocate formalin storage for particular groups, such as amphipods.
	NB: *Formalin should not be used uncritically for storage because it dissolves calcareous shells, etc.*
Insecta	1. Most can be collected and preserved in 70–90% alcohol (as for other hexapods: Collembola, Diplura, Protura). Collembola best in 80–95% isopropyl alcohol, as they can deteriorate in ethyl alcohol.
	2. Larvae and pupae can be fixed in Carnoy's fluid (1 part glacial acetic acid, 6 parts 95% ethyl alcohol, three parts chloroform) or KAA (2 parts acetic acid, 10 parts 95% ethyl alcohol, 1 part kerosene, dye-free) up to 24 h before storage in 80–90% alcohol.
	3. Many winged adults preserved dry: kill by exposure to fumes of ethyl acetate (not for green insects: decolorizes) or potassium cyanide (*CARE!!*) in properly constructed killing bottle, then (a) for small specimens, card or card-point or (b) for large specimens pin and set in style for that order. May be necessary to gut larger specimens of Orthoptera and Phasmatodea.

labels such as 'benthic sample 14a', 'sweep sample 4, transect b' are adequate for reference to a survey by the participants, but largely meaningless in a wider context. The more comprehensive details for permanent labels include the country and more local political regions, latitude and longitude (which may even substitute for country in some marine samples) or a near approximation, nature of habitat (in as much detail as possible: 'under stone in flowing stream', 'on bark of dead *Eucalyptus*', 'in bottom sand at 10 m depth', and so on), date, method of collection, collector's name, and note of any particular survey or study involved, with copy of relevant sample code, if available. Each specimen or sample may be given a reference code as a unique number cross-referenced to the collector's records, but this is not a long-term substitute for fuller data and codes must be 'translated' in due course. Labels must be associated clearly with the specimens to which they refer. They must be written or printed in preservative-proof ink and, for example, inserted inside the specimen container or impaled on the same pin as the specimen. Most museums now have considerable numbers of specimens, especially older ones, whose sole data labels are codes once referable to collectors' notebooks which have long been lost. The specimens therefore usually have minimal scientific value because of this lack of documentation. Labels can be mass-produced by computer, and details completed by hand, and INBio (p. 145) has been experimenting with barcode labels to facilitate data capture by computer scanning. Such streamlining becomes an important logistic concern when very large numbers of specimens are involved. Standards for label quality include paper quality and permanence of marks. Standards for categories and terms for collection data were appraised, for insects, by Noonan and Thayer (1990), who elaborated a suite of features for recording geographical and ecological data, including many descriptive categories suitable for use in data bases.

Data use and retrieval

One important purpose of obtaining identifications of specimens is to appraise and define the samples of invertebrate assemblages as precisely as possible. Another is to be able to assess the 'value' of the samples in terms of the taxa they contain and their relative abundance. This can be accomplished most effectively by incorporating also whatever information on the same taxa may be available in published literature or in the vast storehouse of unpublished information represented by specimens in museum collections and their data labels. It follows that maintenance and enhancement of major invertebrate collections has extremely high importance in documenting the world of invertebrates and facilitating development of strategies for their conservation (Danks 1991). In practice, though, many collections are neglected and specimens continue to rot in many parts of the world. Such losses have been termed 'the silent crisis in systematics' (Cotterill 1995), and increase further the difficulties of making precise identifications. Again from Cotterill, 'Specimens are the material representation of unique information which can be interpreted by present and future biologists'. A prerequisite for such effective data retrieval from collections is effective and skilful curation of the specimens, in itself an activity which urgently needs much more logistic support throughout the world. The sheer volume of specimens in many institutional collections guarantees that only a small proportion will be under active appraisal at any time.

The three highest levels of the nine noted by McGinley (1989) apply, namely (level 7) physical curation complete, species-level inventory (data base) complete; (level 8) as above but individual specimen label data captured; (level 9) as the above two, but additional research data (such as measurements of specimen) captured (see Miller 1991). These levels represent what are, in practice, fully curated specimens with information from them made available for wider use. For contrast, McGinley's lower levels are as follows.

1. Material in urgent/immediate need of proper curation to render it safe from degradation (such as insects on corroded pins).

2. Material which is well preserved but unsorted and unidentified (and, therefore inaccessible for research), typical of many ecological samples.

3. Material sorted to major category and therefore useful for specialist appraisal.

4. Identified material which has not yet been incorporated into the main collection.

5,6. Successive curation of identified specimens but without incorporation into any integrated data base.

As yet very few institutions have attempted comprehensive databasing of their vast main collections, and the taxonomic uncertainties make this premature for many groups because the results may mask complexes of taxa currently treated as single entities. For example, the problems associated with mapping the distribution of a given species include:

1. Taxonomic confusion, as when apparently good taxa are shown to consist of two or more distinct species. Harding (1991) cited the case of a woodlouse (isopod) not being recognized by British workers as distinct from a more common but superficially very similar species.

2. Closely related species, as when species are recognized generally as distinct but formal identification can be made reliably only by experts.

This is common in many invertebrate groups in which specific characters are small, and examination may require dissection or other careful treatment.

3. Overlooked species: those which are known but whose presence is masked by false assumptions. Harding (1991) noted that the damselfly *Lestes dryas* was regarded as extinct in Britain from 1973 to 1982 but was 'rediscovered' in 1983 and is now known from several sites. It is likely that it was present throughout the period of presumed extinction but was not sought because it had indeed died out at some of its former locations (see section on status evaluation, p. 191).

As Nielsen and West (1994) stressed 'The vast amount of information already contained in collections must be mobilised and made more readily available', and this may be particularly important for species which are conservation targets and groups which comprise high components of species diversity. Major conservation applications which can benefit directly from such information include:

1. Assessment of distribution, including changes over time (p. 179).

2. Listing the taxa recorded from a specified geographical region or habitat type.

3. Determining the presence of notable (such as endangered, rare, or taxonomically isolated) species in a region or habitat, and helping to focus searches for such taxa.

4. Documenting increases in the range of exotic taxa, many of which may be important as threats to native species.

However, capturing such data effectively may be difficult. Curation has traditionally been considered the province and responsibility of the museum or other holding institution (Quicke 1993), not of the individual scientists seeking to use the information which may emerge. This has massive ramifications for the appraisal of large samples of invertebrates, because the funding needed to sort, curate and identify the taxa now needs to be an integral part of the survey budget, and may increase the costs substantially.

The tentative nature of species-level taxonomy in many invertebrate groups, linked with the problems of confusion noted above, emphasizes two further needs for practical study:

(1) the need for standard, adequate methods for specimen preparation, and

(2) the importance of responsible deposition and curation of voucher material from all surveys where data retrieval and comparison may be needed in the foreseeable future.

The first of these has already been discussed. Taxonomic characters of many invertebrates can be lost or obscured by careless or inexperienced handling, and the initial mode of preparation can have far-reaching consequences.

Voucher specimens

The topic of voucher specimens is often disregarded by ecologists, despite its importance. A voucher specimen may be defined as one which 'physically and permanently documents data in an archival report by: (1) verifying the identity of the organism(s) used in the study, and (2) by doing so ensures that a study which otherwise could not be repeated can be accurately reviewed or reassessed' (Lee *et al.* 1982). Unless such specimens are available, errors or ambiguities of identification may never be clarified.

It is difficult to generalize over the extent of the voucher material which should be retained. On one hand, long series of unambiguously identified and non-variable common species are usually not needed. On the other, for variable species or possible sibling complexes which might reveal important new information after further study, or series from remote localities, more comprehensive vouchering may be advisable. Another view (Scudder 1996) is that it is unacceptable to discard unwanted specimens on grounds of both costs and ethics. Lee *et al.* suggested that collecting and depositing appropriate vouchers should be recognized as an integral budgetary component of a survey, and Scudder (1996) additionally advocated determining the storage institution before the study commences, recognizing that the bulk samples may have considerable value in other studies of a local fauna. Many granting agencies are still reluctant to provide such funds. But even accessing and handling voucher material is an expense which many museums simply cannot afford, despite the attractions of the material. Many invertebrate surveys produce vast numbers of potential voucher specimens, and their maintenance may detract from activities that the host institution considers to be more important (Quicke 1993). It seems increasingly likely that that requests to house vouchers, as a vital aspect of survey confirmation, will need to be accompanied by provision of funds to house and curate the material for a suitable period (not, necessarily, 'posterity') to remove such pressures on existing institutional budgets.

The amount of preparation needed for voucher specimens may differ according to common use. Foster (1994) noted that coleopterists tend to dry-mount their specimens, by pinning or gluing them on cards, whereas ecologists more commonly preserve material in alcohol. For water beetles, he recommended having access to both kinds of material: a dry collection is easier for direct comparison of specimens, but they are then much harder to dissect and examine critically than alcohol specimens.

More extensive material from surveys, including that of unsorted and undetermined taxa and unsorted samples, should also be considered for archival deposition. Such material may have been gathered at considerable expense but is often discarded. It constitutes 'ecological collections' (Danks et al. 1987) which would facilitate monitoring of habitat changes over time if it could be examined at some future time. As Yen (1993) commented, 'if this kind of collection had been made more widely in the past, we would probably have many more answers to conservation management issues—but it is not too late to make ecological collections for use over the next century'. There are two major reasons for making such ecological collections of invertebrates (Yen 1993).

1. Material not given priority for analysis currently may become of considerable value in the future when specialist attention is available for analysis of a particular group, or their relevance in practical conservation assessment becomes greater.

2. It may be the only opportunity to collect particular taxa before they become extinct, or to sample the invertebrate assemblages at particular sites or at remote or generally inaccessible localities. Retrospective analysis may help to indicate the extent of change, provide information on historical distribution and, perhaps, provide clues as to why changes have occurred.

In addition, such material is collected without additional costs as an integral part of the survey, and the costs of subsequent bulk preservation and storage are likely to be comparatively small in relation to those required for higher level curation.

Voucher material of any sort is important in information transfer because it is, in essence, a necessary component of the data base on which decisions may be based (Hawksworth and Mound 1991).

Addressing the taxonomic impediment for invertebrates

Much of this chapter has emphasized that taxonomic expertise in many invertebrate groups is itself a rare commodity, and that the low level of availability of expert help can be a major impediment to the study of diverse assemblages for conservation. It may not always be easy to discover what help may be available. Various country-based or theme/group-based listings of invertebrate specialists are available, but any prospective participant should be consulted well before the programme is commenced. An initial approach to a museum or local university may often lead to useful contacts or recommendations, but the availability of relevant specialists may even define the target groups for a particular survey. As noted earlier, it is critical that limited expertise be utilized as effectively as possible and liaison between taxonomists and parataxonomists can do much to avoid problems of identification or earlier preparation of material. In addition, the time taken to identify the specimens may be important; as Rosenberg *et al.* (1979) noted 'impact studies usually have inflexible schedules and the availability of taxonomic expertise during the lifetime of the study can determine its success or failure'.

It follows that well co-ordinated workshops and authoritative identification guides (with clear indication of 'problem groups' and the like) for invertebrates, and the development of databases on groups of conservation relevance are of critical importance, and survey material can provide the impetus for such syntheses. As examples from southeastern Australia, the Murray-Darling Freshwater Research Centre has instituted annual workshops on freshwater invertebrates, led by authorities in particular groups, which also have facilitated production of valuable keys for those groups. Second, the water mites collected in freshwater surveys in Victoria were for long simply stored. In due course the accumulated specimens formed the basis for an illustrated guide to generic level for Australian Hydracarina. Such co-ordination and synthesis is needed badly for many invertebrate groups in many parts of the world, even in North America and Europe for some taxa.

Many similar cases could be cited. In general, the availability of such field or more technical identification guides, designed to be helpful to non-specialists, may be critical in determining the accessibility of invertebrates to non-taxonomist users and in raising awareness of invertebrate diversity. As Janzen (1993) emphasized, the need to identify taxa is very different from assessing results of sampling completeness from ecological surveys, but forms the solid baseline information which can help put in train processes which can have practical conservation value. As another example, Ng (1991) discussed the development of a database on the crabs (Decapoda) of Southeast Asia. In Singapore, alone, about 400 species have been recorded and some are valuable ecological indicators of environmental quality. At present, inability to identify the crabs to species level reliably there has led to their neglect, despite widespread recognition of their importance in conservation assessment. Ng foreshadowed the utility of such keys on computer software, and this trend is one of the most important recent advances in improving applicability of systematics to conservation.

The major problems confronting the non-expert embarking on sorting invertebrates to taxonomic category are threefold (after Moldenke *et al.* 1991).

1. The information needed is usually highly scattered rather than collated effectively into a single source.

2. Dichotomous keys, the usual way to proceed toward formal identification, require specialized knowledge of morphology, often invoking specialized terminology peculiar to the group involved. Keys are often incomplete, covering only part of the fauna, simply because they have not been based on sufficiently comprehensive material; and many are old and now of rather little use. Much older material may be difficult to recognize reliably from published information because descriptions of species are often brief and, by more modern standards, inadequate for diagnosis.

3. Taxonomy is a visual skill needing detailed comparison of structural characters to diagnose species. Many keys traditionally used have few or no illustrations, and the users will commonly not have easy access to good reference collections of identified specimens for comparative study.

Integrated taxonomic synopses for many groups are commonly unavailable in any form, let alone one used easily by non-specialists, and their production demands considerable investment of time and specialist interest. The burden of accurate identification need is not lessened because of this, and development of 'user-friendly' identification manuals is a priority in helping to overcome the problem. Some are now available on CD-ROM or HyperCard software systems and the development of computer-driven, image-based taxonomy provides important working tools for conservation biologists. As an example, Moldenke *et al.* (1991) described such an approach to the identification of soil animals. COMTESA (COMputer Taxonomy and Ecology of Soil Animals) is divided into two main parts. The first distinguishes 150 separate functional/taxonomic groups and provides an ecological emphasis designed, in this case, to be of use over North America. The second provides identification to genus and species levels for regions/sites/ecosystem levels. The system can produce user-friendly regional keys which can be amended and updated as required, and the authors viewed one application of COMTESA as improving the quality of identifications and specimen sorting achieved by ecologists and technicians. This is helped by the keys containing considerable redundancy to delineate groups with easily confused forms or where immature stages and adults are dissimilar, and by the facility to enter the key at various levels or go back to earlier stages if ambiguities arise. Related information on the species or groups is also provided.

The DELTA system developed in Australia has also broken new ground in construction of computer recognition systems for invertebrates, and is potentially of very wide significance (Dallwitz 1993).

Any region-based keys will not usually transfer uncritically to other parts of the world, where the fauna is likely to differ, but not all groups of invertebrates can yet be treated in this way anywhere. The great need is to increase the number and usefulness of keys to those groups which are used commonly at the species level as indicator taxa or as frequently documented components of diversity in descriptions or comparisons of assemblages. Selection of such groups is discussed in Chapter 7.

Finally, some modern taxonomic methods have the potential to help overcome some of the traditional problems of assessing invertebrate species richness in samples. The morphological disparity between adults and immature stages of any taxa renders their unambiguous association very difficult, but the relatively quick and inexpensive method of RAPD–PCR (analysis of random amplified polymorphic DNA by polymerase chain reaction), although not yet used widely for invertebrates, may prove particularly useful for this in the future, as well as for separating highly similar species (Ablett 1994). Many invertebrates need special treatment to facilitate good taxonomic treatment, such as by being 'fixed' in some way for dissection or microscopical or histological examination (Table 6.2). Some molecular appraisals depend on ensuring the integrity of the DNA. Ideally, this may entail immediate storage in liquid nitrogen—a treatment only rarely available in the field. Storage, without heating, in absolute ethyl alcohol is often a good alternative.

Taxonomic techniques are changing rapidly as the need to cope with massive diversity with limited logistic resources increases, and their application is leading to renewed appreciation of organismal complexity (Quicke 1993; National Research Council [NRC] 1995), especially through the development of an array of molecular techniques (Heywood 1995). Not least, combinations of molecular genetic techniques with more classical morphological approaches are revealing numerous sibling complexes within what were formerly treated as single species. Although not restricted to invertebrates, some such applications are leading to severe reappraisal of some important indicator and commercial taxa on which conservation or rational harvesting policies have devolved in the past. Two examples of marine indicators, treated more fully by the NRC (1995):

1. The mussel *Mytilus edulis* formed the basis of the extensive pollution monitoring programme in the USA known as 'mussel watch'. It is now known to consist of three distinct species, whose different growth rates result in observed different uptakes of contaminants, so that knowledge of species-specific variations in pollutant uptakes are masked in the overall programme results.

2. The worm *Capitella capitata* was regarded as a widespread indicator species for disturbed, organically enriched sediments, but is now known to comprise 15 or more sibling species which differ in life history characteristics such as generation time, brood size and larval type. Such ecological variations, inevitably, have been overlooked in using the worm to reflect environmental degradation.

Rapid molecular techniques are coming to be an important component of many biodiversity research programmes (NRC 1995), not least because they can help markedly in providing resolution not attainable by more traditional taxonomic criteria, and increase the effective input of an individual worker in clarifying diversity and distribution patterns of organisms. They constitute one of the greatest hopes for understanding invertebrate diversity in all major ecosystems.

Further reading

Magurran, A. E. (1988). *Ecological diversity and its measurement.* Croom Helm, London.

Marshall, S. A., Andersen, R. S., Roughley, R. E., Behan-Pelletier, V., and Danks, H. V. (1994). Terrestrial arthropod biodiversity: planning a study and recommended sampling techniques. *Entomological Society of Canada Bulletin* **26** (Suppl.).

McSorley, R. (1987). Extraction of nematodes and sampling methods. In *Principles and practice of nematode control in crops* (ed. R. H. Brown and B. R. Kerry), pp. 13–47. Academic Press, Sydney.

Resh, V. H. and McElravy, E. P. (1993). Contemporary quantitative approaches to biomonitoring using benthic macroinvertebrates. In *Freshwater biomonitoring and benthic macroinvertebrates* (ed. D. M. Rosenberg and V. H. Resh), pp. 159–94. Chapman & Hall, New York.

Warwick, R. M. (1993). Environmental impact studies on marine communities: pragmatical considerations. *Australian Journal of Ecology* **18**, 63–80.

7 Taxonomy and target groups for conservation studies

Introduction

The practicalities of sampling and sample analysis, particularly the recognition and identification of taxa at finer levels of separation, tend to ensure that not all the groups of organisms in invertebrate surveys are processed for incorporation into analysis, synthesis and decision-making. The dearth of practical identification guides, coupled with many of the existing ones being incomplete, outdated, and unreliable, so that they cannot be used with confidence by non-specialists, comes as a surprise to many biologists familiar with better-known animal groups. There is little realistic short-term prospect of reliable guides becoming available for most invertebrate groups in many parts of the world. Even for the best-known groups in the most completely documented faunas, problems of identification are not infrequent. Although many groups of macro-invertebrates are understood reasonably well—so that in Britain, for example, taxonomy has progressed well beyond the descriptive phase for some groups—this is more usually not the case.

Needs for identification

The practical roles for identification alluded to earlier are: (1) need for consistent, unambiguous recognition of particular species or higher taxon sets, and (2) need for identification, delimitation, or recognition of members of assemblages for use in diversity and species richness measurements, both for given sites and habitats, and for comparison with others where some form of ranking for priority management or reservation is contemplated. Clearly, such identifications must be consistent across sites and sampling occasions. The first of these levels can sometimes be confounded by presence of 'look-alike species' which need to be distinguished. Many of the invertebrates listed on protection schedules in various countries are extremely similar to unprotected species and may be distinguishable only by an expert and, simply because many are listed because they are rare or poorly known, adequate comparative material for diagnosis may be difficult to obtain. It therefore becomes difficult to enforce such legislation effectively, as it is not reasonable in practice to expect wardens, customs officers and others to separate these taxa unambiguously with the limited and sometimes outdated knowledge at their disposal. All species of birdwing butterflies are listed by CITES, for example, simply because some threatened or vulnerable taxa which command high prices from collectors are only distinguishable with difficulty from common species. In fieldwork where such taxa are involved, advice may be needed on possible confusions which could arise. In many instances a specialist will be able to provide a listing of distinguishing features, or comparative illustrations, whereby the one(s) of concern may be differentiated. In other cases, original taxonomic research may be needed to confirm this. However, many taxa listed on schedules for protection remain ambiguous, difficult to diagnose or recognize, and with little prospect of becoming better understood in the near future.

Selection of groups

The criteria of taxonomic knowledge and information available become important in selecting invertebrate groups for study, as important determinants of their utility in meaningful ecological analyses. The high profile of butterflies in insect conservation, for example, arises in large part because of the long-term interest and knowledge gained by collectors, as well as their general popular appeal. Knowledge of some other groups reflects the outcome of specialist interest and the availability of sufficiently definitive taxonomic monographs leading to the publication of field guides or other accounts which make the group accessible to non-specialists. Scientific societies in many countries have initiated, over the years, series of 'handbooks' or similar documents to elucidate, describe, and provide illustrated keys for invertebrate groups in their areas. Thus, in Britain many of the insects are covered by the Royal Entomological Society's *Handbooks for the identification of British insects*, freshwater invertebrates by keys produced by the Freshwater Biological Association, and other groups by the synopses of the British Fauna (Linnean Society). However, other than in some of the more affluent temperate regions such works may not be commercially viable, and equivalent documentation is rare. Many such series have been initiated, but most have been difficult to sustain, or volumes appear very infrequently and at increasingly high prices. Even for Britain, only about 30% of the insect fauna has been treated in this way after some 45 years of the handbooks series so that, as one example, about half the British Hymenoptera remain 'effectively impossible to identify' (Mound and Gaston 1994). Reasons for the difficulty of sustaining such series of publications include:

1. Small markets, so that prices tend to remain high even for simple cost-recovery, and are not an attractive commercial enterprise.

2. Loss of taxonomic expertise through retirements and retrenchment, and its non-replacement, so that ability to produce the books is diminishing.

3. That production of such 'secondary works' is usually not regarded by employers or fellow scientists as important in relation to primary taxonomic research, and is not valued in career advancement. Compilations of this nature are sometimes described as 'not proper science'.

Bibliographic works, such as Sims (1980*a*, *b*) and Hollis (1980), are invaluable in listing many possible sources of relevant information for many parts of the world, many of which are useful starting points in evaluating how much (or how little!) is known about a particular group of invertebrates, and the difficulties of identifying them. As single possible source works for key references to invertebrate identification, these volumes are unrivalled. However, Sims emphasized that there were no suitable major references to some invertebrate groups. Global and regional knowledge for most taxa is highly uneven, and for some there is still substantial reliance on older classic studies which may be very difficult to obtain. Many volumes of the classic 'Fauna of British India' series, for example, have been reprinted without change decades after they were first produced, and some of the insect volumes remain the best available treatments of the groups they cover, although clearly outdated and incomplete. At a broader level, bibliographic information on invertebrates has only rarely been organized comprehensively for any country beyond Europe. A bibliography and data base of some 14 500 references to the terrestrial invertebrates of New Zealand (Ramsay and Crosby 1992) indicates what can be achieved in this arena.

Despite some laudable attempts to increase the resources available for taxonomic documentation and synthesis as a basic need in interpreting patterns of diversity (SA 2000 1994; Heywood 1995), such works will not be available for most invertebrate groups—or, even, the best-known groups for many parts of the world, in the near future. The urgent needs for practical conservation must, therefore, be accomplished without them—that is, without a firm consensus on, or agenda for, priority systematic work.

Levels of taxonomic resolution possible with limited expertise are recognized as a criterion for using some invertebrate groups in preference to others in conservation assessment (New 1993, 1994; Pearson 1994), on the basis that stable, interpretable and well-understood taxonomy provides a solid foundation for other studies—a sentiment often expressed forcefully in recent years, but which is still not appreciated widely enough. Considering marine environmental impact studies, for example, Warwick (1993) included similar comment in his assessment of the relative advantages and disadvantages of *ecological* groups—so that 'Identification of macro-planktonic organisms is moderately easy because of the ready availability of appropriate literature for many areas' (advantage); 'Identification of almost all the meiobenthic taxa to species level presents difficulties even in Europe and North America, and in many parts of the world the fauna is almost completely unknown' (disadvantage). However, Warwick also pointed out the increasing availability of easily used keys to meiobenthic genera, in itself partially a response to a perceived increasing need for improved conservation assessment. Despite the attraction and practical need to determine which invertebrate groups it may be feasible to analyse in surveys, Danks (1996) has emphasized that this restriction can result in taxonomic coverage being confined to groups which provide little practical information about the objectives of a particular study, through being generalist taxa or of only marginal incidence or importance in the habitat.

In selecting possible target groups of invertebrates for use in conservation studies, the best possible advice on what may be feasible for identification is clearly relevant, together with an appraisal of the major literature for the group(s) in the region to determine its usefulness and the ease with which it can be obtained and interpreted in relation to the resources and level of identifications needed. Much of the literature to hand may not be recent. Searching more recent volumes of the relevant sections of the Zoological Record may reveal more up-to-date work and, through the author listings, may perhaps lead to contact with specialists whose advice may be important to the study. For many invertebrate groups, though, that expertise may not be available within the region of the study.

In contrast to the vertebrates, for which many museums and research institutions have staff members who are specialists in each major group—or, at least, in mammals, birds and 'lower vertebrates'—as a minimum complement, the invertebrates are usually served by far fewer staff and lesser resources. Commonly the expertise of such staff, however pre-eminent each may be in his or her chosen group, usually cannot encompass a scope equivalent to 'birds' or 'mammals'. Many museums, for example, employ only one entomologist, who may work professionally on only one order, family or even genus of insects—which nevertheless may contain more species than the whole Mammalia or Aves—but be expected to deal authoritatively with all insects as well as other arthropods and a variety of other invertebrate groups. These dealings will include queries from members of the public, scientists and government agencies. At present, even checklists of invertebrate taxa described in many groups do not exist and most that do still contain varying levels of undetected specific and generic synonyms, and other confusion. Many modern taxonomic revisions of 'popular groups' may reduce as many names to synonymy as the new species which are described. There is considerable need for clarification of the taxonomy of selected invertebrate groups and increasing formal taxonomic effort for these as a prelude to preparation of identification guides. Janzen's (1993) eloquent plea for such 'taxonomic housecleaning' and preparation of usable locally integrated identification guides is applicable very widely.

Priority groups

One way to proceed effectively may be to accept that some invertebrate groups are indeed more tractable and more useful in monitoring and assessment than others, either by prior demonstration from other studies or from the expertise and facilities available, so that those 'other groups'—if they can be delimited with confidence—may not need as much emphasis. Indeed, the conservation literature has for long endorsed the concept of such taxa, as 'indicators' that can be monitored to assess aspects of community or ecosystem quality. However, the choice of groups for study is more complex: zeal from individual specialists acting as advocates for 'their' group may at times mask more objective attempts to select optimal taxa. Choice of target groups for a survey should, ideally, be made to provide as much information as possible in relation to what is known of their ecology. Thus, for the relatively well-known British fauna, Brooks (1993*a*) listed the following as desirable for the target groups.

1. Collectively, to have the potential to inhabit all the habitats to be surveyed within the survey area.

2. The national and, preferably, the local distribution of species in the target group should be known, so that their status (p. 193) can be appraised meaningfully.

3. The biologies of the target species should be sufficiently well known that meaningful conclusions can be drawn about the quality of the habitats surveyed.

4. They should include species that have reasonably exacting habitat requirements, so that the presence or absence of such species can be related to a specific attribute of the survey area.

5. The surveyor must be able to have the species in the target groups accurately identified and should consult acknowledged taxonomic experts for verification of critical species.

6. The target group, ideally, should be accessible to standard sampling procedures, so as to maximize representation in samples.

Much of any protocol such as this reflects the desirability of good background knowledge and, for much of the world, information equivalent to Brooks' criteria 2–5 is unlikely to exist in any definitive form, even for the best-known invertebrate groups. New (1993, 1994, 1995*a*) emphasized the need for discussion on such 'taxon triage' for invertebrate surveys, not least because of the reality that such exercises almost always restrict the variety of taxa interpreted either on the grounds of pragmatism (availability of expertise

Table 7.1

Ranking of criteria for selecting and using indicator taxa in different contexts: seven criteria are ranked from (1) least important to (7) the most important for monitoring and inventory studies (after Pearson 1994)

Monitoring	Inventory
1. Economic potential	1. Economic potential
2. Occurs over broad geographical range	2. Specialization to habitat
3. Patterns of response reflected in other taxa	3. Biology and natural history well known
4. Biology and natural history well known	4. Occurs over broad geographical range
5. Easily observed and manipulated	5. Patterns reflected in other taxa
6. Well known and stable taxonomy	6. Easily observed and manipulated
7. Specialization to habitat	7. Well known and stable taxonomy

and other resources) or scientific rationale or, commonly, both of these. In the broadest context, even some phyla appear to be more useful than others, on such criteria as taxonomic and ecological understanding, and amenability to capture by standard sampling procedures. But, within any such large group particular segregates (such as orders or families) may be more rewarding than others. Consensus at this level would indeed represent major advance in invertebrate conservation planning and in understanding the use of invertebrates in environmental impact studies, not least by focusing restricted expertise on groups of defined value and leading to increased taxonomic and biological understanding of these. With careful selection, adequate management to conserve a suite of nominated invertebrate groups encompassing a wide range of ecological roles and habitats might serve as a comprehensive umbrella for the less-attended taxa (New 1993) and reflect patterns of biodiversity just as meaningfully as total inventories. Murphy (1990), Pearson (1994), and others, have emphasized the need for rigorous interpretation in conservation biology, and objective selection of target taxa for study is an important facet of defining assemblages. Pearson (1994) drew the distinction between taxa selected for indicators of overall diversity (and usable in an inventory) and those selected for monitoring, and noted the relative importance of seven criteria in determining the rank parameter scores to select optimal taxonomic groups with some objectivity (Table 7.1).

Speight's (1986) approach of selecting 'core' and 'satellite' groups—those which should be included in all surveys and those which could be added for particular habitats or purposes—demonstrates another attempt to select taxa objectively for conservation assessment. Indeed, a recommended protocol for combining aspects of intensive and extensive sampling extends Speight's approach more formally (di Castri *et al.* 1991). Inventories should be made at selected sites, including representatives of all major ecosystems and communities in a region, and selected taxonomic groups surveyed on a much wider range of sites (Fig. 7.1). New (1991) discussed the nature of 'flagship' invertebrates, taxa which can be used to foster communication in conserva-

ECOSYSTEM	SITE NO.	1	2	3	4	5	6	7	8	9	10	11	12
							TAXONOMIC GROUP						
MOIST TROPICAL FOREST	1		✓		✓						✓		
	2		✓		✓						✓		
	3		✓		✓						✓		
	4	✓	✓	✓	✓	✓	✓	✓	✓	✓	✓	✓	✓
	5		✓		✓						✓		
DRY TROPICAL FOREST	6		✓		✓						✓		
	7		✓		✓						✓		
	8	✓	✓	✓	✓	✓	✓	✓	✓	✓	✓	✓	✓
	9		✓		✓						✓		
	10		✓		✓						✓		
DESERT	11		✓		✓						✓		
	12		✓		✓						✓		
	13	✓	✓	✓	✓	✓	✓	✓	✓	✓	✓	✓	✓
	14		✓		✓						✓		
	15		✓		✓						✓		

Fig. 7.1 Strategy for combining survey for many taxonomic groups in few sites and few groups in all sites (after di Castri et al. 1991).

tion and later (New 1993) compared the relative importance of parameters for flagship species, indicators, umbrella taxa and keystone species, all of which are important in prioritizing aspects of invertebrate conservation (Table 7.2). That appraisal is clearly open to substantial refinement, but indicates some of the differing priorities of the various emphases fostered by such categories. For example, flagship species must be well known, accessible and engender public goodwill: they are the 'messengers' in spreading awareness of conservation need, and may or may not themselves be target taxa for conservation. Keystone species must have (or be supposed to have) some important definable ecological role; and indicators must be well-known, accessible, and undergo changes in response to definable environmental changes. This analysis excludes 'predictors', which combine many of the desirable features of indicators and umbrella species.

Table 7.2
Functionally significant criteria for selecting invertebrate groups as priorities in conservation* (after New 1993)

Features	Category			
	Indicators	Keystones	Umbrellas	Flagships
Taxonomy well known	+++			+++
High diversity	+			+
Geographically widespread	++			++
Abundant/dominant	++	++	+	++
Accessible to sampling	+++	+	++	+++
Ecology understood	+++	++	++	+
Occupy key ecological role	+	+++	+	
Habitat specific	++	++	+++	++
Respond to change in environment	+++	++	++	++
Engender public sympathy			+	+++

*'+', important to '+++', most important; for particular segregate taxa, many of the blanks, above, can be filled in to varying extents.

Surrogates for species richness estimates

More information is needed urgently, drawing on analyses at various levels of taxonomic resolution, on: (1) what levels can be used as genuine surrogates for full species-level analyses, and (2) what higher groups may adequately reflect the well-being of others not studied directly; that is, of predictors and indicator groups (p. 169) and whether these can be combined effectively.

More specifically, some ecologically diverse groups may be especially useful in such assessments. Hutcheson (1990) summarized earlier references suggesting that beetles (which comprise, perhaps, about 40% of insect species) are generally representative of the richness of an insect fauna. One of the most intensively investigated groups of terrestrial invertebrates in relation to being 'mirrors' of communities is the ants (Hymenoptera, Formicidae), which have a number of advantages over many other taxa. Thus, generic level identification is commonly reasonably straightforward (even though species recognition is not), they are abundant and diverse in many terrestrial environments, participate in a wide range of ecological interactions among which various 'functional groups' (Greenslade 1979) that grossly parallel taxonomy are definable, and many are amenable to simple replicable sampling methods such as pitfall traps (p. 55). At least in some environments, generic diversity may be a valid surrogate for full species diversity (A. Andersen 1995) and there is need to test this more comprehensively in a range of ecosystems. Ants are a major component of arboreal arthropod biomass in many parts of the world and understanding their intricate mosaic patterns is an important aspect of understanding invertebrate diversity there (Majer 1993).

For most sites and habitats, a series of different invertebrate groups may be needed to reflect diversity or richness, rather than relying on any one group alone (di Castri *et al.* 1991; Solbrig 1991). Jones (1993) nominated molluscs, crustaceans and polychaete worms for marine benthos. For some terrestrial environments, Disney (1986) advocated the insect orders Diptera and Hymenoptera because of their taxonomic and ecological diversity, but use of these orders at the species level is at present hampered by poor taxonomic understanding over much of the world. La Salle and Gauld (1993) also emphasized the likely importance of Hymenoptera as a focal group for priority study. At a lower level, a convincing case for using tigerbeetles (Carabidae, Cicindelinae) as indicators of regional biodiversity (Pearson and Cassola 1992) reflects that the faunas of nearly 130 countries are reasonably well known, and that their diversity at a site can be determined reasonably reliably in about 50 h, compared with months or years for many other groups. The advantages suggested for tigerbeetles include good stable taxonomy, well understood biology, conspicuousness in the field, incidence in a broad range of habitats but with many specialized species, and patterns of species richness highly correlated with a variety of other groups. Such criteria have not yet been applied critically to a sufficient range of other taxa. At present, groups recommended by ecologists or systematists as having high importance for conservation assessment are not necessarily tractable taxonomically at the levels needed and, once any consensus is reached, massively increased funding will be needed to render them comprehensively understood and accessible to conservation managers. The current 'dilute' approach of wishing to describe or define all invertebrates as a complete template for invertebrate biodiversity studies is both utopian and an impediment to practical conservation. However, the number of different groups needed to assess patterns of distribution of animal diversity may be large. On a broad scale, Humphries and Vane-Wright (1992) proposed the global analysis of 100 or more groups (genera, tribes or families) of about 200 species each as an initial template. Debate on what such groups should be, or how they are to be selected optimally, is far from completed. However, for many more restricted regions, representative groups can be selected by consensus involving the greatest possible amounts of local specialist knowledge.

Recent attempts to examine possibilities for extrapolation of data derived from one group or system to another (Hammond 1994; Colwell and Coddington 1994) divide into 'hierarchical' and 'non-hierarchical' approaches. The latter are exemplified by extrapolating species richness of group A to group B (butterflies to beetles in Hammond's example) or area (site) A to area (site) B. Hierarchical ratios, in contrast, are of the form:

(1) subgroup to group;

(2) smaller scale to larger scale;

(3) sample to inventory;

(4) habitat to inventory.

The establishment of each potentially useful ratio depends on finding suitable reference groups that can be sampled reliably to produce sufficiently accurate inventory. Choice of sampling methods and focal groups must be tailored to an individual ratio/problem. 'Focal group' (sensu Hammond 1994) is one of three categories which can be used in extrapolating to assess species richness, as follows.

1. A *focal group*, often but not necessarily taxonomically based, is a subdivision of a larger group of interest selected specifically for its qualities as a predictor set.

2. A *reference group* is one used as a basis for extrapolation to a group for which only poorer data are available. Each is likely to be useful only in specified (often, narrow) situations.

3. A *key group* has the principal role to provide a focus for efforts to document and estimate species richness in a given situation. Key groups

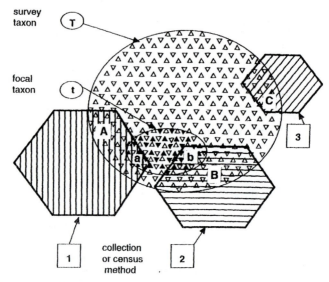

Fig. 7.2 Use of hierarchical taxon ratios and calibrated sampling methods to estimate species richness (Colwell and Coddington 1994).

can serve as standards for comparison, but are not general purpose indicators.

The above terminology for these groups is not yet widespread but reflects the growing interest in, and awareness of, the ways in which invertebrates may be used in attempts to document diversity at many levels.

Hierarchical ratios are important in extrapolation at many levels. Their use at global scale (to estimate global species richness from localized samples of any animal group) is fraught with difficulty because of the many assumptions necessary, but use in better-documented local environments (of more frequent relevance in conservation assessment) can sometimes be justified more soundly. Colwell and Coddington (1994) indicated how use of ratios can be combined with standardized sampling regimes (Fig. 7.2), with the objective of estimating richness of a given taxon (T) at a study site. Each of several sampling methods (1–3) is 'calibrated' for the focal taxon/taxa (t) which has been surveyed completely and which is/are a subset of T, by assessing the proportion of t which is captured by each method. In Fig. 7.2, the first sampling method (1) yields subset 'A' of T and subset 'a' of t, and the richness of T can then be estimated from the assumption that A/a approximates T/t. Analogous estimates can be made from methods 2 and 3, but in this example method 3 is uninformative as none of the focal taxon is captured. Estimates of this nature may be averaged to help eliminate biases inherent in each individual method.

Further reading

Colwell, R. K. and Coddington, J. A. (1994). Estimating terrestrial biodiversity through extrapolation. *Philosophical Transactions of the Royal Society of London B* **345**, 101–18.

Hammond, P. M. (1994). Practical approaches to the estimation of the extent of biodiversity in speciose groups. *Philosophical Transactions of the Royal Society of London B* **345**, 119–36.

Mound, L. A. and Gaston, K. J. (1994). Conservation and systematics—the agony and the ecstasy. In *Perspectives on insect conservation* (ed. K. J. Gaston, T. R. New, and M. J. Samways), pp. 185–95. Intercept, Andover.

Quicke, D. J. L. (1993). *Principles and techniques of contemporary taxonomy*. Blackies Academic and Professional, Glasgow.

Vane-Wright, R. I. (1994). Systematics and the conservation of biodiversity: global, national and local perspectives. In *Perspectives on insect conservation* (ed. K. J. Gaston, T. R. New, and M. J. Samways), pp. 196–211. Intercept, Andover.

8   Monitoring and evaluating status

Introduction

Single species studies have been a major impetus for invertebrate conservation, and will continue to capture the imagination and to test the ingenuity of biologists and managers alike. Studies on assemblages or particular taxonomic groups commonly purport to assess change in diversity or relative abundance over space or time. Much decision-making in both these broad contexts depends on the outcome of status evaluation, and monitoring the changes and trends in abundance and distribution of the species (singular or plural) under study. The problems of monitoring invertebrates, and methods for estimating population size and structure are outlined in this chapter, as they are essential components of many surveys which emphasize conservation studies. Unlike much of the work discussed earlier in this book, this may need to be achieved without killing, harming, or, even, capturing the delicate animals involved.

Monitoring

'Monitoring' commonly implies some form of inspection at intervals, without necessarily capturing or killing the target organisms. In other cases, it incorporates the need for samples taken as described earlier to be interpreted over a time scale well beyond that of a single survey, to detect changes in numbers of a rare species in response to management over a sequence of seasons or generations, or as responses of a taxonomic group or broad-based assemblage to changes in environmental quality. Aquatic communities may be monitored, for example, to assess effects of pollution on the benthos, and changes in benthic composition are thereby an important tool in assessing environmental quality or health.

Monitoring implies, or may imply, long-term commitment to a study over many generations or years. It is thereby often expensive, and the objectives must be defined very clearly at the outset. As Hellawell (1991) noted, 'monitoring' is now an omnibus term which is often applied rather casually to a variety of activities. The major field objectives are as follows (after Goldsmith 1991):

(1) to record long-term environmental change and its ecological effects;

(2 to record response(s) to a changing management factor or regime;

(3) to determine the effectiveness of a particular management regime for species, assemblage or habitat conservation and to refine management as needed—this may incorporate monitoring the effectiveness of policy or legislation and regulatory measures;

(4) to record change, and rate of change of a species, assemblage or habitat; and

(5) to determine the cost-effectiveness of management.

Monitoring is thereby definable broadly as surveillance to detect changes in relation to 'baseline' data or some defined standard(s) such as the incidence, range or population size of a taxon. It can be based on taxa (either single species or larger groups), site factors, or both and in many cases the necessary standards are themselves ill-defined (Hellawell 1991). The published literature on monitoring strategies is now large, but there are some common pitfalls. Hellawell emphasized the need for very clear objectives, including the kinds of analysis needed, and the avoidance of 'open-ended' strategies without clear targets. The scheme shown in Fig. 8.1 is still very common for invertebrates and complex assemblages; field surveys yield enormous amounts of data (based on very large numbers of specimens), and

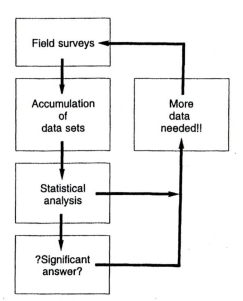

Fig. 8.1 A common sequence of events in ecological surveys, leading to ambiguous results and repetition of work cycles in efforts to improve the inferences (Hellawell 1981).

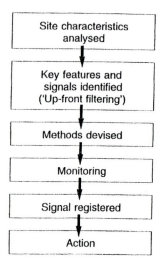

Fig. 8.2 A more precise sequence, based on a clear definition of aims leading to a satisfactory outcome. Monitoring can be repeated rigidly in such a framework (Hellawell 1981).

statistical analysis commonly reveals either an inconclusive answer or that the data are not sufficiently rigorous on which to base conclusions. Either implication leads to the need for yet more data, and lessens the value of the work accomplished.

Figure 8.2, in contrast, exemplifies a more efficient approach wherein the 'key features' (such as presence or defined abundance of particular taxa) and 'signals' (such as the threshold number of individuals or species below which conservation action would be initiated) provide clear directions for a monitoring strategy and any subsequent action (Hellawell 1991).

In general, precise information is needed (or, at least, valuable) in monitoring programmes designed to assess the status, performance, and management of rare invertebrates as conservation targets, but greater ambiguities occur with expansion to monitoring environmental changes by using invertebrates as tools—except where incidence and abundance of easily recognized taxa (such as butterflies in Britain: Pollard 1991; Pollard and Yates 1993) are employed. Even then, interpretation of patterns of change may be very difficult, because its causes can usually be only inferred or assessed in general terms, and range from local to widespread. Nevertheless, surveys and broad-scale distribution mapping of selected invertebrate groups provide one of the major baselines to place monitoring (and status evaluation) of significant species in a more than local context.

Although it is becoming possible, gradually, to design scientifically rigorous monitoring protocols (see, for example, papers in Goldsmith 1991), major practical restrictions such as lack of resources for this over much of the tropics necessitate development of minimalist standardized guidelines which are simple and inexpensive, and able to be used by non-specialists in remote areas (Sparrow *et al.* 1994). Complementarity of sampling methods may thus assume additional importance, to maximize returns for limited effort. Protocols may be needed which produce reasonably rigorous information without the full complexities of multiple replication and stratified sampling designs.

Generally, for conservation purposes, a monitoring programme can have three particularly pertinent outcomes.

1. Estimates of population size and trends for target taxa.

2. Estimates of the demographic parameters for the taxa.

3. Linking density and demography of taxa to habitat/site/microclimate characteristics.

Monitoring may entail:

(1) measuring the presence or absence of particular species;

(2) characterizing community structure by functional groups;

(3) measuring the relative abundance of species; and

(4) undertaking ecological studies of the species and detecting changes in population size.

As Kremen *et al.* (1993) noted, for arthropods, these approaches represent a gradient from least to most costly and difficult. The second approach is data-rich but may be reasonably straightforward to implement because it relies on placing morphospecies (RTUs) to functional group, rather than on precise taxonomic studies. It may be particularly useful for much of the tropics and other regions for which detailed faunistic and taxonomic knowledge is poor, and the approximations introduced by amalgamating ecological categories uncritically may not be important in relation to the positive information gained. However, some uncertainties are almost inevitable by grouping into broad categories.

As a long-term process, monitoring invertebrates is not necessarily intensive. For many seasonal taxa, monitoring may be an annual inspection event undertaken during a short period that the target species is accessible or in a particular growth stage which can be found more easily than others. Despite the need for defining objectives, however, it is common that some of the more interesting results are unexpected and it is preferable that the observations are sufficiently 'solid' for these to be appraised with the benefits of hindsight!

As with survey methods discussed earlier, a variety of methods are used in monitoring invertebrates. Many of the methods for conventional survey are also employed. It may be necessary to cover large areas, to determine the patterns of distribution of taxa, or the responses of sentinel taxa to change. Conversely, the emphasis may be on detecting the fluctuations of a rare species on a very small area of habitat, with no likelihood of extending the survey beyond that, and where any disturbance or mortality to the target species cannot be condoned.

Extensive monitoring is exemplified by surveys to monitor the changes in distribution and abundance of the crown-of-thorns starfish (*Acanthaster planci*) and hard corals on the Great Barrier Reef, during which a total 331 reefs were inspected, with research vessels travelling about 56 000 km (Moran and De'ath 1992). In contrast, the habitat to be monitored may be a small area of rockface or vegetation, or other habitat supporting an elusive and inconspicuous taxon. In many practical exercises, the two approaches are combined, so that small plots monitored in detail are used to build up a synoptic view of a larger area surveyed less intensively, or by different methods, and the kinds of information that results from large-scale surveys tends to be less finely focused than that from small plots. The information recorded is either direct counts or relative judgements based on large amounts of visual information, and there can be substantial subjectivity in some such approaches. Sources of bias include visibility of specimens (when potential target organisms are missed by observers) and accessibility (when target organisms are not available due to various conditions) (Marsh and Sinclair 1989).

As for survey collections, different monitoring methods may lead to different conclusions, and many of the variations have not been evaluated critically. For giant clams (Tridacnidae) in the Philippines, for example, comparison of two survey methods suggested that one led to substantial underestimation of small individuals (Mingoa and Menez 1988). Ranking of methods for surveying coral reef organisms (Weinberg 1981; Gamble 1984) suggested strong differences in reliability. Line transects and point intersect methods

Table 8.1
Coral-reef organism monitoring—ranking of survey methods, with lowest number (1) indicating the best method (after Gamble 1984)

Method	Survey criterion		
	No. species	Relative cover	Density
Individual counting and cover estimate, quadrat	2	1	1
Line transect-species count and intercept length	6	5	4
Point intercept-surface, quadrat	2	6	NA
Point intercept-line, transect	5	7	NA
Point centre quarter method—plotless	6	3	2
Photographic record	1	2	NA
In situ mapping	4	4	3

NA, not applicable.

were not generally reliable, and quadrat-based individual counts and cover estimates were ranked highly (Table 8.1). Such considerations apply widely in visual surveys.

Observer bias

Long-term or geographically widespread monitoring programmes usually involve participation of several people. Their relative skills and observational powers, together with their familiarity with and knowledge of the target species can be an important source of error. Observers on butterfly transects (p. 180) commonly achieve different results over the same routes, and Pollard (1991) regarded the main weakness of his recording method adopted for surveying British butterflies as differences between individual workers in their recording skills. In his long-term survey, this was countered to some extent by the same individual recorders continuing for many years at the same sites. One, partial, counter is to have each survey done independently, but under the same conditions, by at least two observers and adopting the average result.

Estimates of worker variability, due in part to different 'search images' for small organisms, emphasize the needs for field workers on a given project to train together and, wherever possible, to employ the same staff throughout a project. In one such test involving sampling a rocky shore in Britain, Baker and Crothers (1987) placed 39 molluscs (*Littorina obtusata*) into an area of seaweed, 50×100 cm, previously cleared of gastropods, and asked 10 observers to count the snails in the area. Counts ranged from 16 to 48, with a mean of 29.1, standard error 33! It seems that some workers (eight) missed animals among the algae whereas others inadvertently re-counted them. Thus, even with apparently straightforward quantification in a small, simple arena, considerable error may occur. More accurate quantification may be important for management, be it for rare species whose sustainable take for scientific or other purposes may be based on the information, or on a broader commercial scale where monitoring has an important role in guiding sizes of harvesting quotas, bag limits, individual size restrictions for capture, and other regulatory factors which can help to sustain exploitation and safeguard human livelihoods.

Estimating population size and recording distributions

Estimating population size is a key element of monitoring to establish the status of taxa. Techniques for this, and approaches to analysis, are described in many ecology texts, and the practicalities of monitoring invertebrates in this way are often complex (Southwood 1978). Only very rarely is it possible to make total counts of an invertebrate population, and then only on small, circumscribed habitats or sites. Moore (1964), for example, counted male dragonflies at a pond by viewing them through binoculars, but such conspicuous "birdwatchers' bugs" are rather exceptional and, more usually, some subsample of the habitat, delimited by quadrats or transects, or of the population is examined and population size estimated from such information.

Habitat subsamples: transects and quadrats for direct counts

For conspicuous diurnal taxa, such as many butterflies, standardized counts can be made along transects of the sort pioneered by Pollard (1977, 1991; Pollard *et al.* 1986; Pollard and Yates 1993). The methods which have become standard in Britain, and adopted widely as models elsewhere, evolved from 1973 and led to the national Butterfly Monitoring Scheme developing from 1976. In brief the following is a summary of a complex scheme.

1. At each site in the scheme, counts are made along a fixed route from the beginning of April until the end of September each year. The 26 recording weeks encompass the flight periods of all the species likely to be present. The route is selected to include representative habitat types of the area and divided into sections, with the divisions usually reflecting changes in vegetation type. Separate counts are made for each section.

2. Counts are made by an observer walking along the route and recording all butterflies seen in a belt of approximately 5 m width. Most species can be identified without capture, but it is necessary to net and check some specimens.

3. Counts are made only when the weather meets specified conditions.

4. The weekly counts are used to calculate an index of abundance.

Very similar protocols have been suggested for other conspicuous diurnal invertebrates such as dragonflies (Moore and Corbet 1990; Brooks 1993*b*), with emphasis on standardizing survey procedures so that different observers provide comparable data for incorporation into mapping schemes (p. 195) and plotting patterns of seasonal incidence, activity, and abundance. For the well-known British dragonfly fauna, Brooks recommended the following minimum conditions, without which the survey should be considered invalid.

1. The survey should not start earlier than 11 a.m. or later than 1 p.m.

2. The air temperature in the shade should be above 17 °C.

3. There should be at least 50% sunshine. As each new section (in Brooks' survey, a length of river bank with eight separate sections) is entered, the surveyor records whether a shadow is cast. The survey is valid if at least four of the eight sections are recorded as sunny.

4. Wind conditions should be light. Leaves and branches moving are acceptable, but if trees are bending the wind is too strong.

These conditions maximize the chances of the survey coinciding with maximum dragonfly activity, and indicate the kind of detail which can be adopted for a well-understood local fauna, as well as the generality for other areas. Although valuable as a basis for designing studies elsewhere, uncritical transfer of such protocols as the above to other parts of the world may be unwise. Steytler and Samways (1995) found that some territorial dragonfly taxa avoided the hottest times of day in South Africa, for example. Ideally, verification and testing in local surroundings should be undertaken, and refinements introduced as needed. 'Representative counts' are undertaken most usefully at times when the dragonflies are most concentrated and numerous (Schmidt 1985).

While recording dragonflies under the above conditions, the observer walks at a continuous slow stroll, keeping to the river banks, and records every identifiable specimen (whether perched or flying) in front and to each side, but not behind. The sections are completed sequentially, and any 'problem species' which cannot be identified with certainty are grouped together. Moore (1991) noted that two types of error might arise, both affecting accuracy of the sampling. On the one hand individual insects might leave without being counted, after being disturbed or after enforced territorial encounters, and, on the other, individuals could be counted twice—after initial flight and on their return. However, counts of true dragonflies (Anisoptera) can be taken as accurate, and counts of the more cryptic damselflies (Zygoptera) usually exceed 80% accuracy (Moore 1991).

In these cases, and with the caveats noted earlier, population changes from generation to generation and over a flight season are reflected in differences in direct counts at the same site. Because many invertebrates vary widely in abundance from generation to generation, long-term observations may be needed to determine any 'real' decline. Van Swaay (1990) suggested calculating the running average of the number of butterflies or their distribution over a period of 5 or 10 years, so that a running average over 5 years of year 'n' is the average value for years '$n - 2$' to '$n + 2$'. For less mobile taxa, quadrats or transects are used to determine recruitment, mortality (and, hence, turnover) in the population in the same habitat unit between sampling occasions. Such plots can be permanent, marked by pegs, paint marks on rocks, or with grid marks placed for the duration of the study. For sedentary taxa such as barnacles or sponges, photographic recording can be used to save field time if many sites are to be recorded and/or exposure time between tides, or diving time, is limited. Design and designation of fixed plots, and recording techniques for the information have both diversified considerably. Even for mobile organisms, fixed plots can be a valuable adjunct to more extensive monitoring, but the principle of using defined areas of habitat—either as fixed plots or as quadrats of a given size—for monitoring is widespread. The black sea urchin, *Diadema antillarum*, was monitored at monthly intervals in six 25 m^2 quadrats on Caribbean reefs from 1983 to 1992 (Lessios 1995). Population density was measured also on 11 other reefs with annual transects (ten 1.8 m wide transects from shallow water to 17 m depth or the base of the reef), and both exercises were part of an investigation of the dynamics of the urchin after a catastrophic mass death in 1983–1984, which resulted in near-extinction of this important component of Caribbean reef communities (Lessios 1988).

One metre square quadrats, rather than fixed plots, in a range of water depths in Lake St Clair were used to survey unionid mussels to detect changes to native fauna wrought by the exotic zebra mussel (*Dreissena polymorpha*) (Gillis and Mackie 1994). Monthly samples over the summer months comprised hand collections of unionids made by SCUBA divers on 20 quadrats. These collections were supplemented by Ekman grab samples to ensure that juvenile mussels, easily missed in hand sampling, were incorporated. The zebra mussel can colonize native unionids, so that numbers and size frequency were determined by collecting a distinctive native species during SCUBA sampling and enumerating the epizoic fauna on the shells.

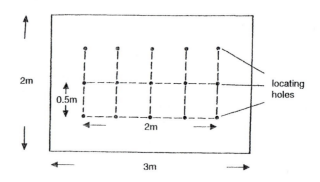

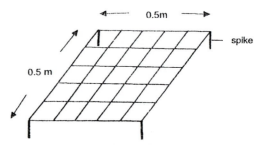

Fig. 8.3 Method of permanent location of quadrat frame on rocky substrates (after Hawkins and Hartnoll 1983).

In sampling from quadrats on sloping rocky seashores, Hawkins and Hartnoll (1983) recommended 2×1 m plots at three levels on the shore. Each quadrat was divided into eight half-metre subquadrats defined by holes drilled into the rock, needed to locate the corner spikes of a divided quadrat frame precisely (Fig. 8.3). Each subquadrat is then recorded individually. In other situations, where gradients may not be so clear, multiple random quadrats are useful—although quadrat size may need to be evaluated in relation to the patchiness of the target organisms. Provided that the taxa are distinctive, photographs give clear evidence of changes in abundance or size, and of the persistence of particular individuals between successive observations.

Transects, either line or belt, are invaluable for sampling along gradients such as away from habitat edges, on sloping bottoms of the littoral zone, or across the intertidal region and, in general, several representative transects are needed in any habitat to determine the consistency of any zones in which the focal taxa are aggregated or concentrated. Data accumulated may need to be defined carefully in relation to boundaries—in a line transect, for example, any organism traversed by the line is usually counted, but in belts of defined width, an organism may alternatively be assessed as 'in' or 'out' under such conditions. Chiappone and Sullivan (1992) measured linear coverage for every centimetre along 50 m transect lines placed on coral reefs in the Bahamas, and recorded every traversed coral with its length along the line, to the nearest centimetre. Such information can be used to reflect species diversity and relative abundance, and percentage cover as parameters which can be compared easily with other sites. In highly heterogeneous environments, line transects may be too 'conservative', in that many representative species not actually contacted by the line will be omitted, and incorporation of 1 m² quadrats added significantly to the reliability of the information (Chiappone and Sullivan 1992).

There are many variations of transect sampling for invertebrates, ranging from interval sampling along broad belts, where the abundance of taxa can be useful in general comparisons or for assessing site values (Baker and Crothers 1987), to quantitative measures at stations along lines. Abundance scale measurements (such as in Table 8.2) are used extensively, for example on shore surveys using the baseline of a tape measure laid down the shore, or a string tagged or marked at known intervals. At each station, totalling about 10 over the entire vertical tide range, the abundance of organisms is recorded in a strip 3 m wide by 30 cm deep. This approach is relatively rapid and two transects per tidal cycle can be documented in many places. The transect strip cuts across small-scale mosaics laterally while keeping within a shallow vertical zone, and exemplifies the consideration needed for scale in designing any such transect sampling regime.

Transect sampling allows for relating numbers of individuals to a known unit of habitat but, without knowledge of the longevity of individuals, there is

Table 8.2
Examples of 'abundance scores' (for cover or abundance) as used in invertebrate surveys: organisms on rocky shores in Britain (after Baker and Crothers 1987)

Barnacles and small winkles:		*Limpets and large winkles:*	
E 500 or more	$0.01/m^2$	E 20 or more	$0.1/m^2$
S 300–499	$0.01/m^2$	S 10–19	$0.1/m^2$
A 100–299	$0.01/m^2$	A 5–9	$0.1/m^2$
C 10–99	$0.01/m^2$	C 1–4	$0.1/m^2$
F 1–9	$0.01/m^2$	F 5–9	$/m^2$
O 1–99	$/m^2$	O 1–4	$/m^2$
R < 1	$/m^2$	R < 1	$/m^2$

Balanus perforatus:		*Dogwhelks, top-shells, anemones:*	
E 300 or more	$0.01/m^2$	E 10 or more	$0.1/m^2$
S 100–299	$0.01/m^2$	S 5–9	$0.1/m^2$
A 10–99	$0.01/m^2$	A 1–4	$0.1/m^2$
C 1–9	$0.01/m^2$	C 5–9/m^2	locally sometimes more
F 1–9	$0.1/m^2$	F 1–4/m^2	locally sometimes more
O 1–9	$/m^2$	O <1/m^2	locally sometimes more
R < 1	$/m^2$	R always <1/m^2	

Mussels, piddocks (score holes):	*Tubeworms, Pomatoceros:*
E >80% cover	A 50 or more tubes $0.01/m^2$
S 50–79% cover	C 1–49 tubes $0.01/m^2$
A 20–49% cover	F 1–9 tubes $0.1/m^2$
C 5–19% cover	O 1–9 tubes/m^2
F small patches, <5% rock cover	R <1 tube/m^2
O 1–9 individuals/m^2, no patches	
R <1 individual/m^2	

Scale: E, extremely abundant; S, superabundant; A, abundant; C, common; F, frequent; O, occasional; R, rare.

no information on turnover between sampling occasions and, hence, of absolute population size.

Video recording

'Domestic' video cameras in underwater housing have been recommended as a means of reducing subjectivity of large-scale counts on coral reefs (Carleton and Done 1995). The technique is reliable and simple, and can be used by people with little previous training in its operation. The camera is operated during swum or towed transects, and video transects can then be analysed by subsamples of the film to note proportional cover, the number of organisms, abundance of selected species, and so on. There are substantial limitations to the taxonomic resolution possible compared with hands-on sampling but, for broad taxonomic categories of reef benthos, reasonably reliable estimates of relative abundance can be accumulated and the visual record can be archived for further analysis. However, demographic and diversity analyses may be limited substantially, and the abundance of rare species may be difficult to estimate unless they are very distinctive.

In clear water (depth 1.5–3 m) high-quality images are obtainable without artificial light at tow or swim speeds of about 1.2 m/s and 0.6 m/s, respectively, with the camera held about 1–1.5 m from the substrate. Slower and closer recording narrows the transect sampled, but may be valuable in facilitating higher taxonomic resolution. More generally, 5–10 m of general footage at a reef site may be a useful documentary adjunct to closer surveys, and reveal taxa not seen by SCUBA inspection (Maragos and Cook 1995). Remote use of video cameras suspended from boats is likely to become more important in such studies.

Photographic monitoring

Low-altitude aerial photographs enable analysis of many features of coral reefs, and are valuable also in indicating sites which may be of special interest for closer surveys (Maragos and Cook 1995).

Closer photographic documentation is valuable in many aspects of monitoring of permanent or representative plots. Done (1992a) noted that stereogram images allow for better interpretation of changes in community status than single images. For his long-term records of coral communities on the Great Barrier Reef following *Acanthaster* attack, Done established 30 permanent transects on two regions of the reef, each marked out with steel pins, and used two 35 mm cameras mounted 30 cm apart to obtain stereogram colour transparencies of contiguous 1 m^2 sections at annual intervals. Over a decade (1980–1990), dramatic status changes occurred: in the two 5-year intervals, 21 and five transects showed degradation, six and 10 retained their general condition and three and 15 grew. Although Done's (1992a) survey extended over 10 years, this was apparently not long enough to clarify the causes of the changes observed, and Done (1992b) emphasized the need for very long-term surveys to document and understand the significance of reef development and to optimize management regimes.

Photographic monitoring may miss covered species and, while it gives a permanent record of plots, can be laborious to evaluate.

Manta tows

The manta tow technique has been used extensively for monitoring coral reef systems. It was developed for studying impact of the crown-of-thorns starfish, and has now been employed in many parts of the tropics (Kenchington 1978). A snorkel diver, as observer and recorder, is towed at a constant speed behind a small boat, with the length of the tow and number of variables (Table 8.3) recorded being standardized. The range of purposes of the technique includes:

(1) general descriptions of large areas of reef;

Table 8.3
Biological variables recorded in monitoring crown-of-thorns starfish (*Acanthaster planci*)
on the Great Barrier Reef, recorded after each 2-min tow
(Moran *et al.* 1989; Moran and De'ath 1992)

Parameter	Scale/category	
No. of *Acanthaster*		
Average size of *Acanthaster*	0–15 cm diameter	(S) (small)
	>15 cm diameter	(L) (large)
No. of feeding scars on coral	0	(A) (absent)
	1–10	(P) (present)
	>10	(C) (common)
Cover of live coral	0%	0
	1–10%	1
	11–30%	2
	31–50%	3
	51–75%	4
	76–100%	5
Cover of dead coral	(as for live coral)	
Cover of sand and rubble	(as for live coral)	

(2)   monitoring broad effects of large disturbances;

(3)   selecting areas for study; and

(4)   identifying broad changes in distribution and abundance of some key
      species (Moran and De'ath 1992).

Tows lasting 2 min are made before recording the accrued information.
The technique (Fig. 8.4) has been likened to aerial reconnaissance in application and has a number of advantages over some other aquatic monitoring
techniques (Moran *et al.* 1989; Moran and De'ath 1992):

(1)   large areas of reef, including entire perimeters, can be surveyed
      relatively quickly, so that taxa with patchy distributions are covered
      adequately;

Fig. 8.4 Principle of the 'manta tow' technique for monitoring coral reefs.

(2) data can be related accurately to particular regions on a reef;

(3) continuous in operation, and the observer can cover large distances with little fatigue;

(4) relatively simple to perform after initial training;

(5) the time that an observer can spend in the water is not limited, as for example, it is with SCUBA equipment;

(6) suitable for remote locations with minimal support, and under reasonably arduous conditions.

Disadvantages, as in any other technique, place limitations on use of manta tows:

(1) the tow path is controlled largely by the boat driver, so some of the track may be inappropriate;

(2) may yield less information than from intensive SCUBA survey of an area, or other recording method;

(3) may not enable the observer to stop and inspect particular sites more intensively;

(4) observer is usually some 2–10 m from the reef, so animals may be overlooked; and

(5) factors such as weather, topographic complexity and observer bias affect the quality of the information gathered.

Many of these drawbacks, of course, recur in any monitoring technique, and need to be appraised carefully. Thus, SCUBA survey counts of *Acanthaster* may yield far higher numbers than from manta tows (Fernandes 1990; Fernandes *et al.* 1990): on average 23% of starfish counted during SCUBA surveys were found in manta tows over the same areas, but ranking of sites by the two methods may correspond, and manta tows can be calibrated to reflect SCUBA survey results (Moran and De'ath 1992). Errors in detection arise from variations in the tow path in relation to reef profiles (Fig. 8.5), but observers can usually scan over a transect of 10–12 m width, depending on slope angles.

Trials on the recovery of artificial targets (ice-cream container lids of 17 × 17 cm, painted brown to resemble starfish) suggested that manta tow estimates of abundance were likely to be unreliable on wide transects (Fernandes 1990).

Several methods may therefore be needed to monitor the same group(s) of invertebrates. Five different methods have been recommended for giant clams in various surveys, for example:

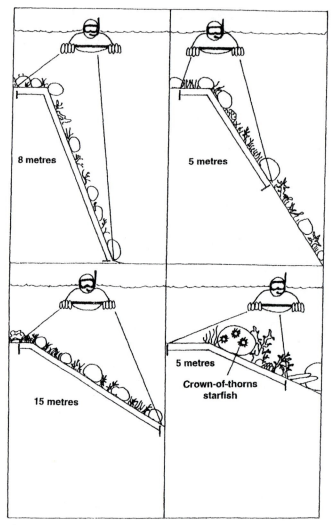

Fig. 8.5 Manta tows: variation of position and width of search path at different points along a reef perimeter (after Moran and De'ath 1992).

(1) belt transects, usually incorporating a line of known length to maintain orientation on a reef;

(2) circular plot surveys;

(3) arial surveys;

(4) modified manta tow surveys; and

(5) flow meter techniques, incorporating a calibrated flow meter to measure the distance travelled by a diver.

Comparative study of the first and last of these in the Philippines (Mingoa and Menez 1988) gave similar estimates of the number of clams, and numbers of individuals/species, but one or both may be biased for certain size categories. The flow meter approach revealed 76% fewer small (2–6 cm length) *Tridacna maxima* and 60% higher large (10–14 cm) individuals than the belt transect.

Mark–release–recapture methods for estimating population size

Absolute population estimates can be gained by some form of mark–release–recapture (MRR) method (Southwood 1978), which incorporates the following steps.

1. A proportion of the population is captured and the individuals marked in some way which renders them identifiable.

2. The marked individuals are released into the same population and allowed to mix freely in it.

3. At some future time a second sample is taken from the population.

4. The number of marked individuals in the second sample is presumed to have the same ratio to total numbers as the total initially marked would have to the original total population.

5. The population size can therefore be calculated.

Such methods do not depend on accurate assessment of sampling units, but can be employed only when individuals can be marked permanently without harming them, or changing their behaviour or susceptibility (such as by the marks rendering them more conspicuous to predators) in the population, and can be recognized unambiguously when recaptured. In practice, marking methods need to be tested for efficacy, and adequate lasting marks may be difficult to devise. Thus, although it is in principle very easy to mark many gastropods by putting paint or plastic strips on their shells, many such marks can be removed easily. Heppleston (1972) painted *Galba* snails with nail polish but 10% of marks were lost after 2 weeks and 15–20% had disappeared after 4 weeks. By contrast, such techniques cannot be used for slugs because of their soft bodies. Alternatives have involved using radioactive isotopes incorporated into foodstuffs, which also can be stored in the consumer. Radioactive phosphorus (^{32}P) taken in by slugs with food accumulates in the nervous system, mucous and salivary glands, the odontophore, and parts of the mantle epithelium (Fretter 1952), and some individuals were still radioactive after 45 days.

Efficacy of marking in any particular context needs to be checked carefully, and any effects of marking calibrated by retaining samples of marked individuals alive to compare their longevity and behaviour with unmarked controls before employing the method for critical population estimation. Murphy (1989) warned of the dangers of rough handling of delicate animals such as small butterflies, and counselled the need for care, including avoiding MRR techniques in some cases. The practical problems of marking thus include:

1. Ensuring that the marks last for the duration of the study.

2. Avoiding any changes of behaviour induced by marks—for example, attachment of labels to insect wings might interfere with blood circulation in newly emerged adults.

3. Natural camouflage may be rendered ineffective—for example, bright colours on normally cryptic snail shells may increase their visibility to predators such as birds. Marks may make individuals of 'collectable' species more conspicuous to unscrupulous human collectors, and thereby increase their vulnerability. Conversely, of course, such permanent marks might protect such individuals because they are no longer perfect specimens for sale or display: Gall (1984) marked a forewing of individuals of the rare Uncompahgre fritillary butterfly (*Boloria acrocnema*) in a population so that the insects were less attractive to commercial collectors.

4. The organism may be damaged by rough handling during capture or marking, by paint sticking legs, mouthparts or wings together or restricting free movement; anaesthesia may lead to changes in metabolism or longevity.

The latter may need to be considered carefully, especially when studying small populations of rare species.

As a prelude to an MRR study of the British satyrine butterfly *Melanargia galathea*, Morton (1982) subjected butterflies to several different marking and capture techniques. Size of mark and colour of mark seemed to have no significant effect on recapture rates. However, repeated disturbance due to capture was associated with reduced recapture frequency. A similar inference was made for the swallowtail *Graphium sarpedon* by Singer and Wedlake (1981); it was possible to mark series of this species without capturing the butterflies, when they congregated to drink at riverside pools. However, this is rather exceptional and, in nearly all cases, capture of the invertebrates for marking is necessary.

In a rather different context paralleling the above, harvesting of marine commercial mollusc crops, rough capture can be an important cause of 'shock', whereby scallops can be damaged by contact with the dredge and suffer deformation of the shells, if they survive (Caddy 1989*a*). Culver (1982) noted that for amphipods and isopods in riffles of North American streams, dislodgement and inability to maintain position in a current was a major cause of mortality, and appendage damage can occur easily in laboratory streams.

Southwood (1978) also discussed the conditions for releasing individuals after marking, to ensure that their behaviour is as normal as can be hoped for. In many studies the animals can be captured, marked, and released quickly—for example, in butterflies marked or numbered on the wings with quick-drying felt-tipped pens—but for others a period of captivity, be it hours or days, may be necessary. Invertebrates should be released in their natural habitats, and liberation at a number of points rather than all together may facilitate the free mixing which is assumed as a condition for valid later analysis. If the animals have a marked periodicity of activity, some workers recommend that release should occur during the inactive period, to help counter artificially heightened activity immediately after release. However, care must be taken not to increase the susceptibility of freed animals, such as by exposing normally nocturnal moths to diurnal insectivorous birds. It may be advantageous to release initially into the confines of a cage which can be removed at the start of the normal high activity period.

The various forms of analysis for MRR data are explained in numerous ecological texts, but all have the basic assumptions that marking has no adverse effects, does not change the accessibility of the organisms to capture, and that mixing of the marked individuals in the larger population does indeed occur. It may also be assumed that the population is closed (p. 194), so that it is not augmented or diminished by dispersal. MRR can be an important tool in monitoring conspicuous invertebrates, and can be used in conjunction with transect or plot-based counts (of butterflies, for example) to clarify changes in population size over a season, to determine changes in sex ratio, and to compare population sizes in different generations and places, as well as providing information on individual longevity.

Ford (1945) summarized methods for multiple marking, so that individuals are given a different mark if captured on each of a series of sampling occasions. Their presence in the population and position in the habitat patch can thus be plotted progressively over their life.

Status evaluation for invertebrate species

Much of the detailed methodology for studying species noted earlier in this book has been developed in efforts to estimate population size and seasonality, commonly of taxa which are of concern as pests or harvestable commodities. As noted earlier, studies of such economically important species have been a major source of information valuable also in practical conservation. The major steps in a conservation programme for a single invertebrate species are summarized in Fig. 2.1 (p. 15). These are of much more general relevance, but emphasize the importance of evaluating status as the major template against which to assess conservation need, and to plan management. This information has been used in many cases to allocate the taxon to one of a hierarchy of categories reflecting urgency of conservation need and, thus, for setting priorities for use of restricted funds and other resources. It follows that this must be done responsibly, and the problems with studying invertebrates noted in Chapter 1 render achieving satisfactory data on status very difficult and, often, ambiguous. Yet the accuracy of assessing status (even according to criteria which are not absolute) and ranking a species in relation to others may determine, simply, whether any practical conservation is possible. The twin practical problems are: (1) defining 'status' and its major components and how these may be quantified, and (2) deciding the geographical scale at which this should be evaluated (New 1995b).

Components of conservation status

These include: (1) taxonomic integrity; (2) rarity; and (3) vulnerability.

Taxonomic integrity

The problem of taxonomic integrity reflects the need for unambiguous recognition and diagnosis of a target species, including subspecies, as this category is now recognized commonly as equivalent to a full species for protective legislation (Opler 1991), provided that the subspecies is accepted as valid by scientific consensus. Perhaps particularly for butterflies, subspecies have attracted considerable attention in conservation because many are localized and, thereby, susceptible to local threats. In ambiguous cases, taxonomic revision may be needed to gain authoritative opinion on the taxonomic status of putatively distinct isolated populations. Recognition features for such focal taxa must be defined clearly. For some, it may be sufficient simply to specify 'individuals from site X' as a geographically distinctive entity.

Rarity

'Rarity' poses problems of definition and assessment because of the numerous ways in which abundance and distribution can be interpreted, and the emotive uses of the term. In general, rarity is assessed in relation to three attributes (Ferrar 1989): habitat specificity (ecological specialization), geographical range (distribution), and population size (abundance). For many invertebrates, the latter two states may equate simply to 'under-recorded', and lack of biological knowledge of most taxa renders assessment of habitat specificity difficult. A small or cryptic invertebrate may be 'difficult to find' rather than genuinely rare, so that a heralded occurrence of a poorly known species may need careful interpretation before conservation measures are implemented.

Practical information needed therefore relates to density and distribution, and many of the approaches discussed in earlier sections may be employed to sample for the species over a broad range, as well as to determine its microdistribution on a given site, and its population size.

Vulnerability

Decline may be strong evidence of the need for conservation action, and dictate the urgency and extent of management needed, such as a recovery programme to build up numbers, perhaps involving captive breeding and/or translocation, rather than solely safeguarding an existing stable situation for a rare species which—although it might exist solely in remnant populations—is no longer threatened or declining. A species may be vulnerable to continuing threats, or less so (perhaps, even, secure) at a level of abundance or geographical range less than previously. Should it again become vulnerable, it is likely to have a higher conservation ranking than before its initial decline(s).

Status evaluation

This also has a strong geographical component, so that conserving an invertebrate species may involve purely local needs, or needs magnified by imposition of political or other administrative boundaries, or conservation over a much wider geographical range. Thus, many invertebrates (together with other animals, and plants) are listed on the 'protection schedules' of particular countries or States even though they may be widespread (and not threatened or vulnerable) elsewhere. Even within a given political area, threats may differ greatly at different sites, and species status evaluation may involve determining if only some populations are at risk or if the species needs protection over a broader range, or over most or all of a restricted range. Localized threats to populations of widespread taxa may assume considerable local importance but may be ranked lower for allocation of scarce resources than, for example: (1) threats to the sole remaining population of a species, or (2) a more widespread threat likely to influence a taxon over a wider range. Simplistically, threats caused by specific events are commonly local—the destruction of particular habitat patches and the extirpation of local populations—whereas threats related to processes, such as global warming or widespread ecological succession, may have influences over much greater areas.

Allocation of most invertebrates to formal conservation status categories, such as in the traditional IUCN Red Data Book listings by the revised criteria described by IUCN (1994b), is very difficult because of the general lack of holistic population dynamics data and knowledge of distributions. For many, information available is limited to presence/absence data at particular sites and the prime aim is simply to detect the taxa and to attempt to designate 'critical habitat' in delimiting the boundaries of a site which may need to be maintained if the species is to thrive. This in itself can be an extraordinarily difficult task for mobile taxa with complex needs. For a rare lycaenid butterfly (*Acrodipsas myrmecophila*) in Victoria, Australia, three full flight seasons observations at the butterfly's only known colony site revealed sight records of only four or five individuals, and extensive searches for the only ant species with which its caterpillars are known to cohabit proved fruitless (Britton *et al.* 1995), although the ant was discovered there in the fourth year! Gaining quantitative data on such taxa is scarcely possible, even if funding is available, and they indicate well the frustrations of attempting Population and Habitat Viability Analysis (PHVA) for invertebrates. Even population structure may be difficult to define. Many populations of threatened invertebrates are assumed to be closed, but many are proving to have a metapopulation system, so that the significance of local scarcity or extinction within a metapopulation based on fragmented habitats may be undefined (Hanski and Thomas 1994), and necessitate a broader appraisal than initially anticipated.

Knowledge of population structure may influence the kind of management needed for a species. This problem is by no means peculiar to invertebrates, but the low mobility of many taxa ensures that the extent of habitat isolation in relation to the likelihood of recolonization is an important facet of conservation planning for species whose continuance depends on interchange between populations.

In short, rare invertebrates can be very difficult to study (Main 1982; New 1995*b*), despite their prominence in conservation activities. Low abundance may obviate choices of conservation treatment or spot-based counts of individuals, and even determining presence or absence may have a high element of chance. The *Acrodipsas* butterfly noted above was seen on only four visits, of more than 50, to the site, in itself an intensity of survey far above that usually undertaken for rare species, especially at remote sites. Attempts to increase frequency of sighting, or to discover early stages, may result in inadvertent habitat destruction, or oversampling, and devices which may lead to death of individuals (such as a Malaise trap—p. 41—for butterflies) should not be used in areas where such susceptible taxa are known to occur.

As with many rare or elusive taxa, statements on whether the species is present can be based only on a given level of detection 'sensitivity'. 'No detection' may indicate extinction or absence, but also that the population is below the sensitivity levels of the survey or sampling methods used. If so, the population may eventually recover to a detectable level, or persist in small numbers. As in attempts to determine whether pest insects have been eradicated (Perkins 1989), use of pheromones or other specific baits may be useful in sensitive detection of taxa which respond to these.

Changes in distribution and abundance are used not only to evidence decline but also as important indicators of conservation success and of the correct management having been used. However, many invertebrates fluctuate naturally in abundance and, to some extent, in distribution over series of generations, and it is rare to be able to separate confidently trends due to management from such normal 'noise', except when these are monitored carefully and attributable directly to specific management provisions. Distribution maps can reveal where species with restricted ranges occur and, in the relatively few cases for which reliable historical data are available, can reveal rates of decline in a fauna—a component of conservation status important in helping to set priorities for taxa which are under particular threat (Thomas and Abery 1995). Detection of decline is difficult, and distribution maps may give only very conservative estimates of more widespread scenarios. Only rarely are records sufficiently long term or comprehensive to show unambiguous trends in distribution and abundance. Data on the British butterflies (Pollard and Yates 1993) are perhaps the best example for any local fauna and, although long-term fisheries records of some molluscs and pelagic crustaceans are also available, these are less standardized and more variable in their comprehensiveness. For the British butterflies, Harding *et al.* (1994) recognized the following activities.

1. Survey. Observations (qualitative and/or quantitative), usually to standard procedures such as transect walks (p. 180) and over a restricted time period, without preconception of what the results should be.

2. Surveillance. Repeated surveys to provide a time series of observations to estimate variability, without preconception of what the results should be.

3. Monitoring. Intermediate surveillance to measure the extent of variation from an established/expected norm.

These activities now involve about 200 different recording schemes for butterflies in Britain (Asher 1992), and are the foundation impetus for surveys elsewhere in the world. 'Recording' has largely replaced collecting specimens (in itself the foundation data of distribution recording) in well known faunas, but this can occur only when: (1) there is no ambiguity over identification, and (2) selective capture and observation is possible. As noted earlier, most groups of invertebrates can be documented properly only after collecting and critical examination, if at all.

Comprehensive recording, either numerical or as presence/absence information, provides the survey information which forms the basis of distribution maps, or atlases for taxonomic groups, and for estimating changes in status. These constitute data bases, which can be used for a wide variety of environment-related mapping purposes, such as correlations of species with topography, geology, or other landscape and biotic features, and biogeographical patterns. Features of a species' status likely to accord an invertebrate relatively high priority for conservation, which also should be determined in a survey of that species, include:

(1) very localized distribution, especially in unstable habitats such as those likely to undergo successional change.

(2) distribution confined to vulnerable or threatened habitats or sites;

(3) occurs on a small number of known sites, perhaps with the number of extant sites less than the historical record, as evidence of decline or vulnerability;

(4) taxa which are not represented, or are only poorly represented or managed, in National Parks or other reserves;

(5) taxa which are 'reputedly rare' based on the best available information or intelligence may need special attention to determine whether they are genuinely rare, or their reputation is an artefact;

(6) taxa which already receive conservation attention, likewise, may need more comprehensive investigation to determine if this is warranted, or assess the success of management.

There is a dearth of information on invertebrates present in protected areas, despite the widespread assumption that many (most) may be secure there. Even for the British butterflies, several species are represented only poorly on national nature reserves, although all are present on lower protection level Sites of Special Scientific Interest (McLean et al. 1994). Although emphasis on recording declines tends to concentrate on rarer species, the decline of common and widespread taxa is also of concern. However, as these are usually still recorded as 'present' in mapping cells, these tend not to be detected so readily. Thomas and Abery (1995) showed that the rapidity of such declines among British butterflies gives little room for complacency over their future safety.

Integrating management for species

The phases of management summarized in Fig. 2.1 are universal, and priorities must be assessed in each individual case in conjunction with ways to determine their success, usually manifest by the target species increasing in abundance or distribution or, at least, by the arrest of decline. Protocols are needed badly for management plans and recovery plans for invertebrate species allocated to any conservation category where such attention is needed, but these are generally in embryonic stages of development. Practical proto-

Table 8.4
Major steps in a pro-forma scheme for conservation of species of Lycaenidae (butterflies) (after Arnold 1983)

Major	Subsidiary phase
1.	Preserve, protect and manage known habitat to provide conditions needed: (a) preserve—prevent further change; (b) maintain larval and adult resources; (c) propose critical habitat (USA); (d) if necessary, clarify taxonomic status of target species.
2.	Manage and enhance population by habitat maintenance and improvement: (a) investigate and initiate habitat improvement as appropriate; (b) Determine physical and climatic regimes needed, and relate to local habitat enhancement; (c) investigate ecology of any tending ant species; (d) investigate ecology of food plant species.
3.	Evaluate above, and incorporate into development of long-term management plan.
4.	Monitor populations to determine status and evaluate success of management.
5.	Increase public awareness of species by education/information programmes.
6.	Enforce available protective regulations and laws, and determine whether additional legal steps are needed; if so promote these.

cols, realistically budgeted, must: (1) have sufficient generality in execution and interpretation for development of a reasonably standard set of procedures, and (2) incorporate sufficient flexibility to respond to different taxa and habitats, and to different time scales. Standard methodology on sampling is an integral aspect of this, and the diversity of activities needed to conserve single invertebrate species is summarized well in Arnold's (1983) tabulation of lycaenid butterfly management needs, which emphasizes the interdependence of sound management and good biological understanding. The details incorporated into the pro forma scheme noted in Table 8.4 serve to protect the habitat and critical resources needed by a species, and to clarify and monitor its status. Subsequently, management and habitat enhancement is pursued to reduce the impact of threatening processes and increase the viability of the species. The value of public education (p. 209) is also stressed, together with the need for judicious protective legislation in some instances, a step which emphasizes that practical conservation extends beyond the realm of science. The portfolio of activities summarized in Table 8.4 exemplifies the diverse needs of a practical species-focused management plan, and—wherever possible—the need to draw on published information and other practical expertise. Much of this involves field assessments, but the likelihood of needing to implement recovery plans for rare taxa also involves aspects of '*ex situ* conservation': captive rearing, husbandry, and release are a suite of themes of accelerating relevance in invertebrate conservation (New 1995*a*).

Further reading

Baker, J. M. and Wolff, W. J. (ed.) (1987). *Biological surveys of estuaries and coasts*. Cambridge University Press, Cambridge.

Goldsmith, B. (ed.) (1991). *Monitoring for conservation and ecology*. Chapman & Hall, London.

Kremen, C., Colwell, R. K., Erwin, T. L., Murphy, D. D., Noss, R. F., and Sanjayen, M. A. (1993). Terrestrial arthropod assemblages: their use as indicators in conservation planning. *Conservation Biology* 7, 796–808.

Magurran, A. E. (1988). *Ecological diversity and its measurement*. Croom Helm, London.

New, T. R. (1997). *Butterfly conservation*. 2nd edn. Oxford University Press, Melbourne.

Pollard, E. and Yates, T. J. (1993). *Monitoring butterflies for ecology and conservation*. Chapman & Hall, London.

Southwood, T. R. E. (1978). *Ecological methods. With particular reference to the study of insect populations*. Chapman & Hall, London.

9 Alternative approaches to species-focused conservation

Introduction

The expense and complexity of single species invertebrate conservation renders it impracticable as the sole—or, even, major—strategy to pursue, because only a minute proportion of the taxa needing conservation could possibly be treated, even though the wide taxonomic spectrum of taxa considered provides a solid framework for development. Funding and expertise for invertebrate conservation is limited, and concentrating on species alone for conservation would rapidly deploy this support with many taxa remaining neglected, and lingering doubts over its most effective use. Emphasis has thus also been placed on the prime need for conservation of any taxa, the protection of natural habitats. Surveys, sometimes of particular target groups, play important roles in selecting optimal areas for protection—or in justifying need for protection of remnant habitats where such a choice is unavailable.

Habitat protection

The alternative practical emphasis to focusing on single species has been to attempt to reserve, or otherwise protect, the widest possible variety of habitats and natural areas in the hope (even, expectation) that most species will thereby be assured of 'somewhere to live' and be sustainable. Yet, as noted earlier, even the best-known invertebrate group (butterflies) in the best-documented region of the world (the United Kingdom) is not satisfactorily represented in high-quality nature reserves, and human pressures and conflicting interests in many other parts of the world render security of natural areas, even if formally protected, extraordinarily difficult or impossible to guarantee. 'Land for conservation', despite its vital importance, is a luxury in areas with burgeoning human population and needs. Reserve areas need to be justified in the strongest practical terms and the attitude and principles of conservation through development fostered wherever possible. In biological terms, areas which can be shown to be significant as centres of endemicity, centres of diversity, 'hotspots' and the like assume priority, especially if such estimations for invertebrates coincide with those for different taxa and additional or other values (such as having traditional significance to local people, provision of income through ecotourism, and harvesting of commercially desirable species such as many butterflies) occur, or can be found and promoted. Invertebrate data are thereby important in helping to select priority areas for reservation, either for the species they contain or as indicators of significant diversity, endemism or complexity.

A major key to sustaining invertebrate assemblages in many parts of the world, as for other taxa, depends on such approaches to sustainable use with income generation for local people, rather than simply 'locking up' areas and creating hostility by excluding people from their traditional ways of life. Management for selected notable taxa which can then function as putative 'umbrella taxa', through helping to assure protection of the habitats on which poorly documented, complex assemblages depend, needs to be explored constructively. Flagship taxa thereby assume massive additional importance beyond their own individual interest, and detailed knowledge of their biology and requirements becomes relevant in broader approaches to practical conservation. The recent plan to conserve Queen Alexandra's birdwing butterfly (*Ornithoptera alexandrae*) in Papua New Guinea (AIDAB 1994) is an important recent example in which attention to one species is designed to safeguard primary forest habitats harbouring numerous lesser-known invertebrate and other biota.

Biological inventories

Biological inventories provide critical information for conservation planning, and selection of particular target taxa as an aid to rapid assessment was noted earlier (p. 164). But, as Kremen (1994) noted, following many earlier commentators, the impracticality of providing exhaustive data for invertebrates renders biogeographically informative assemblages (taxonomic groups) especially important in defining areas of endemism and the like. Kremen (1994) advocated using taxa showing evolutionary radiations within a region which are likely to be 'information rich' for conservation planning in that area. Such groups are likely to be rich in species and to have high endemism, and could be designated for many areas and on a range of geographical and habitat scales (Noss 1990), and with varying degrees of completeness and taxonomic focus. Estimates of diversity and endemism can be made at species level, genus or subgenus level or, with progressive loss of fine-scale focus, at higher taxonomic level.

Thus, on a global conservation scale for the swallowtail butterflies (Papilionidae), Collins and Morris (1985) showed that the faunas of 51 countries had to be considered if at least one viable population of each of the 573 species was to be conserved. The highest ranking country faunas (those with greatest diversity and endemism of swallowtails) are Indonesia and the Philippines. Both are complex archipelagos with much island-level endemism, so that many swallowtails are more narrowly restricted. Within each island, many of the populations or species are more narrowly distributed so that, with adequate knowledge, sites could be selected for each of these. But, despite there being numerous putative protected areas, especially in Indonesia, there is very little detailed information on the incidence of swallowtails in these, so that it is by no means clear whether they are adequate for such representative conservation. Similar problems and patterns manifest for the milkweed butterflies (Nymphalidae: Danainae) (Ackery and Vane-Wright 1984), and emphasize the need for more effective documentation of the incidence of a number of invertebrate groups in protected areas as an avenue to setting priorities for augmenting and securing the present reserves network.

More generally within this theme, Larsen (1994) noted that hardly any butterfly inventories exist for key forest habitats all over Africa, and that these are a priority need. He noted, also, that in any case conservation choice for further reserves is very restricted—the major need, as elsewhere in the tropics (in particular), is urgently to conserve what is left and strategic choice is not practicable; Larsen termed it 'an unaffordable luxury'.

Nevertheless, use of taxic overlays is becoming more frequent in helping to designate areas for priority protection and, by and large, the potential of invertebrates in this process has not been prosecuted adequately. As one recent example, significant endemism in invertebrates is one criterion for helping to enhance the value of endemic bird areas for conservation priority (Thirgood and Heath 1994). Surveys of selected conspicuous or reasonably well-known invertebrate groups in protected areas would be entirely feasible if the requisite funding could be raised. Even approximate measures of species diversity would represent immense advance on present levels of documentation and complement the information from vertebrate and higher plant surveys on which conservation planning has drawn to much greater extents. Invertebrate survey data are, perhaps, especially important in yielding information that can be used to describe, rank, or compare sites or habitats in terms of their species richness or more analytical measurements of diversity, assuming that the samples are based on standard (replicable, comparable) levels of collecting and trapping efficiency (Disney 1986).

The major needs in an 'ideal inventory survey', largely dealt with earlier (cf. Table 2.1), may be recapitulated as follows (after Rosenberg et al. 1979).

1. Clear definition of objectives.

2. Thorough knowledge of background literature and related studies, leading to finer focus, identification of gaps, maximizing existing collections and resources, and avoiding repetition or duplication of effort.

3. Project continuity, including continuity of funding, and adequate lead time.

4. Classification and careful choice of representative habitats (concentrate collecting on representative habitats, describe habitats adequately).

5. Stability of areas during the survey.

6. Adequate collection and processing of samples, include firmly in estimates of time and funding at commencement of project.

7. Identification, curation, disposition of specimens.

8. Accessibility of data from surveys—is it to be disseminated widely and, if so, how?

Sample analysis and application

The analysis of large multispecies samples is a complex exercise whose problems are not restricted to invertebrates (and indeed may be enhanced by frequency of need). Methods of ordination analysis, and calculation and interpretation of diversity indices are well established (Gauch 1982; Magurran 1988, for examples), despite continuing debate over the intricacies of some of these. Interpretation of diversity will remain a great challenge: and methods for extrapolating from limited (or, even, reasonably comprehensive) samples to estimate species richness are themselves diverse, not least because of the realization that all approaches, from accumulation rate curves (p. 131) to non-parametric estimators such as the 'jack-knife' (Heltshe and Forrester 1983), pose complex problems. With the latter, for example, Edwards (1993, in a challengingly titled paper) claimed that, despite stated problems 'it does offer a new and potentially useful approach to the estimation of species richness'.

The use of invertebrates, specifically of beetle assemblages in northeastern England, in conservation assessment was discussed by Eyre and Rushton (1989). 'Rarity' and 'typicalness' were generated for 71 woodland sites (using groundbeetles, Carabidae) and 56 lowland ponds (aquatic Coleoptera). Rarity was calculated from records of each species in the region on a 2×2 km^2 record unit base. Methods of calculating the indices used are summarized in Table 9.1. Typicalness was derived from means and standard deviations of site ordination scores (calculated from DECORANA, Hill 1979), with the distance of each site from the mean in two ordination axes integrated (in s.d.s of the ordination score) as typicalness measurements. For each site, two typicalness measurements were calculated: (1) ordination scores from analysis of all data used, and (2) site scores from ordination of data only from one habitat group. Both data series were ranked and the ranking by the two methods compared by using Spearman's rank correlation method. In general there was no correlation between ranking of sites by rarity indices and by typicalness measurements but, when similarity did occur, it was apparently related to the presence of rare species which influenced measures of typicalness.

Table 9.1

Calculation of 'rarity' and 'typicalness' measurements for invertebrates, for use in conservation assessment (after Eyre and Rushton 1989), based on studies of beetles in northern England

---

Rarity

Six rarity indices calculated for each site, based on 'individual species rarity', i.e. the number of 2×2 km tetrad records in the area

1. Species recorded in 1, 2–3, 4–7, 8–15, 16–31, 32–63, 64 and more, tetrads given scores of 7–1, respectively. Site score is sum of scores for each species and is the 'beetle rarity total'.

2. Similar to above, except scores given are geometric (i.e. 64, 32, 16, 8, 4, 2, 1) instead of 7–1. Sum of these scores is the 'species rarity total' for each site.

3. 'Rarity association' value of a site was calculated using species that scored 2 or more in the above geometric scale, with bias caused by presence of a very rare species compensated by reducing the highest score to the nearest other score. Addition of 3 and 2, above, gives the 'Rarity association total'. With all the above, the totals were divided by the number of species in the list, so quality of sites on a unit basis is reflected by

4. Beetle quality factor (no. $1/n$)

5. Species quality factor (no. $2/n$)

6. Rarity quality factor (no. $3/n$)

Typicalness

Two methods, based on means and standard deviations of site ordination scores (calculated by DECORANA: Hill 1979); distance of each site from the mean in two ordination axes calculated in standard deviations of ordination score, and these distances are typicalness measurements.

1. Site ordination scores from analysis of all data.

2. Site scores from ordination of data within one habitat groups only (habitat defined by TWINSPAN), to remove influence of sites in other habitat groups on ordination in individual habitat groups.

One serious problem with site assessments using invertebrates is in agreeing what the most useful approaches may be. Eyre's and Rushton's beetle study recognized that many invertebrates reflect habitat parameters other than vegetation, so that classification of invertebrate habitats should be complementary to those of vegetation, and measurements of conservation criteria of invertebrates should not be confined by vegetational data. In contrast, Disney (1986) recommended use of diversity measurements in habitats defined on the basis of their vegetation, on the pragmatic grounds that these are a straightforward way to explain invertebrate data to management agencies. As noted earlier (p. 7), invertebrates may subdivide the overall habitat more finely than revealed easily by measurements of vegetation or other single parameters employed commonly by people. With increased study, many invertebrate groups are likely to become valuable in site and habitat evaluation at increasingly sophisticated levels.

As an example of practical site evaluation for conservation in which invertebrates were used, incorporating several of the value parameters designated by Margules and Usher (1985) and Usher (1986), Usher and Edwards (1986) investigated the arthropods of several subantarctic islands in relation to the five criteria used to designate Specially Protected Areas in Antarctica. These are: (1) representative examples of major ecosystems; (2) areas with unique complexes of species; (3) areas which are the type locality or only known breeding locality of the species; (4) areas which contain especially interesting breeding colonies of birds or mammals; and (5) areas which should be kept inviolate as future comparative reference areas. The low species richness of arthropod assemblages in the Antarctic renders obtaining complete (or near-complete) inventories reasonably achievable for a range of different sites. 'Diversity' has only limited relevance in such impoverished faunas, and the first two of the criteria listed above were particularly important. 'Representativeness' was adjudged the most important so that examples of all kinds of community were conserved, and 'uniqueness' ensures that any particularly unusual assemblages are not lost. Similar reasoning is implicit in many rankings in more complex environments, but often without the equivalent level of reliable documentation.

There are thus two major contexts in which invertebrate assemblages participate or are involved in conservation; as for single species, these are as 'targets' or 'tools', with the latter being the more common, at least in formal terms. As Eyre *et al.* (1986) noted, analysis of invertebrate community data can be important in environmental monitoring (where the invertebrates are agents for assessing change, the proviso being that the factor(s) that affect the distribution and/or diversity of the assemblages are understood), environmental impact assessment (at a range of geographical scales, using ordination analysis to determine the quality of individual sites), and conservation (incorporating, especially, attributes of rarity, diversity and typicalness). They emphasized also the need for species-level identifications to validate the use of ordination analysis, and that the most accurate interpretations of numerical classifications and ordinations are produced by people who have knowledge of the data base and of the ecology of the invertebrate group(s) used.

Inventory and monitoring for invertebrates are interrelated in many ways, but differ in their objectives (Kremen *et al.* 1993). Both approaches depend on sound interpretation of the abundance, distribution, and incidence of particular taxa, and changes in these in response to natural or anthropogenic change. Both also rely heavily on use of selected taxa or assemblages for focus. A recommended general scheme for undertaking such studies using defined target groups (Kremen *et al.* 1993) is as follows.

1. Five to 10 higher taxa are chosen for investigation.

2. For each taxon, specialists select a 'target assemblage' using objective selection criteria (species richness, high endemism, other) as far as

possible. If possible, member species should be collectively well distributed and abundant, and display high beta or gamma diversity.

3. Standard ecological sampling is used to test the information value of the assemblages in a limited inventory across an obvious environmental gradient, to show the strength of any basis for accepting or rejecting the target assemblages as biogeographic indicators.

4. Larger-scale inventories, including studies in all major habitats, are then conducted to provide information usable in identifying areas of endemism, select a minimum number of sites to represent a full range of species and habitats, or to perform gap analysis.

Two systematic concepts can be adduced from measures of diversity (Vane-Wright 1994) in selecting priority areas.

1. 'Efficiency' relates to obtaining the greatest biodiversity possible for a given level of investment in acquiring and/or managing sites. In adding new sites to an existing suite of reserves, the principle of complementarity entails adding either:

   (i) the greatest quantity/diversity of previously unprotected taxa, or

   (ii) the greatest biodiversity increment per unit cost. The site with the greatest priority will be the one which adds the largest number of species to those already included in the reserve network (Vane-Wright et al. 1991).

2. 'Flexibility' introduces the need to consider suboptimal alternatives, and entails comparing sites in terms of how they form part of fully representative networks. A site may be 'irreplaceable' (Pressey et al. 1993) if it has unique attributes such as endemic species, and must receive priority for conservation over sites with lower irreplaceability value.

When the species of any group are reasonably well known, and categorized individually for some form of ranking, a summation of the numbers of ranked species can constitute an index of conservation value for the site on which they occur. Thus, the saproxylic beetles of Britain can be ranked to provide an 'index of ecological continuity' (Alexander 1988; Harding and Alexander 1994). Values for a site reflect the number of Red Book Endangered species (three points each), Vulnerable species (two points each) and Rare species (one point each), and combined index values of 20 or more seemed to identify the outstanding assemblages of ancient woodland. Similarly, water beetles may be valuable in helping to rank wetland sites (Foster et al. 1989).

Further reading

Collins, N. M. and Morris, M. G. (1985). *Threatened swallowtail butterflies of the world*. IUCN, Gland and Cambridge.

Gauch, H. G. (1982). *Multivariate analysis in community ecology*. Cambridge University Press, Cambridge.

Spellerberg, I. F. (1993). *Monitoring ecological change*. Cambridge University Press, Cambridge.

Usher, M. B. (ed.) (1986). *Wildlife conservation evaluation*. Chapman & Hall, London.

10 Involving people in invertebrate conservation

Introduction

The major practical barriers to increasing wider interest in invertebrate conservation and conducting effective surveys have been stressed repeatedly in earlier chapters, but devolve into three major categories.

1. The adverse images and public profile or, at least, general apathy with which invertebrates are regarded.

2. The widespread lack of appreciation, even within the community of zoologists and ecologists, of their diversity and fundamental importance in natural ecosystems.

3. The lack of resources, including expertise, for studying invertebrate diversity and biology, and for incorporating this information effectively into broader conservation programmes by standard sampling and analytical protocols.

These categories, and their many subdivisions, emphasize the need to involve people in many walks of life, to improve and foster public sympathy for invertebrates in pragmatic ways, and to enlist whatever help can be mustered to undertake practical aspects of sampling, recording, distribution mapping, helping in well co-ordinated surveys and in protecting and managing sites, as a major collective contribution to sustaining the earth's biota. Such activities can be encouraged in many ways, and at various levels. In addition, wider appreciation of the roles and importance of invertebrates has the potential to foster commitment of more resources to documenting and conserving them.

Enlisting support

Most non-specialist support for invertebrate studies has traditionally come for 'popular' groups, especially butterflies, whereas the relative lack of volunteer work on some other groups has mirrored their more general neglect. At one, enviable, extreme the British Butterfly Conservation Society has more than 10 000 members, and the group's strength is evident in the extensive monitoring and recording schemes it has spawned, with numerous local projects, including practical aspects of habitat management and maintenance, in progress (Harding 1991; Asher 1992; Harding *et al.* 1994). Asher noted the problems of co-ordinating more than 200 butterfly recording projects in Britain, with a range of different objectives, time frames, and levels of compatibility. The British Butterfly Monitoring Scheme has stimulated similar, generally less comprehensive, studies elsewhere. In many countries, naturalists' groups and professional scientific societies focusing on invertebrates play important parts in helping to educate people about these animals, and co-ordinating participation and interest from non-scientists and scientists alike. For example, the Xerces Society, founded in North America in 1971, has played an important part in educating people about invertebrate importance and conservation (Opler 1994). Many of the practical problems of operating a recording scheme (Foster 1994) centre on co-ordination, communication and quality control of the data accumulated. Dissemination of the digested or synthesized information to those who have helped gather it, with adequate acknowledgment, is critical in maintaining interest. Many amateur enthusiasts are somewhat suspicious of the activities of professional scientists, as all too often their efforts seem merely to fuel a 'black hole' from which nothing tangible ever emerges.

On another level, based more evidently on vested interest, the principle of conservation through development provides opportunity for individual people or settlements to participate in practical invertebrate conservation for a financial return. The money raised from controlled and co-ordinated sales of collectable invertebrates, such as ranched or farmed butterflies, may be the key to conserving some primary habitats in many parts of the tropics. If people can derive an adequate or profitable life-style from habitats which have already been changed substantially, the need to destroy further primary forest (for example) for subsistence agriculture is reduced. The principle is at present being tested actively in Papua New Guinea's Northern (Oro) Province (Orsak 1993; AIDAB 1994), through a major international project aimed at conservation of Queen Alexandra's birdwing butterfly, *Ornithoptera alexandrae*.

Larsen (1994), and others, have stressed the need to involve local people intimately in such projects, and that this may be the only practical avenue for gaining sympathy for conservation in environments where obtaining even the most basic human needs must take precedence. Integrated conservation and development projects need to be monitored closely to assess their progress and success. Until now, such monitoring has usually been inadequate (Kremen *et al.* 1994), and few such projects have even had provision for this to occur. Biodiversity monitoring is seen as a desirable—even, necessary—phase of such assessment, and monitoring of indicator groups or assemblages is an exercise in which many people can participate easily. Pearson (1994) stressed, for tigerbeetles (Carabidae: Cicindelinae), the advantage that people can learn rapidly to recognize and sample them with little experience.

Volunteers can play important parts in helping to monitor or assess many aspects of environmental quality, and these roles are becoming increasingly appealing to financially limited government agencies and frustrated scientists at all levels. Conservation has traditionally always appealed to a wide range of people, many of whom are very willing to participate in practical activities which contribute substantially to the well-being of local environments or taxa. Thus, state water pollution biologists in the USA draw heavily on volunteer-generated data (Penrose and Call 1995). Quality of the data is a major concern, because many of the organisms are generally unfamiliar to many people, and three State regulatory agencies have compared volunteer data with ongoing state monitoring programmes, which all involve interpretation of macroinvertebrates in benthic samples to order or family. This level of recognition appears to be achievable reasonably reliably, especially if the spectrum of taxa appraised is limited—for example to the Ephemeroptera-Plecoptera-Trichoptera suite recommended by some assessment groups (Eaton and Lenat 1991), as a rapid qualitative method (sometimes referred to simply as 'EPT'). This approach selects particularly responsive groups to reflect water quality. It may be feasible to select important and characteristic indicator groups within such orders in a given region, which volunteers may learn to recognize easily. In North Carolina, volunteers are encouraged to recognize three distinctive groups of insects which are intolerant to pollution and, therefore, indicators of good water quality. Their major survey focus is on philopotamid caddisflies (recognizable in North Carolina by having orange heads), any stone-cased caddisfly and any large perlid stonefly. Opportunities for liaison with official agencies are numerous, and the resulting cooperation with professional biologists, focus for dissemination and exchange of information (such as by newsletters), and training in collecting, interpreting and managing the data are all important benefits from such exercises (Penrose and Call 1995). Four major factors are important for a recording scheme based on such broad surveys to succeed (Harding 1991):

(1) a volunteer national organizer and/or network of volunteer regional organizers;

(2) volunteer specialists to record information for the scheme.;

(3) readily accessible information guides; and

(4) a practical selection of species to be covered (that is, avoiding groupings of species which require vastly different survey techniques).

Data are usually recorded on standard-field cards, and validated before incorporation into a data base. The products of such surveys, as exemplified by the Biological Records Centre (UK) include maps, publications and data bases for practical conservation, and more intangible benefits such as increased and better-organized scientific knowledge of distribution and changes in species status and habitat condition.

Many distribution recording schemes for invertebrates, local conservation projects, and societies and groups such as those mentioned above, provide opportunity for lay people to learn about, and participate in, practical conservation activities involving invertebrates. Whereas these may not appear, initially, to have the same 'importance' as working with rhinoceros, whales, condors or rare parrots, the target insect or snail may be just as significant as these in representing an even more isolated and ancient lineage whose loss would indeed impoverish global diversity. Many such projects and groups generate informal publications such as newsletters and bulletins, or more formal research programmes, and provide opportunities to participate in field work, such as surveying or recording invertebrates under more experienced guidance, or to help process the resulting samples.

Collaborative research and education is of immense importance in studies on invertebrates, not least to dispel their often poor public images. Changing people's attitudes towards invertebrates is an important aspect of facilitating communication. Yen (1994) emphasized the critical roles for museum and zoo curators in developing greater public awareness of invertebrates. The skills associated traditionally with the personnel of these groups of institutions are complementary, and could lead to very strong alliances and collaboration in facilitating integrated programmes to promote invertebrate conservation. Primarily, combinations of live displays of invertebrates (using adjuncts such as video technology and binocular microscopes to help examination of small organisms) and displays of models and preserved specimens can emphasize their diversity and aspects of their ecology and importance. Such displays are attractive to school children, and involving young people in natural history as a conduit to gaining badly needed expertise in the future is widely seen as vital. Many 'hands on' invertebrate displays are developing (SASI 1993, 1994), and these will surely continue to diversify. Robinson (1993) emphasized the importance of education to overcome peoples' 'vertebrocentric bias' and that appreciation of invertebrates is a major key to education on biodiversity. The increasing interest in some charismatic invertebrates as unusual pets is also an important conduit for fostering interest.

In general, natural history as a hobby seems to have declined strongly in many countries where it was formerly very popular. Projects in which non-professionals can be involved encompass many relevant aspects of invertebrate biology, including: (1) research associated with the collections of museums, such as helping to prepare and curate specimens at various levels; (2) field surveys; (3) gaining basic biological information through observing and rearing trials; and (4) local natural history projects involving active participation by government authorities, schools, community groups (such as the numerous 'Friends' groups who help to protect particular species or sites, and whose continued support on any management committee is an important facet of liaison between scientists and the wider community), and others. Much of the knowledge which has helped to give butterflies such a high profile in insect conservation has come from the 'work' of hobbyists and collectors, and the symbiosis between amateur and professional lepidopterists is a model needed badly for many other invertebrate groups. It is occurring well for some—such as dragonflies, some groups of beetles, grasshoppers and molluscs—and with promotion of other taxa as flagships for conservation and assessment of biodiversity, there is opportunity to foster such interest in many ways. At present, much of the impetus stems from the zeal of individual scientists prepared to take volunteers (who may be asked to pay their own costs) on field excursions, but some organizations encourage such enterprise among their staff. As one example, CSIRO (Australia's leading scientific research body) runs the 'Double Helix Club' through which many young people participate in surveys and biological research, supported by their schools, and aiding scientific teams. Some recent examples are outlined by New (1995a), and include surveys of earthworms in Australia, surveying the spread of dung-beetles introduced to aid breakdown of ungulate dung, and habitat enrichment for a rare birdwing butterfly.

Following from the popularity of butterfly houses (Collins 1987) and similar exhibits, many more diverse displays of invertebrates are gradually appearing. The best of these incorporate many of the educational principles noted earlier, and are important conduits for 'popularizing' invertebrates in many ways. Some participate actively in the captive breeding of taxa of conservation concern, although the number of institutions involved actively in invertebrate conservation is still low. Pearce-Kelly (1993) highlighted the leading role of London Zoo in developing a number of active conservation programmes, in tandem with educational exhibits.

One very positive effect of butterfly houses, in particular, has been to remove the 'barrier' between observers and animals, allowing children and adults to experience at close quarters living organisms they might see otherwise only as dead museum specimens, if at all (Toone 1990). Such familiarization, and overcoming feelings of antagonism towards invertebrates, may be a major avenue to recruiting invertebrate zoologists of future generations, whose roles in studying invertebrates for conservation will surely be of immense importance. Central to this is the commitment to making invertebrates more interesting and appealing to people, and Czechura (1994) identified five immediate issues which need to be considered in developing 'marketing strategies' for these animals.

1. Recognition that not all taxa will inspire general interest, so that existing interest in core groups must be used to popularize other taxa.
2. The overall lack of available information must be addressed, through a

concerted approach to using and creating field guides, non-technical references, displays, and others. Targeting regional or perceptual groups of animals (Czechura noted 'guide to house spiders' rather than 'spiders of Queensland') rather than standard taxonomic monographs may be worthwhile.

3. The lack of common names needs to be addressed, as complicated scientific names are off-putting to many people.

4. The poor images of invertebrates need to be addressed.

5. Because of economic constraints, sharing resources and active cooperation are necessary. Czechura (1994) noted exhibitions of invertebrates which have toured the various Australian state museums and have involved many different contributors and a broadly developed funding base.

Services which might be provided by local museums include access to equipment and libraries (Lott 1994), especially to members of natural history societies. Individual museum or university staff can do much to stimulate interest in invertebrates simply by communicating enthusiasm and practical advice. Continuing pressures on such institutions and erosion of their skills base and facilities is rendering such opportunities increasingly scarce, and is one of the most worrying aspects of catalysing interests in our natural world, especially among young people whose commitment to conservation will be so vital in the decades to come.

Further reading

Kellert, S. R. (1993). Values and perceptions of invertebrates. *Conservation Biology* **7**, 845–55.

Opler, P. A. (1994). Conservation and management of butterfly diversity in North America. In *Ecology and conservation of butterflies* (ed. A. S. Pullin), pp. 316–24. Chapman & Hall, London.

References

Ablett, E. M. (1994). An appraisal of RAPD-PCR: a new molecular tool for the identification of invertebrate species. *Memoirs of the Queensland Museum* **36**, 1–7.

Ackery, P. R. and Vane-Wright, R. I. (1984). *Milkweed butterflies*. British Museum (Natural History), London/Cornell University Press, New York.

Adis, J. (1979). Problems of interpreting arthropod sampling with pitfall traps. *Zoologischer Anzeiger* **202**, 177–84.

AIDAB (Australian International Development Assistance Bureau) (1994). *Queen Alexandra's Birdwing butterfly conservation project Oro Province Papua New Guinea. Feasibility study.* Project design document (December 1993). Canberra,

Alexander, K. N. A. (1988). The development of an index of ecological continuity for deadwood associated beetles. Insect indicators of ancient woodland. *Antenna* **12**, 69–71.

Alberch, P. (1993). Museums, collections and biodiversity inventories. *Trends in Ecology and Evolution* **8**, 372–5.

Andersen, A. N. (1995). Measuring more of biodiversity: genus richness as a surrogate for species richness in Australian ant faunas. *Biological Conservation* **73**, 39–43.

Andersen, J. (1995). A comparison of pitfall trapping and quadrat sampling of Carabidae (Coleoptera) on river banks. *Entomologica Fennica* **6**, 65–77.

Arnold, R. A. (1983). Conservation and management of the endangered Smith's blue butterfly, *Euphilotes enoptes smithi* (Lepidoptera: Lycaenidae). *Journal of Research on the Lepidoptera* **22**, 135–53.

Aron, W., Ahlstrom, E. H., Bary, B. McK., Bé, A. W. H., and Clarke, W. D. (1965). Towing characteristics of plankton sampling gear. *Limnology and Oceanography* **10**, 333–40.

Asher, J. (1992). *A programme for the coordination of butterfly recording in Britain and Ireland*. British Butterfly Conservation Society, Cambridge.

Aucamp, J. L. and Ryke, P. A. J. (1964). A preliminary report on a grease film extraction method for soil microarthropods. *Pedobiologia* **4**, 77–9.

Baker, J. M. and Crothers, J. H. (1987). Intertidal rock. In *Biological surveys of estuaries and coasts* (ed. J. M. Baker and W. J. Wolff), pp. 157–97. Cambridge University Press, Cambridge.

Barker, K. R. (1978). Determining nematode population responses to control agents. In *Methods for evaluating plant fumigants, nematicides and bacteriacides* (ed. E. I. Zehr), pp. 114–25. American Phytopathological Society, St Paul, MN.

Barnett, B. E. (1979). Sorting benthic samples. *Marine Pollution Bulletin* **10**, 240–1.

Basset, Y. (1988). A composite interception trap for sampling arthropods in tree canopies. *Journal of the Australian Entomological Society* **27**, 213–9.

Beattie, A. J., Majer, J. D., and Oliver, I. (1993). Rapid biodiversity assessment: a review. In *Rapid biodiversity assessment* (ed. A. J. Beattie), pp. 4–14. Macquarie University, Sydney.

Blades, D. C. A. and Marshall, S. A. (1994). Terrestrial arthropods of Canadian peatlands, synopsis of pan trap collections at four southern Ontario peatlands. *Memoirs of the Entomological Society of Canada* **169**, 221–84.

Bloemers, G. F. and Hodda, M. (1995). A method for extracting nematodes from a tropical forest soil. *Pedobiologia* **39**, 331–43.

Blomquist, S. (1990). Sampling performance of Ekman grabs—*in situ* observations and design improvements. *Hydrobiologia* **206**, 245–54.

Blomquist, S. (1991). Quantitative sampling of soft-bottom sediments: problems and solutions. *Marine Ecology Progress Series* **72**, 295–304.

Boddeke, R. (1989). Management of the brown shrimp (*Crangon crangon*) stock in Dutch coastal waters. In *Marine invertebrate fisheries, their assessment and management* (ed. J. F. Caddy), pp. 35–62. John Wiley, New York.

Bongers, T. (1990). The maturity index: an ecological measure of environmental disturbance based on nematode species composition. *Oecologia* **83**, 14–9.

Boucher, G. and Lambshead, P. J. D. (1995). Ecological biodiversity of marine nematodes from temperate, tropical, and deep-sea regions. *Conservation Biology* **9**, 1594–604.

Boulton, A. J. (1985). A sampling device that quantitatively collects benthos in flowing or standing waters. *Hydrobiologia* **127**, 31–9.

Bouwman, L. A. (1987). Meiofauna. In *Biological surveys of estuaries and coasts* (ed. J. M. Baker and W. J. Wolff), pp. 140–56. Cambridge University Press, Cambridge.

Brinkhurst, R. O. (1993). Future directions in freshwater biomonitoring using benthic macroinvertebrates. In *Freshwater biomonitoring and benthic macroinvertebrates* (ed. D. M. Rosenberg and V. H. Resh), pp. 442–60. Chapman & Hall, London.

British Museum (Natural History). (1954). *Instructions for collectors*, No. 9A. *Invertebrate animals other than insects*. London.

British Museum (Natural History). (1961). *Instruction for collectors*, No. 4A. *Insects*. London.

Britton, D. R., New, T. R., and Jelinek, A. (1995). Rare Lepidoptera at Mount Piper, Victoria—the role of a threatened butterfly community in advancing understanding of insect conservation. *Journal of the Lepidopterists' Society* **49**, 97–113.

Brooks, S. J. (1993*a*). Guidelines for invertebrate surveys. *British Wildlife* (1993), 283–286.

Brooks, S. J. (1993*b*). Review of a method to monitor adult dragonfly populations. *Journal of the British Dragonfly Society* **9**, 1–4.

Brown, B. (1993). Maine's baitworm fisheries: resources at risk? *American Zoologist* **33**, 568–77.

Brown, B. V. and Feener, D. H. Jr. (1995). Efficiency of two mass sampling methods for sampling phorid flies (Diptera: Phoridae) in a tropical biodiversity survey. *Contributions in Science, Natural History Museum of Los Angeles County*, No. 459.

Burd, B. J., Nemec, A., and Brinkhurst, R. O. (1990). The development and application of analytical methods in benthic marine infaunal studies. *Advances in Marine Biology* **26**, 169–247.

Buskirk, R. E. and Buskirk, W. H. (1976). Changes in arthropod abundance in a highland Costa Rican forest. *American Midland Naturalist* **95**, 288–98.

Caddy, J. F. (1989*a*). A perspective on the population dynamics and assessment of scallop fisheries, with special reference to the sea scallop *Placoplecten magellanicus* Gmelin. In *Marine invertebrate fisheries: their assessment and management* (ed. J. F. Caddy), pp. 559–89. John Wiley, New York.

Caddy, J. F. (1989*b*). *Marine invertebrate fisheries, their assessment and management.* John Wiley, New York.

Cairns, J., Albaugh, D. W., Busey, F., and Chanay, M. D. (1968). The sequential comparison index—a simplified method for non-biologists to estimate relative differences in stream pollution studies. *Journal of the Water Pollution Control Federation* **40**, 1607–13.

Canaday, C. L. (1987). Comparison of insect fauna captured in six different trap types in a douglas-fir forest. *Canadian Entomologist* **119**, 1101–8.

Carleton, J. H. and Done, T. J. (1995). Quantitative video sampling of coral reef benthos, large scale application. *Coral Reefs* **14**, 35–46.

Chandler, G. T., Shirley, T. C., and Fleeger, J. W. (1988). The tom-tom corer, a new design of the Kajak corer for use in meiofauna sampling. *Hydrobiologia* **169**, 129–34.

Chessman, B. C. (1995). Rapid assessment of rivers using macroinvertebrates: a procedure based on habitat-specific sampling, family level identification and a biotic index. *Australian Journal of Ecology* **20**, 122–9.

Chiappone, M. and Sullivan, K. M. (1991). A comparison of line transect versus linear percentage sampling for evaluating stony coral (*Scleractinia* and *Milleporina*) community similarity and area coverage on reefs of the central Bahamas. *Coral Reefs* **10**, 139–54.

Christie, N. D. (1975). Relationship between sediment texture, species richness and volume of sediment sampled by a grab. *Marine Biology* **30**, 89–96.

Clark, W. H. and Blom, P. E. (1992). An efficient and inexpensive pitfall trap system. *Entomological News* **103**, 55–9.

Cockran, W. G. (1977). *Sampling techniques* (3rd edn). John Wiley, New York.

Coddington, J. A., Griswold, C. E., Davila, D. S., Penaranda, E., and Larcher, S. F. (1991). Designing and testing sampling protocols to estimate biodiversity in tropical ecosystems. In *The unity of evolutionary biology* (ed. E. C. Dudley), pp. 44–60. Dioscorides Press, Portland.

Colebrook, J. M. (1979). Continuous plankton records, monitoring the plankton of the North Atlantic and the North Sea. In *Monitoring the marine environment* (ed. D. Nichols), pp. 87–102. Institute of Biology, London.

Coleman, N. (1980). More on sorting benthic samples. *Marine Pollution Bulletin* **11**, 150–2.

Collins, N. M. (1987). *Butterfly houses in Britain. The conservation implications.* IUCN, Gland.

Collins, N. M. and Morris, M. G. (1985). *Threatened swallowtail butterflies of the world*. IUCN, Gland and Cambridge.

Collins, N. M. and Thomas, J. A (ed.) (1991). *Conservation of insects and their habitats*. Academic Press, London.

Colwell, R. K. and Coddington, J. A. (1994). Estimating terrestrial biodiversity through extrapolation. *Philosophical Transactions of the Royal Society of London B* **345**, 101–18.

Common, I. F. B. (1986). A small portable light trap for collecting microlepidoptera. *Australian Entomological Magazine* **13**, 15–9.

Conand, C. and Sloan, N. A. (1989). World fisheries for echinoderms. In *Marine invertebrate fisheries: their assessment and management* (ed. J. F. Caddy), pp. 647–63. John Wiley, New York.

Corbet, P. S. (1966). A method for sub-sampling insect collections that vary widely in size. *Mosquito News* **26**, 420–4.

Cotterill, F. P. D. (1995). Systematics, biological knowledge and environmental conservation. *Biodiversity and Conservation* **4**, 183–205.

Council of Europe. (1986). *European Charter for Invertebrates*. Strasbourg.

Coy, R., Greenslade, P., and Rounsevell, D. (1993). *A survey of invertebrates in Tasmanian rainforest*. Technical Report No. 9. Parks and Wildlife Service, Hobart, Tasmania.

Cranston, P. S. (1990). Biomonitoring and invertebrate taxonomy. *Environmental Monitoring and Assessment* **14**, 265–73.

Cranston, P. S. (1993). Rapid biodiversity assessment in aquatic ecosystems. In *Rapid biodiversity assessment* (ed. A. J. Beattie), pp. 15–20. Macquarie University, Sydney.

Cranston, P. and Hillman, T. (1992). Rapid assessment of biodiversity using 'Biological Diversity Technicians'. *Australian Biologist* **5**, 144–54.

Cranston, P. S. and Trueman, J. W. H. (1997). 'Indicator' taxa in invertebrate biodiversity assessment. *Memoirs of the Museum of Victoria* **56**, 267–74.

Crossley, D. A. and Blair, J. M. (1991). A high-efficiency, 'low-technology' Tullgren-type extractor for soil microarthropods. *Agriculture, Ecosystems and Environment* **34**, 187–92.

Culver, D. C. (1982). *Cave life. Evolution and ecology*. Harvard University Press, Cambridge, MA.

Cummins, K. W. (1962). An evaluation of some techniques for the collection and analysis of benthic samples with special emphasis on lotic waters. *American Midland Naturalist* **67**, 477–504.

Czeckura, G. V. (1994). Is the public really interested in invertebrates? What the Queensland Museum Reference Centre enquiries from 1986–1993 tell us. *Memoirs of the Queensland Museum* **36**, 41–6.

Dallwitz, M. J. (1993). DELTA and INTKEY. In *Advances in computer methods for systematic biology, artificial intelligence, databases, computer vision* (ed. R. Fortuner), pp. 287–96. Johns Hopkins University Press, Baltimore.

Danks, H. V. (1991). Museum collections: fundamental values and modern problems. *Collection Forum* **7**, 95–111.

Danks, H. V. (1996). *How to assess insect biodiversity without wasting your time*. Biological Survey of Canada (Terrestrial Arthropods) Document series, No. 5, Ottawa.

Danks, H. V., Wiggins, G. B., and Rosenberg, D. M. (1987). Ecological collections and long-term monitoring. *Bulletin of the Entomological Society of Canada* **19**, 16–8.

Darling, D. C. and Parker, L. (1988). Effectiveness of Malaise traps in collecting Hymenoptera, the influence of trap design, mesh size, and location. *Canadian Entomologist* **120**, 787–96.

Davenport, M. W. (1985). Artificial substrata: their use, advantages and disadvantages in aquatic invertebrate monitoring. In *Biological monitoring in freshwaters* (ed. R. D. Pridmore and A. B. Cooper), pp. 259–71. Water and Soil Directorate, Wellington. Miscellaneous Publication No. 83.

de Laguna, J. B. (1989). Managing an international multispecies fishery, the saharan trawl fishery for cephalopods. In *Marine invertebrate fisheries, their assessment and management* (ed. J. F. Caddy), pp. 591–612. John Wiley, New York.

di Castri, F., Vernhes, J. R., and Younes, T. (ed.) (1992). Inventorying and monitoring biodiversity. A proposal for an international network. *Biology International*. Special Issue No. 27, 1–28.

Didden, W., Born, H., Domm, H., Graefe, U., Heck, M., Kùhle, J., Mellin, A., and

Römbke, J. (1995). The relative efficiency of wet funnel techniques for the extraction of Enchytraeidae. *Pedobiologia* **39**, 52–7.

Dietrick, E. J. (1961). An improved backpack motor fan for suction sampling of insect populations. *Journal of Economic Entomology* **54**, 394–5.

Digweed, S. C., Currie, C. R., Cárcamo, H. A., and Spence, J. R. (1995). Digging out the 'digging-in effect' of pitfall traps: influences of depletion and disturbance on catches of ground beetles (Coleoptera, Carabidae). *Pedobiologia* **39**, 561–76.

Disney, R. H. L. (1982). Rank methodists. *Antenna* **6**, 198.

Disney, R. H. L. (1986). Assessments using invertebrates, posing the problem. In *Wildlife conservation evaluation* (ed. M. B. Usher), pp. 271–93. Chapman & Hall, London.

Disney, R. H. L., Erzinclioglu, Y. Z., de C. Henshaw, D. J., Howse, D., Unwin, D. M., Withers, P., and Woods, A. (1982). Collecting methods and the adequacy of attempted fauna surveys, with reference to the Diptera. *Field Studies* **5**, 607–621.

Doeg, T. and Lake, P. S. (1981). A technique for assessing the composition and density of macroinvertebrate fauna of large stones in streams. *Hydrobiologia* **80**, 3–6.

Done, T. J. (1992*a*). Phase shifts in coral reef communities and their ecological significance. *Hydrobiologia* **247**, 121–32.

Done, T. J. (1992*b*). Constancy and change in some Great Barrier Reef coral communities, 1980–1990. *American Zoologist* **32**, 655–62.

Drake, C. M. and Elliott, J. M. (1982). A comparative study of three air–lift samplers used for sampling benthic macroinvertebrates in rivers. *Freshwater Biology* **12**, 511–33.

Drift, J. van der (1951). Analysis of the animal community in a beech forest floor. *Tijdschrifte vor Entomologie*, **94**, 1–168.

Dropkin, V. H. (1980). *Introduction to plant nematology*. Wiley, New York.

Dunn, M. (1989). Bibliography of information on pitfall trapping. *Young Entomologists Association Quarterly* **6**, 41–2.

Eaton, L. E. and Lenat, D. R. (1991). Comparison of a rapid bioassessment method with North Carolina's qualitative macroinvertebrate collection method. *Journal of the North American Benthological Society* **10**, 335–8.

Eberhardt, L. L. and Thomas, J. M. (1991). Designing environmental field studies. *Ecological Monographs*, **61**, 53–73.

Edwards, C. A. (1991). The assessment of populations of soil-inhabiting invertebrates. *Agriculture, Ecosystems and Environment* **34**, 145–76.

Edwards, C. A. and Fletcher, K. E. (1971). A comparison of extraction methods for terrestrial arthropod populations. In *Methods for the study of productivity and energy flow in soil ecosystems* (ed. J. Phillipson), pp. 150–85. Blackwell Scientific, Oxford.

Edwards, R. L. (1993). Can the species richness of spiders be determined? *Psyche* **100**, 185–208.

Eggleton, P. and Bignell,D. E. (1995). Monitoring the response of tropical insects to changes in the environment: troubles with termites. In *Insects in a changing environment* (ed. R. Harrington and N. E. Stork), pp. 473–97. Academic Press, London.

Ehrlich, P. and Ehrlich, A. (1981). *Extinction: the causes and consequences of the disappearance of species*. Gollancz, London.

Eleftheriou, A. and Holme, N. A. (1984). Macrofauna techniques. In *Methods for the study of marine benthos* (ed. N. A. Holme and A. D. McIntyre), pp. 140–216. Blackwell Scientific, Oxford.

Elliott, J. M. (1977). Some methods for the statistical analysis of samples of benthic invertebrates. Freshwater Biological Association, Scientific Publication. No. 25. Ambleside.

Elliott, J. M. and Bagenal, T. B. (1972). The effects of electrofishing on the invertebrates of a Lake District stream. *Oecologia* **9**, 1–11.

Elliott, J. M. and Drake, C. M. (1981*a*). A comparative study of seven grabs used for sampling benthic macroinvertebrates in rivers. *Freshwater Biology* **11**, 99–120.

Elliott, J. M. and Drake, C. M. (1981*b*). A comparative study of four dredges used for sampling benthic macroinvertebrates in rivers. *Freshwater Biology* **11**, 245–61.

Elliott, J. M. and Tullett, P. A. (1978). *A bibliography of samplers for benthic invertebrates*. Freshwater Biological Association, Occasional Publication. No. 4. Ambleside. (Supplement, 1983, Publication No. 20).

Ellis, D. V. (1988). Quality control of biological surveys. *Marine Pollution Bulletin* **19**, 506–12.

Ellis, D. V. and Cross, S. F. (1981). A protocol for inter-laboratory calibrations of biological species identification (ring tests). *Water Research* **15**, 1107–8.

Elmgren, K. (1973). Methods of sampling sublittoral soft bottom meiofauna. *Oikos* (Suppl. 15), 112–20.

Elton, C. S. and Miller, R. S. (1954). The ecological survey of animal communities with a practical system of classifying habitats by structural characters. *Journal of Ecology* **42**, 460–96.

Erwin, T. L. (1982). Tropical forests, their richness in Coleoptera and other arthropod species. *Coleopterists' Bulletin* **36**, 74–5.

Eversham, B. C. (1994). Using invertebrates to monitor land use change and site management. *British Journal of Entomology and Natural History* **7** (Suppl. 1), 36–45.

Eyre, M. D. and Rushton, S. P. (1989). Quantification of conservation criteria using invertebrates. *Journal of Applied Ecology* **26**, 159–71.

Eyre, M. D., Rushton, S. P., Luff, M. L., Ball, S. G., Foster, G. N., and Tropping, C. J. (1986). *The use of invertebrate community data in environmental assessment*. Agricultural Environment Research Group, University of Newcastle upon Tyne.

Fernandes, L. (1990). Effect of the distribution and density of benthic target organisms on manta tow estimates of their abundance. *Coral Reefs* **9**, 161–5.

Fernandes, L., Marsh, H., Moran, P. J., and Sinclair, D. F. (1990). Bias in manta tow surveys of *Acanthaster planci*. *Coral Reefs* **9**, 155–60.

Ferrar, A. A. (1989). The role of red data books in conserving biodiversity. In *Biotic diversity in southern Africa* (ed. B. J. Huntley), pp. 136–47. Oxford University Press, Cape Town.

Finnamore, A. T. (1994). Hymenoptera of the Wagner natural area, a boreal spring fen in central Alberta. *Memoirs of the Entomological Society of Canada* **169**, 181–220.

Ford, E. B. (1945). *Butterflies*. Collins, London.

Foster, G. N. (1994). Operating a recording scheme. *British Journal of Entomology and Natural History* **1** (Suppl. 7), 46–57.

Foster, G. N., Foster, A. P., Eyre, M. D., and Bilton, D. T. (1989). Classification of water beetle assemblages in arable fenland and ranking of sites in relation to conservation value. *Freshwater Biology* **22**, 343–54.

Fraser, J. H. (1979). The history of plankton sampling. In *Zooplankton sampling*, pp. 11–18. UNESCO, Paris.

Frazer, J. F. D. (1973). Estimating butterfly numbers. *Biological Conservation* **5**, 271–6.

Fretter, V. (1952). Experiments with P^{32} and I^{131} on species of *Helix*, *Arion* and *Agriolimax*. *Quarterly Journal of Microscopical Science* **93**, 123–46.

Fry, R. and Lonsdale, D. (ed.) (1991). *Habitat conservation for insects—a neglected green issue*. Amateur Entomologists' Society, Middlesex.

Gadagkar, R., Chandrashekara, K., and Nair, P. (1990). Insect species diversity in the tropics, sampling methods and a case study. *Journal of the Bombay Natural History Society* **87**, 337–53.

Gall, L. F. (1984). The effects of capturing and marking on subsequent activity in *Boloria acrocnema* (Lepidoptera, Nymphalidae) with a comparison of different numerical methods that estimate population size. *Biological Conservation* **28**, 139–54.

Gamble, J. C. (1984). Diving. In *Methods for the study of marine benthos* (ed. N. A. Holme and A. D. McIntyre), pp. 99–139. IBP Handbook No. 16. Blackwell Scientific, Oxford.

Gaston, K. J. (1992). Regional numbers of insect and plant species. *Functional Ecology* **6**, 243–7.

Gaston, K. J. and May, R. M. (1992). Taxonomy of taxonomists. *Nature* **356**, 281–2.

Gaston, K. J., New, T. R., and Samways, M. J. (ed.) (1994). *Perspectives on insect conservation*. Intercept, Andover.

Gauch, H. G. (1982). *Multivariate analysis in community ecology*. Cambridge University Press, Cambridge.

Gaydecki, P. A. (1984). A quantification of the behavioural dynamics of certain Lepidoptera in response to light. Ph. D. thesis, Cranfield Institute of Technology (cited by Muirhead-Thomson 1991).

Gerking, S. D. (1957). A method of sampling the littoral macrofauna and its application. *Ecology* **38**, 219–26.

Gibson, R. W. (1975). Measurement of eriophyid mite populations on ryegrass using ultrasonic radiation. *Transactions of the Royal Entomological Society of London* **127**, 31–2.

Gillis, P. L. and Mackie, G. L. (1994). Impact of the zebra mussel, *Dreissena polymorpha*, on populations of Unionidae (Bivalvia) in Lake St. Clair. *Canadian Journal of Zoology* **72**, 1260–71.

Godan, D. (1983). *Pest slugs and snails. Biology and control*. Springer-Verlag, Berlin.

Goldsmith, B. (ed.) (1991). *Monitoring for conservation and ecology*. Chapman & Hall, London.

Gorny, M. and Grum, L. (ed.) (1993). *Methods in soil zoology*. Elsevier, Amsterdam/Polish Scientific Publishers, Warsaw.

Gourbalt, N. and Warwick, R. M. (1994). Is the determination of meiobenthic diversity affected by sampling method in sandy beaches? *Marine Ecology* **15**, 267–79.

Grassle, J. F. and Maciolek, N. J. (1992). Deep-sea species richness: regional and local diversity estimates from quantitative bottom samples. *American Naturalist* **139**, 313–41.

Greenslade, P. J. M. (1979). *A guide to ants of South Australia*. South Australian Museum, Adelaide.

Grizzle, D. E. and Stegner, W. E., (1985). A new quantitative grab for sampling benthos. *Hydrobiologia* **126**, 91–5.

Groombridge, B. C. (ed.) (1992). *Global biodiversity, status of the earth's living resources*. World Conservation Monitoring Centre, Cambridge/Chapman & Hall, London.

Haarlov, N. (1947). A new modification of the Tullgren apparatus. *Journal of Animal Ecology* **16**, 115–21.

Hammond, P. M. (1991). Insect abundance and diversity in the Dumoga-Bone National Park, N. Sulawesi, with special reference to the beetle fauna of lowland rainforest in the Toraut region. In *Insects and the rainforests of South-East Asia* (ed. W. J. Knight and J. D. Holloway), pp. 197–254. Royal Entomological Society, London.

Hammond, P. M. (1994). Practical approaches to the estimation of the extent of biodiversity in speciose groups. *Philosophical Transactions of the Royal Society of London B* **345**, 119–36.

Hanski, I. and Thomas, C. D. (1994). Metapopulation dynamics and conservation, a spatially explicit model applied to butterflies. *Biological Conservation* **68**, 167–80.

Harding, P. T. (1991). National species distribution surveys. In *Monitoring for conservation and ecology* (ed. B. Goldsmith), pp. 133–54. Chapman & Hall, London.

Harding, P. T. and Alexander, K. N. A. (1994). The use of saproxylic invertebrates in the selection and evaluation of areas of relic forest in pasture-woodlands. *British Journal of Entomology and Natural History* **1** (Suppl. 7), 21–6.

Harding, P. T., Asher, J., and Yates, T. J. (1994). Butterfly monitoring I—recording the changes. In *Ecology and conservation of butterflies* (ed. A. S. Pullen), pp. 1–22. Chapman & Hall, London.

Hawkins, S. J. and Hartnoll, R. G. (1983). Changes in a rocky shore community, an evaluation of monitoring. *Marine and Environmental Research* **9**, 131–81.

Hawksworth, D. L. and Mound, L. A. (1991). Biodiversity databases: the crucial significance of collections. In *The biodiversity of microorganisms and invertebrates: its role in sustainable agriculture* (ed. D. L. Hawksworth), pp. 17–29. CAB International, Wallingford.

Heath, J. and Scott, D. (1977). *Instructions for recorders*. Biological Records Centre, Monks Wood Experimental Station, Huntingdon.

Hellawell, J. M. (1978). *Biological surveillance of rivers*. Water Research Centre, Stevenage.

Hellawell, J. M. (1991). Development of a rationale for monitoring. In *Monitoring for conservation and ecology* (ed. B. Goldsmith), pp. 1–14. Chapman & Hall, London.

Heltsche, J. F. and Forrester, N. E. (1983). Estimating species richness using the jackknife procedure. *Biometrics* **39**, 1–11.

Henderson, C. F. and McBurnie, H. V. (1943). Sampling technique for determining populations of the citrus red mite and its predators. *United States Department of Agriculture Circular* No. 671, 1–11.

Heppleston, P. B. (1972). Life history and population fluctuations of *Lymnaea truncatula* (Müll.), the snail vector of fascioliasis. *Journal of Applied Ecology* **9**, 235–48.

Herman, P. M. J. and Heip, C. (1988). On the use of meiofauna in ecological monitoring, who needs taxonomy? *Marine Pollution Bulletin* **19**, 665–8.

Heron, A. C. (1979). Plankton gauze. In *Zooplankton sampling*, pp. 19–25. UNESCO, Paris.

Heywood, V. H. (ed.) (1995). *Global biodiversity assessment*. UNEP/Cambridge University Press, Cambridge.

Hill, M. O. (1979). *DECORANA—a FORTRAN program for detrended correspondence analysis and reciprocal averaging.* Cornell University, Ithaca, New York.

Hinkley, S. D. and New, T. R. (1997). Pitfall trapping for surveys of ant assemblages, lessons from a study at Mount Piper, Victoria. *Memoirs of the Museum of Victoria* **56**, 369–76.

Hollis, D. (1980). *Animal Identification. A reference guide.* Vol. 3. *Insects.* British Museum (Natural History), London/John Wiley, Chichester.

Holloway, J. D. (1976). *Moths of Borneo with special reference to Mount Kinabalu.* Malayan Nature Society, Kuala Lumpur.

Holloway, J. D. (1977). *The Lepidoptera of Norfolk Island, their biogeography and ecology.* W. Junk, The Hague.

Holme, N. A. and McIntyre, A. D. (ed.) (1984). *Methods for the study of marine benthos.* IBP Handbook, No. 16, Blackwell Scientific, Oxford.

Hulings, N. C. and Gray, J. S. (1971). A manual for the study of meiofauna. *Smithsonian Contributions to Zoology* No. 78.

Humphries, C. J. and Vane-Wright, R. I. (1992). Systematic evaluation of the global network of protected areas, objectives, alternatives, prospects and proposals. Draft paper presented to IVth World Congress on National Parks and Protected Areas, Caracas, Venezuela [see Vane-Wright, *et al.* 1994].

Hunter, P. J. (1968). Studies on slugs of arable ground. I. Sampling methods. *Malacologia* **6**, 369–77.

Hurlbert, S. H. (1984). Pseudoreplication and the design of ecological field experiments. *Ecological Monographs* **54**, 187–211.

Hutcheson, J. (1990). Characterization of terrestrial insect communities using quantified, Malaise-trapped Coleoptera. *Ecological Entomology* **15**, 143–51.

IUCN (1994*a*). *The IUCN red list of threatened animals.* IUCN, Gland.

IUCN (1994*b*). *The IUCN red list categories.* IUCN, Gland.

IUCN (1996). *1996 IUCN red list of threatened animals.* IUCN, Gland.

James, R. J., Lincoln Smith, M. P., and Fairweather, P. G. (1995). Sieve mesh-size and taxonomic resolution needed to describe natural spatial variation of marine macrofauna. *Marine Ecology Progress Series* **118**, 187–98.

Janzen, D. H. (1973). Sweep samples of tropical foliage insects, effects of seasons, vegetation types, elevation, time of day, and insularity. *Ecology* **54**, 687–708.

Janzen, D. H. (1993). What does tropical society want from the taxonomist? In *Hymenoptera and biodiversity* (ed. J. La Salle and I. D. Gauld), pp. 295–307. CAB International, Wallingford.

Janzen, D. H. and Pond, C. M. (1975). A comparison, by sweep sampling, of the arthropod fauna of secondary vegetation in Michigan, England and Costa Rica. *Transactions of the Royal Entomological Society of London* **127**, 33–50.

Janzen, D. H., Hallwachs, W., Jimenez, J., and Gámez, R. (1993). The role of parataxonomists, inventory managers, and taxonomists in Costa Rica's National Biodiversity Inventory. In *Biodiversity prospecting* (ed. W. V. Reid,

S. A. Laird, R. Gámez, A. Sittenfeld, D. H. Janzen, M. A. Gollin, and C. Juma), pp. 223–54. World Resources Institute, Baltimore, USA.

Jaramillo, E., McLachlan, A., and Dugan, J. (1995). Total sample area and estimates of species richness in exposed sandy beaches. *Marine Ecology Progress Series* **119**, 311–4.

JCCBI (Joint Committee for the Conservation of British Insects) (1986). Insect re-establishment—a code of conservation practice. *Antenna* **10**, 13–8.

Jones, A. (1993). Horses for courses: pragmatic measures of marine invertebrate biodiversity in response to capacity and need. In *Rapid biodiversity assessment* (ed. A. J. Beattie), pp. 69–74. Macquarie University, Sydney.

Kalinowska, A. (1993). Gastropoda. In *Methods in soil zoology* (ed. M. Górny and L. Grüm), pp. 197–202. Elsevier, Amsterdam/Polish Scientific Publishers, Warsaw.

Kellert, S. R. (1993). Values and perceptions of invertebrates. *Conservation Biology* **7**, 845–55.

Kelso, J. R. M. (1987). Unpublished mss., cited by Resh and Jackson, 1991.

Kempson, D., Lloyd, M., and Ghelardi, R. (1963). A new extractor for woodland litter. *Pedobiologia* **3**, 1–21.

Kenchington, R. A. (1978). Visual surveys of large areas of coral reefs. In *Coral reefs, research methods* (ed. D. R. Stoddart and R. E. Johannes), pp. 149–62. UNESCO, Paris.

Kethley, J. (1991). A procedure for extraction of microarthropods from bulk soil samples with emphasis on inactive stages. *Agriculture, Ecosystems and Environment* **34**, 193–200.

Kingston, P. F. and Riddle, M. J. (1989). Cost effectiveness of benthic faunal monitoring. *Marine Pollution Bulletin* **20**, 490–6.

Kirk, W. D. J. (1984). Ecologically selective colour traps. *Ecological Entomology* **9**, 35–41.

Kitching, R. L. (1993). Towards rapid biodiversity assessment—lessons following studies of arthropods of rainforest canopies. In *Rapid biodiversity assessment* (ed. A. J. Beattie), pp. 26–30. Macquarie University, Sydney.

Knudsen, J. W. (1966). *Biological techniques*. Harper and Row, New York.

Kolasa, J. (1993). Turbellaria. In *Methods in soil zoology* (ed. M. Górny and L. Grüm), pp. 158–62. Elsevier, Amsterdam/Polish Scientific Publishers, Warsaw.

Kozstarab, M. and Shaefer, C. W. (ed.) (1990). *Systematics of North American insects and arachnids: status and needs*. Virginia Agricultural Experiment Station Information Series 90–1, Blacksburg, Virginia.

Kremen, C. (1992). Assessing the indicator properties of species assemblages for natural areas monitoring. *Ecological Applications* **2**, 203–17.

Kremen, C. (1994). Biological inventory using target taxa: a case study of the butterflies of Madagascar. *Ecological Applications* **4**, 407–22.

Kremen, C., Colwell, R. K., Erwin, T. L., Murphy, D. D., Noss, R. F., and Sanjayan, M. A. (1993). Terrestrial arthropod assemblages, their use as indicators in conservation planning. *Conservation Biology* **7**, 796–808.

Krouse, J. S. (1989). Performance and selectivity of trap fisheries for crustaceans. In *Marine invertebrate Fisheries, their assessment and management* (ed. J. F. Caddy), pp. 307–26. John Wiley, New York.

Lambshead, P. J. D. (1993). Recent developments in marine benthic biodiversity research. *Oceanis* **19**, 5–24.

Langley, J. M., Kett, S., Al-Khalili, R. S., and Humphrey, C. J. (1995). The conservation value of English urban ponds in terms of their rotifer fauna. *Hydrobiologia* **313/314**, 259–66.

La Salle, J. and Gauld, I. D. (1993). Hymenoptera: their diversity, and their impact on the diversity of other organisms. In *Hymenoptera and biodiversity* (ed. J. La Salle and I. D. Gauld), pp. 1–26. CAB International, Wallingford.

Larsen, T. B. (1994). Butterfly biodiversity and conservation in the Afrotropical region. In *Ecology and conservaton of butterflies* (ed. A. S. Pullin), pp. 290–303. Chapman & Hall, London.

Lattin, J. D. (1993). Arthropod diversity and conservation in old-growth Northwest forests. *American Zoologist* **33**, 578–87.

Lee, W. L., Bell, B. M., and Sutton, J. F. (1982). *Guidelines for acquisition and management of biological specimens.* Association of Systematics Collections, Lawrence, Kansas.

Lenat, D. R. (1988). Water quality assessment of streams using a qualitative collection method for benthic macroinvertebrates. *Journal of the North American Benthological Society* **7**, 222–33.

Lessios, H. A. (1988). Mass mortality of *Diadema antillarum* in the Caribbean: what have we learned? *Annual Review of Ecology and Systematics* **19**, 371–93.

Lessios, H. A. (1995). *Diadema antillarum* 10 years after mass mortality: still rare, despite help from a competitor. *Proceedings of the Royal Society of London B* **259**, 331–7.

Loneragen, N. R., Wang, Y.-G., Kenyon, R. A., Staples, D. J., Vance, D. J., and Heales, D. S. (1995). Estimating the efficiency of a small beam trawl for sampling tiger prawns *Penaeus esculentus* and *P. semisulcatus* in seagrass by removal experiments. *Marine Ecology Progress Series* **118**, 139–48.

Long, B. and Lewis, J. B. (1987). Distribution and community structure of the benthic fauna of the north shore of the Gulf of St. Lawrence described by numerical methods of classification and ordination. *Marine Biology* **95**, 93–101.

Long, B. G. and Wang, Y. G. (1994). Method for comparing the capture efficiency of benthic sampling devices. *Marine Biology* **121**, 397–9.

Lott, D. A. (1994). The role of local museums in taxonomic support. *British Journal of Entomology and Natural History* **7** (Suppl. 1), 58–60.

Magurran, A. E. (1988). *Ecological diversity and its measurement*. Princeton University Press, Princeton, New Jersey.

Main, A. R. (1982). Rare species, precious or dross? In *Species at risk, research in Australia* (ed. R. H. Groves and W. D. L. Ride), pp. 163–74. Australian Academy of Science, Canberra.

Majer, J. D. (1987). Dealing with data from extensive invertebrate surveys. In *The role of invertebrates in conservation and biological survey* (ed. J. D. Majer), pp. 53–64. Department of Conservation and Land Management, Western Australia.

Majer, J. D. (1993a). Costs of biodiversity assessment. In *Rapid biodiversity assessment* (ed. A. J. Beattie), pp. 35–9. Macquarie University, Sydney.

Majer, J. D. (1993b). Comparison of the arboreal ant mosaic in Ghana, Brazil, Papua New Guinea and Australia—its structure and influence on arthropod diversity. In *Hymenoptera and biodiversity* (ed. J. La Salle and I. D. Gauld), pp. 115–41. CAB International, Wallingford.

Majer, J. D. and Recher, H. F. (1988). Invertebrate communities on Western Australian eucalypts: a comparison of branch clipping and chemical knock-down procedures. *Australian Journal of Ecology* **13**, 269–78.

Maragos, J. E. and Cook, C. W., Jr. (1995). The 1991–1992 rapid ecological assessment of Palau's coral reefs. *Coral Reefs* **14**, 237–52.

Marchant, R. and Lillywhite, P. (1989). A freeze-corer for sampling stony river beds. *Bulletin of the Australian Society for Limnology* **12**, 41–8.

Margules, C. R. and Usher, M. B. (1981). Criteria used in assessing wildlife conservation potential: a review. *Biological Conservation* **21**, 79–109.

Marsh, H. and Sinclair, D. F. (1989). Correcting for visibility bias in strip transect aerial surveys of aquatic fauna. *Journal of Wildlife Management* **53**, 1017–24.

Marshall, S. A., Anderson, R. S., Roughley, R. E., Behan-Pelletier, V., and Danks, H. V. (1994). *Terrestrial Arthropod Biodiversity: planning a study and recommended sampling techniques*. Entomological Society of Canada, Ottawa (Bulletin, Supplement).

Martin, J. E. H. (1977). *Collecting, preparing and preserving insects, mites and spiders*. Agriculture Canada, Publication 1643, Ottawa.

Masner, L. and Goulet, H. (1981). A new model of flight interception trap for some hymenopterous insects. *Entomological News* **92**, 199–202.

May, R. M. (1990). How many species? *Philosophical Transactions of the Royal Society of London B*, **330**, 293–304.

Mazanec, Z. (1978). A sampling scheme for estimating population density of the Jarrah Leaf Miner, *Perthida glyphopa* (Lepidoptera: Incurvariidae). *Journal of the Australian Entomological Society*, **17**, 275–85.

McArdle, B. H. (1990). When are rare species not there? *Oikos* **57**, 276–7.

McElligott, P. E. K. and Lewis, D. J. (1994). Relative efficiency of wet and dry extraction techniques for sampling aquatic macroinvertebrates in subarctic peatland. *Memoirs of the Entomological Society of Canada* **169**, 285–9.

McGinley, R. (1989). Entomological collections management—are we really managing? *Insect Collection News* **2**, 19–27.

McIntyre, A. D. (1971). Deficiency of gravity corers for sampling meiobenthos and sediments. *Nature* **231**, 260.

McIntyre, A. D. and Warwick, R. M. (1984). Meiofauna techniques. In *Methods for the study of marine benthos* (ed. N. A. Holme and A. D. McIntyre), pp. 217–44. Blackwell Scientific, Oxford.

McIntyre, A. D., Elliott, J. M., and Ellis, D. V. (1984). Introduction. Design of sampling programmes. In *Methods for the study of marine benthos* (ed. N. A. Holme and A. D. McIntyre), pp. 1–26. Blackwell Scientific, Oxford.

McLean, I. F. G., Fowles, A. P., Kerr, A. J., Young, M. R., and Yates, T. J. (1994). Butterflies on nature reserves in Britain. In *Ecology and conservation of butterflies* (ed. A. S. Pullin), pp. 67–83. Chapman & Hall, London.

McSorley, R. (1987). Extraction of nematodes and sampling methods. In *Principles and practice of nematode control in crops* (ed. R. H. Brown and B. R. Kerry), pp. 13–47. Academic Press, Sydney.

Mesibov, R., Taylor, R. J., and Brereton, R. N. (1995). Relative efficiency of pitfall trapping and hand-collecting from plots for sampling of millipedes. *Biodiversity and Conservation* **4**, 429–39.

Metcalfe, J. L. (1989). Biological water quality assessment of running water based on macroinvertebrate communities: history and present status in Europe. *Environmental Pollution* **60**, 101–39.

Miller, S. E. (1991). Entomological collections in the United States and Canada. Current status and growing needs. *American Entomologist* (1991), 77–84.

Milne, W. M. (1993). Detachable bags for multiple sweep net samples. *Antenna* **17**, 14–5.

Mingoa, S. S. M. and Menez, L. A. B. (1988). A comparison of two benthic survey methods. *Marine Biology* **99**, 133–5.

Moldenke, A., Shaw, C., and Boyle, J. R. (1991). Computer-driven image-based soil fauna taxonomy. *Agriculture, Ecosystems and Environment* **34**, 177–85.

Moore, N. W. (1964). Intra- and interspecific competition among dragonflies (Odonata): an account of observations and field experiments on population density control in Dorset, 1954–60. *Journal of Animal Ecology* **33**, 49–71.

Moore, N. W. (1991). The development of dragonfly communities and the consequences of territorial behaviour: a 27-year study on small ponds at Woodwalton Fen, Cambridgeshire, United Kingdom. *Odonatologica* **20**, 203–31.

Moore, N. W. and Corbet, P. S. (1990). Guidelines for monitoring dragonfly populations. *Journal of the British Dragonfly Society* **6**, 21–3.

Moore, C. G., Mathieson, S., Mills, D. J. L., and Bett, B. J. (1987). Estimation of meiobenthic nematode diversity by non-specialists. *Marine Pollution Bulletin* **18**, 646–9.

Moran, P. J. and De'ath, G. (1992). Suitability of the manta tow technique for estimating relative and absolute abundance of crown-of-thorns starfish (*Acanthaster planci* L.) and corals. *Australian Journal of Marine and Freshwater Research* **43**, 357–78.

Moran, P. J., Johnson, D. B., Miller-Smith, B. A., Mundy, C. N., Bass, D. K., Davidson, J., Miller, I. R. and Thompson, A. A. (1989). *A guide to the AIMS manta tow technique*. Australian Institute of Marine Science, Townsville.

Morton, A. C. (1982). The effects of marking and capture on recapture frequencies of butterflies. *Oecologia* **53**, 105–10.

Mound, L. A. and Gaston, K. J. (1994). Conservation and systematics—the agony and the ecstasy. In *Perspectives on insect conservation* (ed. K. J. Gaston, T. R. New, and M. J. Samways), pp.185–95. Intercept, Andover.

Muirhead-Thomson, R. C. (1991). *Trap responses of flying insects*. Academic Press, London.

Murphy, D. D. (1989). Are we studying our endangered butterflies to death? *Journal of Research on the Lepidoptera* **26**, 236–9.

Murphy, D. D. (1990). Conservation biology and scientific method. *Conservation Biology* **4**, 203–4.

Murphy, P. W. (ed.) (1982). *Progress in soil zoology*. Butterworths, London.

National Research Council (1995). *Understanding marine biodiversity*. National Academy Press, Washington, D.C.

New, T. R. (1984). *Insect conservation: an Australian perspective*. W. Junk, Dordrecht.

New, T. R. (1991). *Butterfly conservation*. Oxford University Press, Melbourne.

New, T. R. (1993). Angels on a pin: dimensions of the crisis in invertebrate conservation. *American Zoologist* **33**, 623–30.

New, T. R. (1994). Conservation assessment of invertebrate assemblages, is there a place for global level taxon-focussing? *Memoirs of the Queensland Museum* **36**, 153–57.

New, T. R. (1995*a*). *Introduction to invertebrate conservation biology*. Oxford University Press. Oxford.

New T. R. (1995*b*). Evaluating the status of butterflies for conservation. *Proceedings of the International Symposium on Butterfly Conservation*. Osaka, Japan, 1994, 4–21.

New, T. R. and Thornton, I. W. B. (1992). The butterflies of Anak Krakatau, Indonesia: faunal development in early succession. *Journal of the Lepidopterists' Society*, **46**, 83–96.

Ng, P. (1991). Development of a systematics database for southeast Asian crabs. *Research Trends* **3**, 6–7.

Nicholls, J. H. and Thompson, R. M. (1988). Quantitative sampling of crustacean larvae and its use in stock size estimation of commercially exploited species. *Symposia of the Zoological Society of London* **59**, 157–75.

Nielsen, C. O. (1952). Studies on Enchytraeidae. I. A technique for extracting Enchytraeidae from soil samples. *Oikos* **4**, 187–96.

Nielsen, E. S. and West, J. G. (1994). Biodiversity research and biological collections: transfer of information. In *Systematics and conservation evaluation* (ed. P. L. Forey, C. J. Humphries, and R. I. Vane-Wright), pp. 101–21. Clarendon Press, Oxford.

Noonan, G. R. and Thayer, M. K. (1990). Standard fields and terms for databases about insects. *Insect Collection News 4*, pp. 9.

Norris, R. H. and Georges, A. (1993). Analysis and interpretation of benthic macroinvertebrate surveys. In *Freshwater biomonitoring and benthic macroinvertebrates* (ed. D. M. Rosenberg and V. H. Resh), pp. 234–45. Chapman & Hall, New York.

Noss, R. F. (1990). Indicators for monitoring biodiversity: a hierarchical approach. *Conservation Biology* **4**, 355–64.

Noyes, J. S. (1989). A study of five methods of sampling Hymenoptera (Insecta) in a tropical rainforest, with special reference to the Parasitica. *Journal of Natural History* **23**, 285–98.

O'Connor, F. B. (1962). The extraction of Enchytraeidae from soil. In *Progress in soil zoology* (ed. P. W. Murphy), pp. 279–85. Butterworths, London.

Oliver, I. and Beattie, A. J. (1993). A possible method for the rapid assessment of biodiversity. *Conservation Biology* **7**, 562–8.

Oliver, I. and Beattie, A. J. (1996). Designing a cost-effective invertebrate survey: a test of methods for rapid assessment of biodiversity. *Ecological Applications* **6**, 594–607.

Opler, P. A. (1991). North American problems and perspectives in insect conservation. In *The conservation of insects and their habitats* (ed. N. M. Collins and J. A. Thomas), pp. 9–32. Academic Press, London.

Opler, P. A. (1994). Conservation and management of butterfly diversity in North America. In *Ecology and conservation of butterflies* (ed. A. S. Pullin), pp. 316–24. Chapman & Hall, London.

Orsak, L. (1993). Killing butterflies to save butterflies: a tool for tropical forest conservation in Papua New Guinea. *News Bulletin of the Lepidopterists' Society* (1993), 71–80.

Parsons, D. G., Dawe, E. G., Ennis, C. P., Naidu, K. S., and Taylor, D. M. (1983). Sampling of commercial catches for invertebrates in Newfoundland. *Canadian Special Publications of Fisheries and Aquatic Sciences* **66**, 39–51.

Pearce-Kelly, P. (1993). The real value to zoos of invertebrate conservation breeding programmes, with special reference to the invertebrate department at the London Zoo. In *Invertebrates in Captivity*, pp. 30–4. SASI, Tucson, Arizona.

Pearson, D. L. (1994). Selecting indicator taxa for the quantitative assessment of biodiversity. *Philosophical Transactions of the Royal Society of London, B* **345**, 75–79.

Pearson, D. L. and Cassola, F. (1992). World-wide species richness patterns of tiger beetles (Coleoptera: Cicindelidae): indicator taxon for biodiversity and conservation studies. *Conservation Biology* **6**, 376–91.

Peck, S. B. and Davies, A. E. (1980). Collecting small beetles with large-area 'window traps'. *Coleopterists' Bulletin* **34**, 237–9.

Penczak, T. and Rodriguez, G. (1990). The use of electrofishing to estimate population densities of freshwater shrimps (Decapoda, Natantia) in a small tropical river, Venezuela. *Archiv für Hydrobiologie* **118**, 501–9.

Penrose, D. and Call, S. M. (1995). Volunteer monitoring of benthic macroinvertebrates: regulatory biologists' perspectives. *Journal of the North American Benthological Society* **14**, 203–9.

Perkins, J. H. (1989). Eradication: scientific and social questions. In *Eradication of exotic pests* (ed. D. L. Dahlsten and R. Garcia), pp. 16–40. Yale University Press, New Haven.

Phillips, D. J. H. and Segar, D. A. (1986). Use of bio-indicators in monitoring conservative contaminants: programme design imperatives. *Marine Pollution Bulletin* **17**, 10–17.

Platt, H. M. and Warwick, R. M. (1983). *Free-living marine nematodes. Part 1. British enoplids*. Cambridge University Press, Cambridge.

Pollard, E. (1977). A method for assessing changes in the abundance of butterflies. *Biological Conservation* **12**, 115–34.

Pollard, E. (1991). Monitoring butterfly numbers. In *Monitoring for conservation and ecology* (ed. F. B. Goldsmith), pp. 87–111. Chapman & Hall, London.

Pollard, E. and Yates, T. J. (1993). *Monitoring butterflies for ecology and conservation*. Chapman & Hall, London.

Pollard, E., Hall, M. L., and Bibby, T. J. (1986). *Monitoring the abundance of butterflies 1976–85*. Nature Conservancy Council, Peterborough.

Poore, G. C. B. and Wilson, G. D. F. (1993). Marine species richness. *Nature*, **361**, 597–8.

Praagh, B. D. van (1992). The biology and conservation of the Giant Gippsland Earthworm, *Megascolides australis* McCoy 1878. *Soil Biology and Biochemistry* **24**, 1363–7.

Pressey, R. L., Humphries, C. J., Margules, C. R., Vane-Wright, R. I., and Williams, P. H. (1993). Beyond opportunism, key principles for systematic reserve selection. *Trends in Ecology and Evolution* **8**, 124–8.

Price, P. W. (1988). An overview of organismal interactions in ecosystems in evolutionary and ecological time. *Agriculture, Ecosystems and Environment* **24**, 369–77.

Quicke, D. J. L. (1993). *Principles and techniques of contemporary taxonomy*. Blackie Academic and Professional, Glasgow.

Ramsay, G. W. and Crosby, T. K. (1992). Bibliography of New Zealand terrestrial invertebrates 1775–1985, and guide to the associated information retrieval database BUGS. *Bulletin of the Entomological Society of New Zealand* **11**, 1–440.

Rees, H. L. (1984). A note on mesh selection and sampling efficiency in benthic studies. *Marine Pollution Bulletin* **15**, 225–9.

Reisch, D. J. (1959). A discussion of the importance of screen size in washing quantitative marine bottom samples. *Ecology* **40**, 307–9.

Resh, V. H. (1979). Sampling variability and life history features, basic considerations in the design of aquatic insect studies. *Journal of the Fisheries Research Board of Canada* **36**, 290–311.

Resh, V. H. and Jackson, J. K. (1993). Rapid assessment approaches to biomonitoring using benthic macroinvertebrates. In *Freshwater biomonitoring and benthic macroinvertebrates* (ed. D. M. Rosenberg and V. H. Resh), pp. 195–233. Chapman & Hall, New York.

Resh, V. H. and McElravy, E. P. (1993). Contemporary quantitative approaches to biomonitoring using benthic macroinvertebrates. In *Freshwater biomonitoring and benthic macroinvertebrates* (ed. D. M. Rosenberg and V. H. Resh), pp. 159–94. Chapman & Hall, New York.

Resh, V. H., Norris, R. H., and Barbour, M. T. (1995). Design and implementation of rapid assessment approaches for water resource monitoring using benthic invertebrates. *Australian Journal of Ecology* **20**, 108–21.

Ridgway, R. L., Silverstein, R. M., and Inscoe, M. N. (ed.) (1990). *Behaviour-modifying chemicals for insect management*. Marcel Dekker, New York.

Robinson, M. H. (1993). Invertebrates: the key to holistic bioeducation. In *Invertebrates in captivity*, pp. 1–11. SASI, Tucson, Arizona.

Roper, C. F. E. (1977). Comparative captures of pelagic cephalopods by midwater trawls. *Symposia of the Zoological Society of London* **38**, 61–87.

Rosenberg, D. M., Danks, H. V., Downes, J. A., Nimmo, A. P., and Ball, G. E. (1979). Procedures for a faunal inventory. In *Canada and its insect fauna* (ed. H. V. Danks), pp. 509–32. *Memoirs of the Entomological Society of Canada* **108**.

Rounsefell, G. A. (1975). *Ecology and utilization and management of marine fisheries*. Mosby, St Louis.

Russell-Smith, A. and Stork, N. E. (1994). Abundance and diversity of spiders from the canopy of tropical rainforests with particular reference to Sulawesi, Indonesia. *Journal of Tropical Ecology* **10**, 545–58.

Rutledge, P. A. and Fleeger, J. W. (1988). Laboratory studies on core sampling with application to subtidal meiobenthos collection. *Limnology and Oceanography* **33**, 274–80.

SA (Systematics Association) (1994). *Systematics Agenda 2000: Charting the biosphere*. Technical Report, Washington, DC.

Saila, S. B., Pikanowski, R. A., and Vaughan, D. S. (1976). Optimum allocation strategies for sampling benthos in New York Bight. *Estuarine and Coastal Marine Science* **4**, 119–28.

Salt, G. and Hollick, F. S. J. (1944). Studies of wireworm populations. 1. A census of wireworms in pasture. *Annals of Applied Biology* **31**, 53–64.

Samu, F. and Lövei, G. L. (1995). Species richness of a spider community (Araneae), extrapolation from simulated increasing sampling effort. *European Journal of Entomology* **92**, 633–8.

Samways, M. J. (1994a). *Insect conservation biology.* Chapman & Hall, London.

Samways, M. J. (1994b). A spatial and process sub-regional framework for insect and biodiversity conservation research and management. In *Perspectives on insect conservation* (ed. K. J. Gaston, T. R. New, and M. J. Samways), pp. 1–28. Intercept, Andover.

SASI (Sonoran Arthropod Studies Inc.) (1993). *Invertebrates in captivity 1993* (SASI/ITAG Conference), Tucson, Arizona.

SASI (Sonoran Arthropod Studies Inc.) (1994). *Invertebrates in captivity 1994* (SASI/ITAG Conference), Tucson, Arizona.

Schmidt, E. (1985). Habitat inventorization characterisation and bioindication by a 'representative spectrum of Odonata species (RSO)'. *Odonatologica* **14**, 127–33.

Scudder, G. G. E. (1996). Terrestrial and freshwater invertebrates of British Columbia: priorities for inventory and descriptive research. Research Branch, B.C. Ministry of Forests and Wildlife Branch, B.C. Ministry of Environment, Lands and Parks, Working Paper 09/1996. Vancouver.

Shelton, A. M. and Trumble, J. T. (1991). Monitoring insect populations. In *Handbook of pest management in agriculture* (ed. D. Pimentel), pp. 45–62, Vol. II. CRC, Boca Raton.

Sheppard, D. (1991). Site survey methods. In *Habitat conservation for insects— a neglected green issue* (ed. R. Fry and D. Lonsdale), pp. 205–8. Amateur Entomologists' Society, Middlesex.

Sims, R. W. (ed.) (1980a). *Animal identification. A reference guide.* Vol. 1. *Marine and brackish water animals.* British Museum (Natural History), London/John Wiley, Chichester.

Sims, R. W. (ed.) (1980b). *Animal identification. A reference guide.* Vol. 2. *Land and freshwater animals (not insects).* British Museum (Natural History), London/John Wiley, Chichester.

Singer, M. C. and Wedlake, P. (1981). Capture does affect probability of recapture in a butterfly species. *Ecological Entomology* **6**, 215–6.

Solbrig, O. T. (1991). *From genes to ecosystems, a research agenda for biodiversity.* IUBS Monograph, Paris.

South, A. (1965). Biology and ecology of *Agriolimax reticulatus* (Müll.) and other slugs: spatial distribution. *Journal of Animal Ecology* **34**, 403–17.

Southwood, T. R. E. (1978). *Ecological methods. With particular reference to the study of insect populations.* Chapman & Hall, London.

Southwood, T. R. E., Moran, V. C., and Kennedy, C. E. J. (1982). The assessment of arboreal insect fauna: comparisons of knockdown sampling and faunal lists. *Ecological Entomology* 7, 331–40.

Sparrow, H. R., Sisk, T. D., Ehrlich, P. R., and Murphy, D. D. (1994). Techniques and guidelines for monitoring Neotropical butterflies. *Conservation Biology* 8, 800–9.

Speight, M. C. D. (1986). Criteria for the selection of insects to be used as bio-indicators in nature conservation research. *Proceedings of the Third European Congress of Entomology*, Part 3, pp. 485–8. Nederlands Entomologische Vereniging, Amsterdam.

Spence, J. R. and Niemela, J. K. (1994). Sampling carabid assemblages with pitfall traps: the madness and the method. *Canadian Entomologist* 126, 881–94.

Stark, J. D. (1985). Analysis and presentation of macroinvertebrate data. In *Biological monitoring in freshwaters* (ed. R. D. Pridmore and A. B. Cooper), pp. 273–303. Water and Soil Directorate, Wellington. Miscellaneous Publication No. 83.

Stephenson, W. and Cook, S. D. (1980). Skewness of data in the analysis of species-in-sites-in-times. *Proceedings of the Royal Society of Queensland* 91, 37–52.

Stewart, A. J. A. and Wright, A. F. (1995). A new inexpensive suction apparatus for sampling arthropods in grassland. *Ecological Entomology* 20, 98–102.

Steytler, N. S. and Samways, M. J. (1995). Biotope selection by adult male dragonflies (Odonata) at an artificial lake created for insect conservation in South Africa. *Biological Conservation* 72, 381–6.

Stork, N. E. (1988). Insect diversity: facts, fiction and speculation. *Biological Journal of the Linnean Society* 35, 321–37.

Stork, N. E. (1994). Inventories of biodiversity: more than a question of numbers. In *Systematics and conservation evaluation* (ed. P. L. Forey, C. J. Humphries, and R. I. Vane-Wright), pp. 81–100. Clarendon Press, Oxford.

Sutherland, W. J. (ed.) (1996). *Ecological census techniques: a handbook.* Cambridge University Press, Cambridge.

Swaay, C. A. M. van (1990). An assessment of the changes in butterfly abundance in the Netherlands during the 20th century. *Biological Conservation* 52, 287–302.

Sweney, W. J. and Jones, A. E. (1975). Methods for sampling foliage and insect populations of the beech forest canopy. *New Zealand Journal of Forestry Science* 5, 119–22.

Taylor, L. R. and Brown, E. S. (1972). Effects of light-trap design and illumination on samples of moths in the Kenya highlands. *Bulletin of Entomological Research* 62, 91–112.

Taylor, L. R., Brown, E. S., and Littlewood, S. C. (1979). The effect of size on the height of flight of migrant moths. *Bulletin of Entomological Research* **69**, 605–9.

Thirgood, S. J. and Heath, M. F. (1994). Global patterns of endemism and the conservation of biodiversity. In *Systematics and conservation evaluation* (ed. P. L. Forey, C. J. Humphries, and R. I. Vane-Wright), pp. 207–27. Clarendon Press, Oxford.

Thomas, A. W. and Thomas, G. M. (1994). Sampling strategies for estimating moth species diversity using a light trap in a north eastern softwood forest. *Journal of the Lepidopterists' Society* **48**, 85–105.

Thomas, C. D. and Abery, J. C. G. (1995). Estimating rates of butterfly decline from distribution maps: the effect of scale. *Biological Conservation* **73**, 59–65.

Thomas, J. A. (1983). The ecology and conservation of *Lysandra bellargus* (Lepidoptera: Lycaenidae) in Britain. *Journal of Applied Ecology* **20**, 59–83.

Thomas, M. C. (1995). Invertebrate pets and the Florida Department of Agriculture and Consumer Services. *Florida Entomologist* **78**, 39–44.

Toone, W. D. (1990). Butterfly exhibitry. *International Zoo Yearbook* **29**, 61–5.

Topping, C. J. (1993). Behavioural responses of three linyphiid spiders to pitfall traps. *Entomologia Experimentalis et Applicata* **68**, 287–93.

Townes, H. (1962). Design for a Malaise trap. *Proceedings of the Entomological Society of Washington* **64**, 253–62.

Trueman, J. H. H. and Cranston, P. S. (1997). Prospects for the rapid assessment of terrestrial invertebrate biodiversity. *Memoirs of the Museum of Victoria* **56**, 349–54.

Underwood, A. J. (1981). Techniques of analysis of variance in experimental marine biology and ecology. *Annual Review of Oceanography and Marine Biology* **19**, 513–605.

UNESCO (1979). *Zooplankton sampling*. Paris.

Upton, M. S. (1991). *Methods for collecting, preserving and studying insects and allied forms*. Australian Entomological Society Miscellaneous Publication, No. 3. Brisbane.

Usher, M. B. (ed.) (1986). *Wildlife conservation evaluation*. Chapman & Hall, London.

Usher, M. B. and Edwards, M. (1986). The selection of conservation areas in Antarctica, an example using the arthropod fauna of antarctic islands. *Environmental Conservation* **13**, 115–22.

Vane-Wright, R. I. (1994). Systematics and the conservation of biodiversity: global, national and local perspectives. In *Perspectives on insect conservation* (ed. K. J. Gaston, T. R. New, and M. J. Samways), pp. 197–211. Intercept, Andover.

Vane-Wright, R. I., Humphries, C. J., and Williams, P. H. (1991). What to protect? Systematics and the agony of choice. *Biological Conservation* **55**, 235–54.

Vane-Wright, R. I., Smith, C. R., and Kitching, I. J. (1994). Systematic assessment of taxic diversity by summation. In *Systematics and conservation evaluation* (P. L. Forey, C. J. Humphries, and R. I. Vane-Wright), pp. 309–26. Clarendon, Oxford.

Vannucci, M. (1979). Loss of organisms through the meshes. In *Zooplankton sampling*, pp. 77–86. UNESCO, Paris.

Walter, D. E., Kethley, J., and Moore, J. C. (1987). A heptane flotation method for recovering microarthropods from semiarid soils, with comparison to the Merchant-Crossley high-gradient extraction method and estimates of microarthropod biomass. *Pedobiologia* **30**, 221–32.

Warren, M. S. (1993). A review of butterfly conservation in central southern Britain: II. Site management and habitat selection of key species. *Biological Conservation* **64**, 37–49.

Warwick, R. M. (1988). The level of taxonomic discrimination required to detect pollution effects on marine benthic communities. *Marine Pollution Bulletin* **19**, 259–68.

Warwick, R. M. (1993). Environmental impact studies on marine communities: pragmatical considerations. *Australian Journal of Ecology* **18**, 63–80.

Watt, A. D., Ward, L. K., and Eversham, B. C. (1990). Invertebrates. In *The greenhouse effect and terrestrial ecosystems of the UK* (ed. M. G. R. Cannell and M. D. Hooper), pp. 32–7. London, HMSO.

Weinberg, S. (1981). A comparison of coral reef survey methods. *Bijdragen tot de Dierkunde* **51**, 199–218.

Welch, P. S. (1948). *Limnological methods*. McGraw-Hill, New York.

Wells, S. M., Pyle, R. M., and Collins, N. M. (1983). *The IUCN invertebrate red data book*. IUCN, Gland.

Williams, C. B. (1945). Recent light trap catches of Lepidoptera in U.S.A. analysed in relation to the logarithmic series and the index of diversity. *Annals of the Entomological Society of America* **38**, 357–64.

Williams, D. D. and Feltmate, B. W. (1993). *Aquatic insects*. CAB International, Wallingford.

Wilson, E. O. (1987). The little things that run the world (the importance and conservation of invertebrates). *Conservation Biology* **1**, 344–6.

Winterbourn, M. J. (1985). Sampling stream invertebrates. In *Biological monitoring in freshwaters* (ed. R. D. Pridmore and A. B. Cooper), pp. 241–58. Miscellaneous Publication No. 83. Water and Soil Directorate, Wellington.

Wright, J. F. (1995). Development and use of a system for predicting the macroinvertebrate fauna in flowing waters. *Australian Journal of Ecology* **20**, 181–97.

Wu, R. S. S. (1982). Effects of taxonomic uncertainty in species diversity indices. *Marine Environmental Research* **6**, 215–25.

Yamamoto, M. (1975). Notes on the methods of belt transect census of butterflies. *Journal of the Faculty of Science, Hokkaido University, Zoology* **20**, 93–116.

Yen, A. L. (1987). A preliminary assessment of the correlation between plant, vertebrate and Coleoptera communities in the Victorian mallee. In *The role of invertebrates in conservation and biological survey* (ed. J. D. Majer), pp. 73–88. Department of Conservation and Land Management, Perth.

Yen, A. L. (1993). Some practical issues in the assessment of invertebrate biodiversity. In *Rapid biodiversity assessment* (ed. A. J. Beattie), pp. 21–5. Macquarie University, Sydney.

Yen, A. L. (1994). The role of museums and zoos in influencing public attitudes towards invertebrate conservation. In *Perspectives on insect conservation* (ed. K. J. Gaston, T. R. New, and M. J. Samways), pp. 213–29. Intercept, Andover.

Yen, A. L. and Butcher, R. J. (1994). *An overview of the conservation status of non-marine invertebrates in Australia*. Australian Nature Conservation Agency, Canberra.

Index

Printed in the United States
858000001B

9 780198 500117